Distributed by:
South Asia Books
P.O. Box 502
Columbia, MO 65205

WHEN FATHERS RAPE
(A Socio-Psycho-Legal-Global Study)

WHEN FATHERS RAPE
(A Socio-Psycho-Legal-Global Study)

Manish Sharma

A.P.H. PUBLISHING CORPORATION
5, ANSARI ROAD, DARYA GANJ,
NEW DELHI - 110 002

Published by

S. B. Nangia
A.P.H. Publishing Corporation
5, Ansari Road, Darya Ganj,
New Delhi-110002
☎ 3274050

ISBN 81-7024-739-X

1996

© Author

Typeset at
NEW APCON
25/2, Panchsheel Shopping Centre,
New Delhi 110 017
☎ 6460802

Printed in India at
Efficient Offset Printers
New Delhi-110 035

**DEDICATED TO THE GREAT
GOD,
WHO MADE ME LOVE HUMANITY,
AND THUS, DETEST RAPE.**

PREFACE

Abla Nari Hai Teri Yahi Kahani,
Anchal Main Hai Doodh Aur Ankhon Main Pani.

When the legendary poet Matheli Sharan Gupt wrote these lines in the beginning of the 20th century, he had the image of the women of his times. The one who had the 'Pardah' and the 'Burka' as her identity and not her face; the gate of the house as her limits and not the world, the negativism of the world towards her as her pain and the suffocatory attitude of the world to her as her suffocation. Touched by the agony and tears of the fair sex, the poet in Matheli's heart shrieked aloud-Hapless Woman, the same story, Milk in the breast and water in the eyes....

It is a tregedy, that a feminist like me, in the concluding years of the twentieth century, amidst Nalini Singhs and P.T. Ushas; Smita Patils and Shabana Azmis; Indira Gandhi and Sarojini Naidu could only find these two lines to start his book. For the subject of my book is parental rape and I have travelled through the tears of the woman who milks the world and hasn't even the father's arm for a support.

The word 'sex' invokes different reactions. Some people are very shy of sex. The moment you start a talk on the subject, and it doesn't matter whether the subject is good or bad, they would become extremely nervous, start sweating and try to escape the group. If they sit in the presence of a member of the opposite sex their condition is horribly funny to look at. The fun increases if the other member recognise their shyness and is naughty enough to tease them through it. Some people are confident of sex. They will talk freely with boys and girls; whatever the case may be, they'll love going to parties and discos and you can always find them talking about romance and dates! Others are interested in sex. They'll have a lot of girl friends or boy friends; their telephones would appear to be made only for blank calls; their walls, letter pads and notebooks would be stuffed of hearts big and small. The one silver lining in these clouds is that sometimes this group produces excellent poets! Few are obsessed of sex. They'll have speedy bedroom changes and mate replacements and their minds would be stuffed of this passion. But some are MAD of sex. And, it is this group, that has caused the tears of the women, shrieks of the women activists, setting of women commissions and the biggest crime in the history of mankind. These men are rapists and their crime..... RAPE.

It has been the moral and humanitarian demand of the civilizations of all times and all places that women should not be forced to sexual intercourse. As such, moralists and saints from times immemorial have outlined a thousand and one limits with regards to sex. And our highly esteemed Vedas have even gone to the extent of dividing our sexual life into four stages with the Brahmacharya barring even the thought of the opposite sex whereas the last stage Vanaprastha outlines husband and wife to live in forest as friends. However, two-way accepted sexual intercourse is a part of personal life and the law does not and should not interfere. So, while blank calls and love letters invite fascination, interest or good humour even changing beds and sexual diseases are considered immoral but in no way a crime. In any way, we can not expect everyone, however admirable it maybe, to spend his whole life with a single wife (infact, this statement would become a capital joke in the west!)

However, what brings tears is the fact that there are some whose sexual passion is not confined just to changing beds but extended to tearing clothes.

Rape; is the biggest crime committed by the human world. Even when I am writing this piece, my pen has jerked many–a time thinking that while I am sitting with a relaxed posture on my chair, comfortably sliding my pen on the sheets of paper, thousands are being raped in the bedrooms of beasts and barbarians.

What rape is, is better understood if you enter a rape-victim-help institute. The moment you see women with shocked eyes turned to stone, pale faces and stillness of expression that's synonymous with the meaningless life; all your collected agony drops in the form of tears. May be you have known even without entering a rape institute, what it means, when you see a Shabana Azmi or a Smita Patil or a Neena Gupta in a scene where their character is raped and insulted. Their acting is so superb and so realistic that the fiction appears as a fact and the fact pulls out from the depths of your emotions and the passage of your eyes, a line of tears. As creative artists are not created, similarly one is born a feminist. To me,

Preface

being a feminist (though neutral enough to criticize the women, where they share the wrong), is to be in line with God. From the beginning, I have been a feminist and it is a fact, I am proud of. When, at a point in my teenage and I don't know when, I started understanding rape, I recognised it as a crime done by the men of Satan. When my writings assumed serious forms, when I recognised the real duty of a writer as an entertainer cum educationist and when my writings started flowing from the pages of my diaries and notebooks to those of magazines, I felt the thirst to write a piece that could shake the world and make them realise what a horrible word rape is–not the way the world takes the horrible aspect of it but the way it is.

God listened my prayer and wrote a day on my name.

The final hour came on the 16th of February in the form of a newspaper report. I don't know whether to call it a golden day or a black one. While it laid the foundation of what you shall begin reading just now: It made Delhi a black city. That morning while the Sun dawned and dawns every morning, the real sun has never ever arisen from that day.

I got up in the morning as usuals and reached the living room. After exchanging essential courtesies with my parents, I felt the need to quench my morning thirst for a newspaper and picked up 'The Hindustan Times'. As I reached the third page, I read the following heading: MAN HELD FOR RAPING DAUGHTER.

My heart shivered as a single leaf on a tree facing the piercing winds of autumn. The erected structures of morality, humanity and extremity started falling in front of me. I felt as if for centuries we had been driving our caravan of civilization on the floors of human yearning and beastly appetite. At that juncture, if anybody would have talked of India as a land of unique culture where there are Vedas and the Upanishads, I would have felt that he is talking nonsense. Or.... maybe today we talk of India of the past in this manner. Tomorrow maybe, we shall say, India has moved ahead in time with a linear advancement in rape. From rapes, to minor rapes to kid and infant rapes to PARENTAL RAPE .....

Within five minutes, I had decided that I would be doing a research on parental rapes. I was necessarily depressed because being a journalist and writer my duty and creative obsession both made me deeply affected, towards the blackest menace in society and the need to comment on it. Gandhiji had said that Rape is the biggest crime committed by man. I felt at that juncture that how would the great Mahatama have reacted to parental rape. Maybe February the 26th, had the legendary Mahatama been alive, would have started a fast unto death. It's good that the book has been written, otherwise the soul of Gandhiji would have come and cried saying that he was ashamed to be an Indian and that he had achieved independence for a country whose citizens after centuries of civilization and loads of great books hadn't been able to cut themselves off the animal world.

Within hours, the skeleton of this mega research had been framed. It had to be a mammoth analysis and not a thousand word article; involving all sections of society–the VIP's the experts, the women organisations, the common man and viewing all aspects of the problem. Thus was born my JURASSIC PARK, a journey where instead of dinosaurs out of control are uncontrollable human beasts. WHEN FATHER RAPE is a mega analysis seeing the problem from the individual, psychiatric, social, jurisdictive, cultural, moral, criminal and .... GODLY aspects. The ways to describe this analysis are also varied from case studies, interviews, analytical discussions, opinion poll and related studies and theoretical and practical illustrations. It also takes an international view of the problem, discussing about laws throughout the world in a very systematic and diversified manner, thus helping the reader to understand in full the problem and the solution, through a round-the-globe-study.

The way this book was created, the way I have written it, the way I begun it and the way I completed it; I have always thought and I have always believed that something divine made me write it. That it was written for a great cause. And that great one who made me write it was GOD. I know it would invoke laughter or sympathy in my readers towards me but a day shall come when I will be taken seriously.

The book has a very extensive content list that explains the need and importance of each part of the book in the outmost possible detail. A particular part has been defined, and further subdivided to the highest limit of diversification, informing in detail what its pages offer. The contents in themselves are a synopsis of the book.

There is no need therefore, to comment on the chapters here, as it would be an avoidable repetition.

There is however one thing that needs to be commented upon.

Preface   *xi*

In the international perspective, section II and III, before stating the laws of the different countries of the world, the nation is introduced through a 'Introduction File', subdivided into three parts-'Profile', 'The History and Times' and 'Looking Back-Looking Beyond'.

Some of my readers might feel that all this is a useless contribution, that was not needed and is a deviation from the real issue. However, if this is an opinion of any reader, he must try to read the law of any country without reading its introduction file. The reader shall at once realise that he is unable to understand in full the law, and thus is not in a position to make a correct assessment.

Why does this happen? It happens because the law of every country is related to its society, culture, heritage, politics and ideologies. Without understanding the same, the law can not be understood, as it originates from the social ethos.

Why are we reading the laws of the different countries in the first place? They are after all, just statements. I could have made a thousand permutations on rape law. If we are studying laws of different countries, we must first be able to place them in the context of their nation, only then can we hope to extract any benefit.

A word about the book as a whole. 'When Fathers Rape', appears to be a conglomerate of 14 parts and an appendix. It appears that all these parts are separate entities in themselves and any part can be left at will. It is a capital mistake, as this is a book requiring a deep reading of very page, if a correct assessment of the incestual rape menace is to be made with the help of this creative work.

Reading this book, you would find extensive discussions on kid and infant rapes and minor rapes. Don't be surprised that why so, if the title suggests only a deal with parental rapes. The main current of the book is definitely about parental rapes. But parental rapes, as I explain in part-I, can not be discussed separately. Parental rapes are the biggest and the most barbarian part of the rape menace. But it's not something that's completely isolated and so can not be studied in isolation.

One question that readers might ask me is that why such a lengthy research on parental rapes if only some cases in news? My answer is that earthquakes and volcanoes are not thought about when they are at the door but when they are coming towards the door. Again, the solutions in the book are for rapes at large and not just for parental rape.

Execution as a probable punishment and solution to rapes is an important discussion of the book. I wouldn't talk about it here but request my dear readers to attentively attend to the pages concerned with it. However, I would do say one thing that please don't come up and say that people should not be executed in case of rape, as wrong accusations can also be made. Death sentence for other crimes have been passed from the origin of democracy from 1947 and even the most esteemed judge can not deny that in the history of crime and punishment there have been many people falsely accused of a crime and sentenced to death.

One other factor that arose in the book and that needs to be examined is that why are rapes increasing (or decaying) in quality? Some of the eminent persons interviewed replied that rapes are increasing because of the increase in population and more connection of the public with law and media. That goes for the magnitude increase of rape. But why in quality? Why have they become public? Why have Sivapatis been dragged on streets naked with the mute law as the blind spectator? Why, why....WHY? This question cuts arose your mind. And the answer is that we have, over these years, morally degraded to an extent that's beyond explanation. Because some facts are stranger than fiction and some facts are beyond comprehension. While we are moving closer in linear distances through aeroplanes, jets and rockets; the distance between man and morality is moving continually farther. And... we don't have a Lord Krishna to save a Draupadi.

This book is not an epic though it deals with a problem that concerns the whole society and is superhuman in a way. This mega research is nothing but an introduction to the problem, inviting society to react positively and actively to a problem that threatens to destroy the culture of our country.

If I say, that there is nothing left to discuss about parental rapes outside this book; it shall be the biggest joke of the century and for the one to come. But this book might end parental rape. Because what's needed really to combat rape is conscience enough for a renaissance. And the book has words enough to stir your conscience.

Preface

The book also tends to change culture, so that more meaning to the line MERA BHARAT MAHAN can be added.

With all the benefits the research has given me in the form of an author of a research on a new subject, it has shaken me to the core. The tragedy behind this book is immense and I still wish that the house of Jeet Singh wouldn't have existed or a society like ours would have barred the entry of animals in its human world.

With all the black the book exposes, it is not by any means a negative work. Rather it is a book that exposes the blackest black to increase the meaning of the whitest white. I hope and I have a feeling that a lot of positive good shall be served through this book.

I have in the book more than once commented on the punishments metted out to the culprits, with questions on the viability of these punishments. But never should I be understood to insult the court.

Nobody esteems or understands the importance of courts more than I do. However, our constitution gives freedom of speech that also extends to the law. Moreover, my discussions on substitutions to existing punishment is a discussion on possibility and not something which I begin with the words that 'It should in all respects be done'. I can only say that the esteemed judges shall also appreciate my work as a praiseworthy effort of a sincere Indian.

In a country, where Hindus alone worship 33 crores Gods and Goddesses happening of a parental rape is a catastrophe, Our Sanskrit shlokas have echoed with lines like-Janani Janmbhoomhishcha.... (the earth is our mother); Yatra Naryastu Poojyante Ramante Tatra Devatah, Yatreytasto Na Poojyante Sarvastrafalah Kriya (where women are prayed, stay Gods, where they are not is the failure of every fruit of life). Why then, is the mother of the whole world being raped as a daughter?

Isn't it tragic that daughters are raped where Maa Kali is worshipped as a goddess mother...?

116, Defence Enclave **MANISH SHARMA**
Vikas Marg,
Delhi-92

ACKNOWLEDGEMENTS

As integral parts of the book, Dr. Anandi Lal (Psychiatrists), Dr. Promilla Kapur (Psychologist), Dr. L.K. Bhutani (Sexologist), Dr. M.Z. Khan (Sociologist), Mrs. Yamin Hazarika (D.C.P. and Ex-Chief of Women Cell, Delhi) and Mrs. Jayanti Patnaik, (Chairperson, National Commission for Women), for giving exclusive interviews to me, enabling me to form many important parts of the book and guiding me the right direction with their eminence and experience.

Mr. Bhati, Registrar of Indian Law Institute and Prof. Mr. Ahmed Sidiqqui, Dean, Faculty of Law, Jamia Milia Islamia, for being instrumental in getting me the permission to go to the ILI Library, where I researched for Indian Penal Code on rape and USSR rape law and part of British law on rape.

The Staff of ILI Library.

Ms. XYZ, whom I met in ILI Library, a law student, who guided me on certain things.

Mr. Chen Shuang, 3rd Secretary, Embassy of China, for allowing me to visit Chinese Cultural Centre Library at Chankyapuri, that enabled me to get the Chinese Law on rape.

The outstanding 'British Council Library' and 'American Centre Library' where I researched for these countries' laws and did the complete research for Section V of Part 13.

Mr. Pema L. Dorji, Secretary, Embassy of Bhutan, for sending me a copy of Bhutan's Law on rape.

Dr. Mehndi, Incharge of Press Affairs, Embassy of Iran, for allowing me to visit Iran Culture House Library.

Mr. Balali, Librarian of the Iran Culture House Library.

Mr. M. G. Ghadiri, Embassy of Iran, for sending me copies of Iranian women magazine - Mahjubah and published papers written by authoritative Islamic scholars on Islam and Women, enabling me to write the paper entitled 'Islam and Women', (Part 13, Section III, Group A).

Mr. M. A. Ghazi for giving me the outline of Islamic Law on rape.

Mr. Evangelos Theophilou, Attache, Embassy for Greece, for informing me about Greek Criminal law against rape.,

Mr. Arvind, Secretary, Embassy of Ethiopia, for informing me that Ethiopia as no law on rape, leading to a sharp contrast point for part 13.

Mr. Cheleseyeb, Information Secretary;

Mr. Nazarkin, Chief Librarian, Cultural Faculty Library;

Mr. Olef Bondar, Information Secretary; for information on Russian symbolics, valid after 1991 revolution in Russia.

I would like to thank Mrs. Vaijayanti Tonpe, Editor, Children's World who gave me my first break in writing by publishing my poem, "What Should I become", in the July 1992 issue. Her encouragement by introducing me in the profession and by further maturing my talent through successive publications of my MSS, steered me through all odds, and was a guiding force towards this achievement.

My first principal - teacher at Nursery, Mrs. Subash, psychologically inculcated my interest in studies and broke my submissiveness and shyness, alongwith Ms. Minu, my kindergarten teacher. Meaningless as they might be to others, these teachers are instrumental for laying my foundation in my kid days in the right manner.

My thanks are due to to Mr. S.P.S. Jain and Mr. Navdeep Jain, for typing my MSS.

I am thankful to my parents, my younger brother Mohit, my grandfather, and all my relatives, friends, near and dear one especially my

Acknowledgements

uncle Mr. K. N. Bhargava, Controller of Finance, Jamia Milia, for pushing me ahead with the eternal force of encouragement.

My last but surely not the least, thanks are due to the editorial staff my publishers, who found the book worthy for publication and the publisher who converted their assent and wish to reality. My publishers and editors enabled my work to reach the readers, thus fulfilling the elementary purpose of this vast study.

CONTENTS

Preface vii
Acknowledgements xv

Part One : The World of Parental Rapes : Where Humans do not Exist 1-20

Jeet Singh Rape Case 1
Parminder Kaur alias Deepa rape case 10
Gandhi Nagar (East Delhi) rape case 12
Self Proclaimed God, Ram Avtar Shastri Case 12
Subrata Rai rape case 12
Keshav Chand rape case 12
Home Ministry's Under Secretary rape case 12
Analysis on father's blackmailing 12
Comments of Mrs. Jayanti Patnaik, NCW Chairperson 14
1982 minor rape case : apathy in the jurisprudence 15
High Court case involving reduction of sentence on controversial grounds 16
People's comments during the opinion Poll Survey 17
The Special Committee question 18
Men Hatred of Victims : An introductory survey 19
Birth of Phoolan Devis 19
Conclusion 20

Part Two : In Search of a Culprit 21-28

Extensive analytical discussion on how to deal with a culprit, most especially in the rape perspective.
Introduction 23

What I am searching?	24
Reopening of Jeet Singh Case	24
Focus on culprit's crime-making of a true chargesheet	25
The subconscious antithetical establishment	26
The search for the culprit in the man; The right criminological philosophy	26
Why can't culprits be sympathized	27

Part Three : The Psychiatric View — 29-36

Exclusive interview with Dr. Anandi Lal to investigate the medical aspects of the problem and traumas of the victims. An analysis of the psychiatric part of the analysis.

The psychiatric definition of rape	31
Psycho impacts on the victims	31
Madness : A possibility in rape	32
Fits and Rape	32
Case Study : From a psychiatrist's file	32
Raped Daughters, Parents' reactions	33
Reactions of an incestually raped girl	33
Suicide : A possible consequence of Rape	34
Punishment to a culprit : A psychiatrist's opinion	34
Psychiatrist's reaction to the High Court case (Part One)	35
Medicinal Brain's consultation in law making	35
Men Rapes	35
Importance of highlighting victim's traumas	36

Part Four : The Psychological View — 37-56

Based on an exclusive interview with Dr. Promilla Kapur, World renowned psychologist; followed by the writer's analysis.

Contents xxi

The Three Part Break Up

Introduction	39
Interview	40
Writer's analysis	47

Subjective Break Up

Sexual evaluation of the female progeny	40, 47
Rape of a Daughter-Reasons	41, 49
Exemption of a father's punishment	42
Punishment structure	42, 51
Psycho Treatment	42
Sexual Perversion	42, 53
Damage to a raped daughter's psycho structure	43
Hatred of Sex	44, 53
When the culprit-father returns	44
Question of a daughter's consent to sexual relationship with the father : Pro View	45
Question of a daughter's consent : Anti View	55
Birth of a child from a raped daughter's womb–The relationship chaos	45, 5
Reactions of a wife to her culprit husband	46, 54
Reasons, yearning and temptation : The Order and The Chaos	47, 55

Part Five : The Police View 57-68

Exclusive interview with Ms. Yamin Hazarika, D.C.P. and Ex-chief of Women Cell Delhi. Investigation of the reaction of Police to the case of rape. A look into the legal reactions to rapes and parental rapes.

Reaction of police to rape and women exploitation	59
Criminological difference in other women crimes and rape	59
Curb of Police, Increase of Rape : The Great Paradox	59
Mental Condition of Victims : A Police View	60
Stigma and Rape	60

Parental Rape–From a Police Officer's eye 61
Punishment structure 62
Execution Question 63
Unnecessary Paranoia 63
Suspicion and Belief 63
Pseudo Family Bond 64
Father's Bail, Victim's Security and Police Protection 65
General Public's awareness and concern 65
Self Protection of females 66
Rape : Suggestions from an officer 66
Stigma : The Writer's Standpoint 66
Crime against Women in Delhi : Statistical Chart 68

Part Six : The Sociological View   69-89

Based on an exclusive interview with Prof. (Dr.) M.Z. Khan, eminent sociological writer and H.O.D., Social Work, JMI, followed by the writer's analysis. An investigation into the sociological implications of rape alongwith an understanding of the imbroglio and a search for a solution, from a sociological microscope.

Introduction 71
The Morality Issue 73
The Execution Debate 75
Strengthening the Family Stride 83
Sex permissiveness and Rape 86
Has the father-daughter relationship broken apart 87
Superstitions and Rape 88
Social Implications of Rape 88
Conclusion 89

Part Seven : The Sexological View   91-108

Based on an exclusive interview with Dr. L.K. Bhutani, Prof. and Head of the

Department of Dermatology and Venerology, All India Institute of Medical Sciences. An investigation in depth into the complete human sexual behaviourism and the study of human psyche through sex. Alongwith extensive analysis by the writer.

Introduction	93
Why aren't men raped?	94
The sexological difference between spouse and father-daughter sexuality	96
The man in the cave : An idea to estimate the power of sex	97
Does rape occur in animals?	98
Terrifying extension of parental rape : Can a wife be raped by her husband?	100
Man's sexual fantasy	102
The infant death	106
The glimmer of hope	107

Part Eight : The Opinion Poll 109-113

Public opinion survey on the punishment that should be offered to culprits.

Poll introduction, explanation of survey conducting and abbreviations	111
Category-I : Students	112
Category-II : Men Professionals	112
Category-III : Women Professionals	113
Category-IV : Housewives	113
Category-V : All categories	113

Part Nine : Dissecting the Poll 115-124

A complete discussion of the parental rape issue on the basis of what the poll delivers.

Execution : The Indian Paradox	117
The Pregnancy Theory	117

Ramayana : The cultural guiding light and immediate effect	118
Inharmony in law and public opinion : A big democratic question	119
Reformatory Measures : As a joke	119
Prevention of Rape	120
Slums : The sex furnace	120
Can reformatory measures (prevention) prevent parental rapes?	121
The delicate issue of parental incest awareness	122
Custodial Rape : Democracy and Faith in custody	123
Ordinary Rape : The tragic immunization	124

Part Ten : After Thought : Do Culprits Need to Be Thought About   125-136

The question of hypocritic culprits and related issues.

The abnormality of a sex culprit	127
Frustration : 'Should' it lead to rape.....?	128
Rape as a punishment (? !)	129
Execution : The Positive Clause	130
– Open execution	131
– Ordinary execution	131
Is execution a charity?	131
Execution : The Negative Clause	133
The Social Change : An effective outlet	133
Parental Rape : Insufficient Law, study needed	135
When will Supreme Court Grant the Fundamental Right to live?	136

Part Eleven : The Homosexual Element   137-143

Sex : The rule of nature and its breaking	139
Homosexual mate : The difficulty	140
Sex slaves and homosexual satisfaction	140
Child as a perpetual, safe and trusted slave	140
Homosexual incestual abuse : A reality	140

Contents

The Taboos of cultural India : Paradoxical Bridge	140
- Family Issue	141
- Homosexuality and Rape	141
Effects of homosexual parental abuse : The much deeper bruise	142
Conclusion	143

Part Twelve : Critical Issues   145-163

A complete programme by the writer to help in the implementation of the three system approach to eradicate the menace of rape- punishment, prevention and victim counselling and treatment in the post rape situation.

THE PUNISHMENT CONSENSUS   147-148

The right punishment for a culprit on the basis of the extensive study on the father related incest.

THE VICTIM'S DEFENCE   148-155

The Trauma File-   148

    Complete scan of the traumas imparted to victim. On the basis of it, need stressed for a proper counselling to the victim to save her from the post stress that takes many forms of far reaching negative effects on the individual, society and cultural ethos.

The 17 point programme   153

    Presentation of a 17 point programme for victim that must be established by law, alongwith the proper punishment to the culprit, so that this programme prevents the victim from her inner stress caused by the psychological chaos as a counter reaction to her sexual violation, and also the outer stress of social stigma, both contributing to a breakdown of all the faculties, structures and systems of her body.

  . A charter of points and amendments suggested for inclusion in the country's penal code on rape.

THE PREVENTION CLAUSE — 155-163

Introduction — 155

Endurance and Indifference–The distinction between fighting and Kneeling — 155

The First Clause : Sex Education — 157

- Need for Education on Sex — 157
- The suffocated and contracted Indian sex behaviourism — 157
- The 16 point benefit charter — 158
- The 11 point implementation charter — 160
- The Govt. and NGO fund and assistance — 161

The Second Clause : Moral Education — 161

Need and Importance to Society and Individual

The Third Clause : Govt. Intervention — 162

- Introduction — 162
- 5 Point proposal — 162

The Fourth Clause : NGO Intervention — 163

NGO's importance and separate and combined participation in an effective process on rape eradication.

Summing Up — 163

Part Thirteen : The International Perspective — 165-294

A complete study of rape through an international scan on the crime. Punishment structure of India and other countries alongwith proper introductions of each and critical survey of each nation's law. Discussion on common issues and discussion of cases from the international files of crime.

SECTION-I : INTRODUCTION — 167-169

How did law emerge? — 167
Need of Law — 168

Contents   *xxvii*

Need for international studies regarding criminological issues	168
The complete framework of Part 13	169
SECTION-II : INDIA	**170-181**
The Introduction File	**170**
Profile	170
The History and Times of India	171
Looking Back Looking Beyond	173
The Law File	**174**
A Critical Survey	**179**
Poll explanation	179
Parental rape	180
The flexibility of Indian Law	180
Marital Rape	181
Sufficiency of penetration in conviction	181
Custodial rape–Trying to fill a vacuum	181
SECTION-III : RAPE LAWS ACROSS THE GLOBE	**182-279**
A. The Islamic Nations	**182-211**
Group Introduction	182
Women and Islam	182-190
- Prologue	182
- The Essay	183-190
Women–A general survey	183
The woman–man differences	185
(Physiological, Anatomic,	185
Sexual, Maternal)	186
Islam–The Man/Women equality	186
Islam–The female/male differences	188
Religion Accusation	190
Conclusion	190
The Divine Islamic standpoint on Father-Daughter Sexuality	190-193

Introduction	190
(God, Man and Ethics,	190
Quran and Sexuality)	191
Mahram Table-I (Males)	192
Mahram Table-II (Females)	193
The inference from Mahram and Quran	193
IRAN	**193-204**
The Introduction File	193
Profile	193
The History and Times of Iran	195
Looking Back	
Looking Beyond	197
The Feminine Glass	197
(Women in Iranian Constitution, Women and Wakalah, Statistics of success)	197-199
The Law File	**201**
Islam as the Iranian Law Vehicle	201
The peculiar rape law of Islam	202
Rape Law	
(Mahram, Illicit Sex, Rapes;	202
International Terminology)	203
A Critical Survey	**204**
Amendment needed and conclusion	
PAKISTAN	**204-211**
The Introduction File	204
Profile	204
The History and Times of Pakistan	205
Looking Back	
Looking Beyond	207
The Law File	**210**
A Critical Survey	**210**
The ugly Distortions : Reasons and Implications.	
B. THE CONTINENTAL CULTURES	**211-218**
Group Introduction	211

Contents

GREECE	211-218
The Introduction File	211
Profile	211
The History and Times of Greece	213
Looking Back Looking Beyond	214
The Law File	217
A Critical Survey	218
The Execution Paradox	218
The Paradoxical phrase : "forcible extramarital coition"	218
C. SOMERSAULT REGIMES	219-229
Group Introduction	219
RUSSIA	219-229
The Introduction File	219
Profile	219
The History and Times of Russia	221
Looking Back Looking Beyond	224
The Law File	226
A Critical Survey	228
The right understanding of the inferior human being treatment and social inequality issue	228
Execution : A compliment	229
D. SUPERPOWERS AND DEVELOPED REGIMES OF THE WEST	229-253
Group Introduction	229
USE	230-244
The Introduction File	230
Profile	230
The History and Times of the States	231
Looking Back Looking Beyond	234

The Law File	237
Rape in USA	237
Sex offences excluded from the rape category	237
(Indecent Exposure, Indecent Assault, Corruption of a minor and Prostitution)	
The America Jurisprudence on Sexual Assault	238
23. Mere words and mere preparation distinguished	238
24. Sexual Assault	239
25. Of man against woman	239
26. Against unchaste woman	240
27. Of man against man	240
The United States Code, Chap. 99 on rape	241
A Critical Survey	243
Statutory and Forcible rape	243
Victim counselling and attention	243
Sexual assault; Placing assault in the fluid of definition	243
Unchaste women and rape	244
GREAT BRITAIN	244-253
The Introduction File	244
Profile	244
The History and Times of United Kingdom	245
Looking Back	
Looking Beyond	248
The Law File	250
Rape	250
Incestual Rape	252
A Critical Survey	253
Incestual Rape :	
(a) The Pro's and Con's of High Authority handling	253
(b) The Punishment Paradox	253
(c) Why is incest by consent a crime?	253

E. SOCIO-COMMUNIST REGIMES	254-261
Group Introduction	254
CHINA	254-261
The Introduction File	254
Profile	254
The History and Times of China	255
Looking Back Looking Beyond	257
The Law File	258
Special Meanings for Terms and Special Terms in Chinese Jurisprudence	258
Fixed Term Imprisonment	258
Death Penalty	259
Rape : The Chinese Jurisprudence	260
A Critical Survey	261
Rape leading to death and rape-murder : The Chinese Achievement	261
Reform and Reduction Clause	261
F. ROYAL REGIMES	261-271
Group Introduction	261
BHUTAN	262-271
The Introduction File	262
Profile	262
The History and Times of United Kingdom	263
Bhutan's Ballot of Existence	263
Looking Back Looking Beyond	264
The Law File	265
Special Bhutanese Terms	265
Rape Act, enacted by Bhutan National Assembly	265
(Definition, Rape, Gang Rape, Raping a married person, Gang Rape of a married person, Raping a minor, Gang Rape of a minor, Injury, Rape and Murder, Gang	

Rape and Murder, Reporting, Requirement of Proof, False Accusation)	265-269
A Critical Survey	269
Bhutan's dual law	269
Money as a punishment : The uniqueness with a foresight	270
Culprit and Medical Bill Payment	270
Rape-Death and Rape-Murder	271
False accusation : The Right Approach	271
G. AFRICAN REGIMES	271-277
Group Introduction	271
ETHIOPIA	273-277
The Introduction File	273
Profile	273
The History and Times of Ethiopia	274
Looking Back Looking Beyond	275
The Law File	277
A Critical Survey	277
The International Synthesis	278
SECTION-IV : DEVELOPMENT OF THE CRITICAL LAW THOUGHT	279-286
Discussion of important comparative issues.	
Outline	279
1. Marital Rape	279
The Comparative Discussion	281
Suggestions to India	281
2. Execution	281
The Comparative Discussion	282
Suggestion to India	282
3. Incestual Crimes	282
The Comparative Discussion	283
Suggestion to India	283

4. Man Rapes	283
The Comparative Discussion	284
Suggestions to India	284
5. Homosexuality : The Pro and Contra View	285
The Comparative Discussion	286
Suggestion to India	286

SECTION-V : THE INTERNATIONAL CASE BOOK OF RAPE 286-294

1. Execution and Rape (From USA Jurisprudence)	286-289
Case Facts	286
The Case	287
The Comments Conglomerate	288
Naked Questions	289
2. Culprit and his prior Romance Relationship with the victim (From USA Jurisprudence)	290-292
Case Facts	290
The Case	290
The Comments Conglomerate	290
Universal suggestions	291
3. Male Consent Issue in Sexual Relationships (From U.K. Jurisprudence)	292-294
Case Facts	292
The Case	292
The Comments Conglomerate	292
Dressed up India	294

Part Fourteen : When I'll Become a Father   295-299

Appendix   301-307

The black hole of death   303
    Wrong Philosophies and the dangers   303
    Naturalism   303
    Predestination   305

Hobbes and Mandeville Schools of thought : Global dangers in ethical perspective	306
Utopia : Why can't this divine dream be realised	307
Bibliography	309
Index	313

Part One

THE WORLD OF PARENTAL RAPES :
WHERE HUMANS DO NOT EXIST

THE WORLD OF PARENTAL RAPES : WHERE HUMANS DO NOT EXIST

The Madhuban Road in East Delhi leads to a Suburban area called 'Phatak'. In this area runs a railway line and the crossing has given the place its name. The railway line runs a little above the land level, downwards being a small stretch of dirty water. At the very end where the water has collected is a house whose dirty environs match the black water outside. This place and this house has suddenly become the talk of the town. Because this house stands testimony to the fact that the civilization is transcending towards the doom. This is the house of Jeet Singh Chauhan, arrested for raping his two minor daughters.

The dusty caravan of civilization and the wheel of time stand testimony to the reality that what God gave as blessing, man turned to tears. The woman's power to give birth has for centuries, given her tears, distress and banishment. Just because the woman bears and man begets, the woman is supposed to protect her chastity. If rape breaks this chastity, the man still moves with his head high, while the woman has to choose the darkest, corner to weep. If it was necessary for society to run with one sex domination, it should have been the woman who would have ruled. After all civilization exists because woman makes it to exist.

Four five year old kids are raped, even infants are raped. But this has become an 'everyday' news to us. It shocks us, even makes it difficult to sip the morning tea but when something becomes an everyday activity, it tends to immune us. And it has succeeded to do so with the majority of our society.

From an infant to an adult, the girl is not safe anymore. There are people to rape her even when she doesn't know how to write the alphabet.

But, earlier the girl felt secured within the four walls of her house. When hundreds of eyes watch her critically and hundreds of hands yearn to touch her, the girl comes to the house, locks the door and feels relieved and safe. She feels only her house is a human world, rest seems to be animals moving around. But what can she do when she sees her real father folding his heavy hands around her and raping her ....? Does it seem an exaggeration to you? You would not say that if you learn the history of the daughters of Jeet Singh Chauhan.

The story of Chauhan's molestation of his daughter might only be the second or third of its kind but it has at last, broken the staunch faith, that a father-daughter relationship is a relation that can't be broken by rape and molestation. There now exists only brother-sister relationship which has not been shattered by rape, but when those who share in giving birth to a girl, shatter her existence, it only remains to be seen how much time civilization would take to decline, to give contributions of real brother rape cases to the newspaper headlines.

Chauhan's house is at the end of Ganesh Nagar-II. The story of his devilish act that has shocked thousands of feminists and women was told with great concern by Om Prakash Parashar, an elderly Sanskrit teacher in Govt. Model School No. 2 at Shakarpur, who lives in Ganesh Nagar and also owns a shop here. He is the Chairman of the area society called "Manav Kalyan Samiti". He moved to this area in 1974. "All the houses of this area were numbered by me", he says with a smile. His house is situated at a corner that has been named "Parashar Chowk". He knows the Chauhan family, since they arrived.

The story that has reached the public is very distorted, broken and at many points unreal. Parashar and the neighbours told the real story that is extremely shocking and unbelievable.

About seven years ago, Jeet Singh knocked at Parashar's house at five 'O' clock in the morning saying that he had just broughtout his wife back from the village and she died. He needs four hundred rupees. Parashar had only three hundred at the moment, which he willingly gave to Jeet Singh, sharing his emotional concern.

After some time Parashar went to Chauhan's house and saw that his wife had indeed died. But something in the wife's appearance struck him. The woman's hair were oiled and combed, she had a bindi on her forehead, she was bathed and wearing clean and "Pressed clothes". 'How could anyone die wearing so neat a dress and in so neat an appearance, especially when she had just come back from village'?, struck Parashar again and again. He came back home and told the whole incident to his wife. His wife went immediately into the house and the same thing struck her too. She investigated the whole body but couldn't find any marks suggesting murder. But she still couldn't understand the clean appearance. Even the bindi was at its right place and she was looking like a bride ready for marriage. Just then the police arrived. They also started investigating the whole body. At this Parashar's wife said that when the woman is dead, what can be obtained by searching her body like that. The police replied by saying that because they had received a phone call that she has been murdered they would do everything to satisfy them. The police, in the end, registered a natural death. But the whole neighbourhood believes that Chauhan's wife was killed by him because he had started sexually assaulting his daughter when his wife was alive to which she objected and therefore met her end.

Chauhan's eldest daughter committed suicide by consuming poison in 1989. But the people have not wholly believed that it was suicide. Some of them believe that Chauhan had forced her to take poison. Parashar says that a rumour that was in the air many days after the eldest daughter's death was that she had seen her mother's murder in front of her eyes. And because she objected to her molestation and her mother's murder, she was forced to take poison and take a leave from this world.

Chauhan remarried 2-3 years back. His second wife was from some eastern province and couldn't understand the Hindi language well. But she was simple and nice in nature. The first few months of the marriage passed very smoothly but then strains in the marriage started coming to the surface. Chauhan started disbelieving his wife. He often scolded her and tried to dominate her in every respect. Once, the woman came to Parashar's Shop to buy something. After 2 minutes Chauhan also came there to see whether his wife and indeed gone for shopping. At this point, Parashar paused and smiled, saying that Chauhan was himself a characterless, valueless person but still could suspect an innocent woman!

But then suddenly, two-three months back, the second wife also disappeared. She ran away somewhere and has since then not been seen.

The younger sister had been molested for the past two years. Obviously Chauhan could not molest his daughter always keeping it a secret from his second wife. She at last came to know about it and indignated at such shameless behaviour, left the scene.

The younger sister resisted the repeated attacks on her virginity for a very long time. She at last told her elder brother about it. The elder brother and his cousins locked the father in the room beating him and warning him not to repeat such heinous acts. Even the girl explained to her father not to sexually harass her, stressing the piety of their relationship, but nothing could deter Chauhan from satisfying his yearning through his daughter. At last, when the girl could not resist it anymore, she went to the Shakarpur Police Station on 24th Feb. at 9.30 p. m. and reported the whole affair. The Police arrested Jeet Singh Chauhan. But there is also one more reason for the girl going to the Police Station asking them to arrest her father. The youngest daughter who is twelve years old, suddenly realised that her sister was seventeen and very soon might be married off. Then her 'turn' would come. She could look for no means to escape the nearing trauma. So she encouraged her sister to go to the police.

Jeet Singh Chauhan has not ben released on bail because of a very simple reason. Nobody is willing to give the money. The relatives are relieved to see him behind the bars and so are the neighbours. Parashar, in his capacity as Chairman has asked nobody to give money for Chauhan's bail because 'Chauhan has broken all rules of morality and conduct' and doesn't deserve such a help from his neighbours. There is also one more reason. "The neighbours are, in their heart of hearts very furious with Chauhan", Parashar told me "if he is released now and comes here, the people would most possibly pelt stones at him. They might even stone him to death. It's better that he doesn't come now".

Jeet Singh Chauhan has been from the beginning a man of no morals and virtues. He earlier used to work in a petrol pump at Ashram from where he was dismissed for his wrong behaviour with women. His house is full of tenants and many a times his behaviour with his tenants' wives or their female relatives had also been very objectionable.

Chauhan is also a man to be feared. He kept any tenant in his house even without bothering about his credentials. Even thieves have stayed in his house. But no one could leave his house without giving him the full rent. He even fought with his tenants many a times, inviting police to his door.

Parashar calls Chauhan a 'demon'. "Is there anything human about him"?, he asks with great concern, "He doesn't bathe for days on end. He has molested his daughters. He is terrifying to people. He just has the shape of man, his being is that of an animal".

"Even if the girl would have come to us, for help, instead of going to the Police", Parashar says, "I would have taken some men from my Samiti and gone with her to the Police Station. I could have gone to the highest authority for justice". He is ready to help the girl in any way he can. He even proposes to look for a good match for the girls and marry her off before her father is released to save her from further trauma. "I am ready to work for the girl with my body, spirit and soul", he adds with a sense of duty. Being one of the oldest residents, the chairman of the society and an active member in the working and development of the area, he takes the whole neighbourhood as his children and his concern is that of a father. He had boycotted Chauhan a long time back totally and so will the others, he says, once Chauhan returns back. At the same time, he regrets that the society being a mixed union of people, there will be people of Chauhan's mentality who even if they are few shall mix with him and a total boycott is thus impossible.

Chauhan has many tenants living with him. One of them a young man, not more than twenty, was a class fellow of his elder son in school. He now operates a Red Line No. 320 running on the Shahdara-Kendriaya Terminal Route. When I questioned him how he felt about the whole affair and what were his feelings towards the father and daughter, his answers were hesitating and meant to shield Chauhan, mainly out of his fear. Chauhan who has been described as a terrifying, characterless man and whose acts have made these acquisitions facts about his personality was again and again described as a "Nice Person" by him, "who talked to him pleasantly". When asked whether he would have gone to the Police had he known about the affair, he immediately replied, "Yeh Uska Apna Mamla Hai. Hum Beech Mein Kyon Paden? (It is his affair, why should I meddle in between?). When my conversation with this bus driver was going on, one of Chauhan's relatives who had just come that day and was sitting nearby said - "who knows whether all this is truth?" I replied saying that how could he suspect that a daughter could make such an allegation against his father (if Chauhan can be defined one). He immediately fluttered– "Agar Ladki Jhoot Nahin Bolegi, To Baap Bhi Aisa Kyon Karega?" (If the girl wouldn't say a lie, why would the father do such a thing to her?).

Throughout the conversation with the bus driver and Chauhan's relatives one realises a common factor. Both are trying to shield Jeet Singh Chauhan. They can suspect the truth in the poor girl's allegations but they cannot spare a moment to suspect Jeet Singh, when all his past stands as an evidence against him. This shielding factor out of ego, fear or male domination has made rape a shameful act for the victim rather than the culprit. Where culprits are sided with and victims criticized and suspected, what else can be hoped for. Further this bus driver and other people (excluding Mr. Parashar as a notable exception) said that they wouldn't go to the police themselves because "it was not their affair". In these menial suburbs, people are interested to know in detail about the in's and out's of other's affairs but when it comes to saving someone out of her trauma, in a flash they can reply - "It's not our affair". It's extremely disgusting. This stigma, this fear makes things so different. May be if people would have objected, actively and not passively, the father would have been arrested sooner. And who knows even her elder sister would have been prevented from taking (or compelled to take) poison. What is the use of being furious enough to pelt stones now when two innocent lives have been shattered but dreaming about such things in such a society would be living in a fool's paradise.

Just a few houses away from Chauhan's house stands Baptist Convent School. A unique blending indeed. The school teaching moral virtues and code of right individual conduct and the best way to lead life and in the neighbourhood a house that stand as a testimony to the most heinous crime that can be committed. What a combination of virtue and vice. Strange indeed.

The Principle of the school Mrs. Amrita Singh feels that J.P. Chauhan didn't know the real cause of living and so could go to such heinous extent.

"Why did it have to happen in our locality only"?, she says with great concern, "I am shocked to the core. Nobody knows were we are leading to. Today its father raping a daughter, tomorrow it shall be brother raping sisters. Where shall be poor girl go?" And her eyes moisten for a moment.

"Nobody tells the students about it", she tells me, "but still they have come to know about it. The girls are very scared. They feel afraid of everybody-strangers, elders, friends and.....", she adds with great difficulty, "even father." She feels that such incidents can have an extreme adverse effect, especially on the immature minds of young students.

When I asked her if the girl would have been young enough and would have come for admission in the school after this incident, would she have been granted entry into the premises; she replied at once "Why not? Of Course. She is not guilty. She was forced into loosing her virginity. She has all rights to study. I will welcome her as my daughter". Her open mindedness and maternal love even makes her feel that no parents would have objected if the girl would have been admitted in the school.

While people like Chauhan's relatives and tenants with their egos, fears and stigmas indignate you, people like Mrs. Amrita Singh and Mr. Om Parkash Parashar fill you with great happiness. At least, the girl has someone in society to look forward to emotional support. What if they are exceptions. Like the eminent film writer Salim said "A candle kept on a mountain shall give little light but light that can be seen from very far away". Such active supports might be very less but to the girls they shall seem like a million candles of warmth that shall enable her to travel through the piercing cold of reality.

I tried many times to meet the girls but failed. She kept on avoiding me. Nobody has seen her in the neighbourhood since that incident. Her family members say that she goes early in the morning and comes late in the night. It was of course disappointing for a journalist not being able to meet the main victim of his case study, but the girl's absence and her deliberate avoiding is of course understandable. To a woman, rape is the most shameful thing. And for the girls who is the victim in a rape that has been done by her father, the trauma and shame is extremely large. The feeling that she has suffered sexual molestation for two years and the whole affair has become public will be a fact that shall compel her to refrain from public absence as much as is possible. As Mr. Parashar, says, "She has become the talk of town. People talk about her. Whenever, anyone who knows her will see her, he shall point out at the girls and say–She is the same girl. How can the girls live with such defamed public attention. She can't walk with her head high. She can't look into anybody's eyes. Is there any option left for her but to hide?". Very true indeed.

But there's another problem that the girl is facing. She stands in the danger of being killed. "Is the daughter safe once the father is released?" Mrs. Singh asks, "the girls shall be killed by somebody, someday", she says with an air of surety and grave concern. "The man who can't think about moral values of being a father, who is out of control while staying at home, can do anything". And indeed that is very true. Chauhan can't be expected to be ashamed of what he has done. His indignation would of course be with the girl and might kill her for sending him to jail. Though

Parashar doesn't feel so, claiming that even if Chauhan is kept for three years in jail, the girl shall be married off; might fill us with some hope but the danger doesn't end.

And what has the police done, really? Just because the father is in Jail, the police think they have done their job. Infact, the police's indifference to the whole affair can be cited from the fact that when I asked the Shakarpur Police authorities about the address of the girl, I was given the wrong one. When I ringed again, after great search could the police furnish me with the right address. When the police forgot the incident after some days, their seriousness can't even be imagined. Indeed, the girls is in grave danger but who shall do anything?

The whole family of Chauhan is shattered and broken. What can one really say about Chauhan. His ancestors were kings like Prithviraj Chauhan who fought battles to victory. And he could not even fight his yearning to get victory enough for retaining one of the most pious relationships in the world. Father in Jail, mother dead, sister hiding and weeping, elder brother negligent and disinterested in family matters, there remains the 12 year old girl and the seven year old brother. Breaking Mr. Parashar's statement to a slightly different tone, any society is a group of families. Every family has the father as its head. But when the father is characterless and victim of yearning and lust, what can be expected of him and his family? "When the head of the family", asks Mr. Parashar, "looks like a human being, but actually is an animal walking on four legs, can you hope anything ...? Indeed, we can't. Chauhan is responsible for his elder daughter's suicide (if ......), Younger's shattered life, family break-down and family disgrace. Suddenly his seven year punishment looks very small. He has indeed committed a crime unforgivable by God or any real justice on earth.

On May 23, 1994, one of the worst cases of physical and sexual torture came to light. Hindustan Times began the report by saying - "At the tender age of 12 Parminder Kaur Alias Deepa, a native of Basti Abdullapur, Ludhiana, has already made a journey to hell".

Deepa was born of an alcoholic, unemployed father and a mentally deranged mother. While a girl seeks protection in her father and cousins, to Deepa they became the agents of Satan who made her life a living personification of hell.

Her father's elder brother's sons started raping Deepa at the age of five. Her father also started having an intercourse with her every night. With a mentally deranged mother who could not understand Deepa's agony and everyone else as her virginity breakers, Deepa could break her sorrow to no one. The poor girl was left all alone to bear the trauma of repeated rapes.

After a few years, Deepa started suffering from epilepsy. She became an unwanted burden for her father. Since his sexual lust with her had been over, he abandoned her at a place called Malerkotla. There two constables saw her and admitted her to the Rajkiya Mahila Uttar Raksha Graha. There her sexual torture ended and physical torture began.

The four employees of the Mahila Raksha Griha - Champa, Sushila, Seema and Sushma gave unexplicable torture to Deepa. All the worst forms of physical torture which must be accompanied by the worst ethical decline of the torturer, were given to her.

One night Deepa was wrongly accused by Champa of stealing a tea packet. She was stripped of clothes and hair, slapped, beaten and tortured with iron rods and burning woods. The women "branded" her all over her back, thighs and private parts. She was then thrown into a nullah.

After coming back to the Women Home, all on her own, after an hour, the four women threatened her to go away or face death. The poor girls had no way left but to leave the place. She was fully naked and could only find a vest to protect her virginity.

While walking in extreme pain, she was seen by rikshaw puller. He brought her an undergarment and got an FIR registered.

When I read this case study in "The Hindustan Times" I was shocked. For a long time, I felt as if all my sense and wisdom had turned numb. I could not react, for all my faculties had been over powered by a terrifying coldness. After all in what society are we living? Are we the sons of Adam who pray Satan? Are we the products of the worst passions forming the world of unethical consciousness, with ethics and morals only a superficial cover?

Sexual intercourse at the age of 5 years leads to highly destructive damage to a girl's sexual, psychological and mental framework. Forced sexual intercourse accompanied with its sense of insult and forced loss of virginity is to the girl like a bomb exploding within, making the whole life of the female a vast chaos. All this when combined with the fact that the girls was raped by 4 people consecutively, three of whom were brothers and the fourth one father, the individual who had beget her, the case becomes one of the worst specimens in the laboratory of crime. To top it all, the girls was already suffering from epilepsy. Her case is a "fact stranger than fiction". If I would have written a story involving a character synonymous with Deepa, you would have termed it a melodrama.

My sympathy with Deepa is very very deep. But deeper is my bewilderment that the homo sapien is capable of such a deep decline.

July 20, 1994 broke the news of yet another rape case where forty year old father raped her 12 year old daughter in Gandhi Nagar Jhuggis in Delhi.

On August 2, 1994, on reading the news, that a Self Proclaimed God Ram Avtar Shastri raped his daughter, one realised how much has the poison of hypocrisy and sexual fantasy eaten the structure of civilization. Is this the definition of God today?

On April 15, 1995, Subrata Rai, Manager of an Iron Foundry at Shakarpur and resident of Preet Vihar was arrested for raping his daughter for the past three years.

The girl had been studying in a boarding school from where she was called back to Delhi by her father. Little did she know that it was for making her his wife. When the girl could bear it no longer and started suffering from abdominal pains, she broke this terrible and humiliating secret to a friend. The girl's school teacher was told of the whole affair. Subrata Rai was arrested by the East Delhi Police.

April recorded two other cases of parental rapes. On 22nd April, a man Keshav Chand was arrested for raping his daughter. On 27 April, Under Secretary in Union Home Ministry Karam Chand Thakur was arrested for sexually abusing his eight year old daughter for a year.

In all these rape cases, one notices the tact of black mailing used by the fathers to rape their daughter. While this pious relationship is destroyed to bits by the parent's sexual abuse, the poor daughter somehow endures her pain to preserve the sanctity of this holy relationship.

Jeet Singh, Deepa's father and Subrata Rai have raped their daughters for years. When the law decides such cases, it should by no means forget, that it is not a single rape but hundreds of rapes imparted to the girl at regular intervals. While Jeet Singh paid no regard that one of his daughter committed suicide, Subrata Rai could not be pitied by her daughter's request that she be not treated as a wife because she is suffering from abdominal pains. If Deepa's father stopped raping her when he discovered her epilepsy, it was only to discard all his duties towards her and abandon her.

Wherever a father rapes his progeny for years together, he is able to do so because he knows that the daughter would not go against him, he being her father. Thus series of rapes accompanied by this blackmail in the name of relationships, is a naked proof of a father's crime. In once case study, which I am compelled to keep a secret, a father threw open her daughter to his friends for oral sex, while he himself 'enjoyed' from her.

The victim's side is a kaleidoscope of innumerable traumatic emotions, making her a surviving and not a living form.

Parental rape is beyond doubt a very traumatic event. One glance at the interview with Dr. Anandi Lal suggests the mental traumas and physical problems including chances of suicide, fits and madness that a patient undergoes in rape cases which of course increases to a very large extent in parental rapes. Here the prime most reason for increase in trauma is the shock that the relation whom the girl looked for protection, raped her. It's indeed the end of her life. After that is only dragged existence. Where breath of the girl only suggests that she has life, otherwise her appearance is that of a lifeless form.

Socially too, parental rapes can have very adverse effects on society. Any rape distorts the right growth of the society's culture. So when parental rape occurs, accompanied by breaking of a father-daughter relationship and peoples' staunch faith in it, the right growth in culture is broken and shaken. A parental rape because of the shock and fear it generates in public in general and girls in particular is socially, extremely disturbing. When a father-daughter relationship, one of the very big social knots is broken with the cause being as large as rape, which no sufferer and those emotionally connected can pass off just as an 'event', the effects are very large. The social danger by parental rape will appear more to the surface if 10-25 more such cases appear. But, of course, we wish for the reverse to happen.

Looking at parental rapes in particular and rapes in general (as, of course, a parental rape cannot be talked of in complete isolation. After all it's nothing but the most tragic division of Rape); the first thing that comes to one's mind is "the National Commission for Women". The commission was constituted on 31st January 1992 and "it works for entire women's issues and concerns as a high powered, autonomous, apex body of women at national level".

The first thing that comes to the mind is that what is the commission doing exactly for combating rape, most especially parental rapes. Jayanti Patnaik, the soft spoken, determined chairperson says that, "the commission is taking rapes, especially child rape very seriously. In the first year of the commission's existence a seminar was held where rape as a problem was discussed. Parental rapes were also discussed in detail. Recommendations of the conference were passed to concerned cells of the Govt. and the committee of experts is still working on the menace of rape".

She agrees that rape as a problem has increased, which she feels is partly due to heavy increase in population and partly because of more consciousness and awareness among public to report such cases to police and the commission.

But, as she herself admits, there are many cases not being reported to the police. The existence of the National Commission for Women is known only to the cream of the society. Majority of the people especially those in the extreme interiors and tribals do not even have the slightest hint of the presence of such a commission. So what is the commission doing to make its existence known to every citizen of the country?

"The first thing", she says, "is that whenever we go to the states we pressurise the CM's to form State Commissions who can look into the local problems very well. We also get acquainted with the Govt. body in the state - CM's and Officials, MGO's ... the entire system to see how Govt. network in state can extend help to the people". The comission, she informs, also does a lot of publicity through the media-press and T.V. ads. The commission as a regular feature meets press people especially on its state visits. For state visits, the commission also circulates a questionnaire. But she adds with a smile that the N.C.W. has teething problems also. The most specific want of the Chairperson is that one page in every newspaper everyday or at least once in week should be devoted to only women problems. In this way, she feels, media shall extend the commission's

The World of Parental Rapes.............. 15

message and share it's concerns. "Because", she confesses, "we can't do everything. By contacting, intervening and pressurizing the Govt. we are trying to get the women justice".

She feels that even though women Crime Control Cells and Women Commission is present, people have the courage to do rapes, even public rapes mainly because of the stigma attached. The general fear that marriage shall not be able to take place, if the girl's rape case becomes public is prevalent among the majority that prevents them from complaining to the police. "So many parents", she says, "tell the girl, 'Ab jo ho gaya, so ho gaya, Chup rah jayo varna shadi nahin hogi (Now what has happened, has happened. Remain quite. Otherwise marriage won't take place) prevents reports coming to us". "But", she agrees, "to an extent it is true also. The women's position in society is such.

She also feels that apathy in the system is also responsible for it. "A lack, an absence of immediate action and care", makes the whole difference, she confesses.

When we talk of punishments for rape cases and the judiciary's decisions regarding these heinous crimes, a lot of controversial decisions come to the surface. The apathy in the judicial system and absence of a hundred percent involvement is evident.

Two cases of minor rapes were told with great concern by Mrs. Jayanti Patnaik.

The first of these is the 1982 rape case in Madhya Pradesh. An M.B.B.S. doctor raped 5 girls which included his own niece. When he raped an 8 year old, the girl's father overheard what they were discussing. He mustered all his courage and went to the Sessions Court. He never got justice. He then went to the High Court. The High Court fined 3,000/- rupees and said that, *'the character of the doctor was all right'*, because he was a *Govt. Doctor'*, and so he will gain nothing by punishing him. The poor man at last appealed to the Supreme Court. The S.C. fined the man 25,000/- rupees and life imprisonment. By that time, 10 years had elapsed. In April 1992, when the Commission had just come into being, the father wrote to the Commission complaining that the man has not been arrested The N.C.W. immediately intervened leading to the arrest of the culprit.

The apathy in the judicial system is very disturbing to any right tracked mind. The High Court's verdict that the man had a good character when he had raped 6 girls is unbelievably shocking. If this means good character, then what is defined as a bad characteristic in Society?

But perhaps more frustrating is the recent case involving the rape of a four year old kid, brought to the High Court a few months back. In this case the punishment was 'reduced' and the reason given was that because the culprit becomes the victim of it's own lust, there should not be too high a punishment.

It is a totally wrong insight into the problem. If a culprit becomes the victim of its own lust, the most stringent punishment should be given. For murder, dacoitary, loot or any crime a motive might be there. Circumstances and acute need might compel a man to murder or commit burglary. But can any thing in life compel anyone to rape? Can hunger, thirst, panic and fear make one a rapist? Rape, by any one, is done to satisfy his yearning. Morever, rape is not just a "sexual intercourse without consent". Rape means the most horrible punishment given to any victim. Her existence with her self-insult, fear and trauma becomes so shattered that she dies one death everyday. Rape, infact invites the most stringent of punishments. At least no culprit's sentence, in any rape case, in any way, should be reduced.

The law consisting of judiciary and the police; and medical experts and psychiatrists travel two absolutely different paths regarding punishments to culprits in rape cases. A glance at "The Psychiatric View" of the problem and "The Police View", of this menace can suggest to anybody how different the two view points are. So, while the D.C.P. says that, "we can't hang a person for rape", Dr. Anandi Lal feels, "that if one equates the suicidal implication of the patient, even death sentence to the culprit will appear less".

The reason for the different viewpoints is extremely simple. The law is also deeply concerned with the menace. But the judiciary and police with their law books and handcuffs are only able to travel between crime and punishment. They hear a crime, hear evidences, listen to eye-witness quote particular parts from law books and pass a sentence. They however forget that every rape-case requires the reading of a lengthy and complicated book–the heart of the victim. They fail to travel through the traumas of the victim, which psychiatrists do in deep detail. Thus the cold-reasoning of law and warm understanding of a doctor give rise to contrasting decisions. The law mostly goes on the quantity and facts of rape, the psychiatrists and

The World of Parental Rapes..............

experts on quality and depth. The woman who is raped is a 'Victim' to the law and a 'patient' to the doctor. This makes all the difference.

The common gentry's worth and fury is great towards rape culprits. The fury might be passive in nature but definitely is there. As the opinion poll indicates, 21.1% of total voters go for "execution" in ordinary (teenage and above) rape cases while 43.2% go for death penalty in kid and infant rapes while the public fury is maximum in parental rapes with as large as 58.5% going in for execution. In this, 13.5% have even gone for open trial execution.

The public's worth will be understood through the comments by some people, while I took their opinion poll. The poll and its detailed study is included separately in sections 8 and 9 of this analysis.

Samir Khonsla, an employee of the Punjab State Electricity Board; Vishwa Bandhu of Vedic Mission at Nehru Street and Anil Juneja of the Central Reserve Police Force feel that like Pakistan and other Muslim countries, people committing rape especially parental rapes should be killed in front of thousands of people. "The Punishment given to rape culprits should be such that the society sees it and fears to do such a thing", Anil says, "if a person is locked up in Tihar Jail, who shall know about it. Only those few who read papers. Moreover effect and terror for wrong doing is created only in open trials." Anil doesn't express faith in imprisonment in rape cases. He feels a person who rapes, commits a heinous crime. He comes out to do the same thing. According to him, if rape punishments are to be made more stringent, execution is the only solution. Lengthening of imprisonment is no solution. "If imprisonment was any solution, a culprit can learn in 7 years also. What shall we gain by increasing three or five years of his punishment?"

Some are even more severe. Poorna an M.A. student in the Delhi School of Social Work and J. Singh, an employee of DU both feel that rape culprits should be 'castrated'.

Rajneesh, a B. Com. student of K.M.C. feels that relaxation of punishments for minor culprits should not be there.

Subash Gitare, a journalist, who runs a magazine "Lok Dasta", feels that the culprit in parental rapes should be isolated, so that he realises that he has done something wrong. A Botany Hons, student of Hindu, Vishal, also goes for life imprisonment in parental rapes citing the same reason. Neelam Shukrapani, an employee of the Delhi School of Social Work feels that in parental rapes, the Victim should be given the right to divorce her parents as children do in Western Countries.

Rajesh Narang a B. Com. Final year student (Correspondence) feels that in parental rapes, option should be given to the daughter to decide the punishment.

However, there are some who feel that punishment is no solution to the problem. Nihar Ranjan Senapati, an Engineer in Ahuja Engg. at Faridabad feels that punishments are no solution to rape cases. Reformatory measures should be taken to control rape as a menace and cure rape culprits. He goes for sex education and awareness about rape as a big crime. He says that children of today are to become fathers tomorrow. If they are told today about the menace of rape and a hatred for this heinous crime inculcated in their mind, why would they rape their daughters when they become fathers tomorrow? Two postgraduate students feel that while dealing with rape culprits, just punishments studying the total sociological and psychological factors of the problem should be given. However, the persons suggesting reformatory measures are much, much less compared to those who suggest the stringent most punishment (Opinion Poll).

Ram Kumar, an employee in State Bank of India (DU Branch) feels that like T.V. shows family planning ads regularly. Similarity it should show ads on the rape menace as a regular feature. He and Mr. Vishwa Bandhu agree that media has a very large role to play. And, should expose the problem as much as it can. Vishwa Bandhu feels that every rape case should come on front page; even headlines, if possible, leading to shame for the culprit and terror and detestation for common man.

A question now arises–should a committee be set up to look into parental rapes? After all such a problem is new and nowhere does the law make a special provision for dealing with parental rapes. When laws regarding rapes were made, nobody had parental rapes in mind. So how can the same law without amendment deal with parental rapes? Individually, sociologically, psychologically and jurisdictively, parental rapes are miles apart from an ordinary rape, though both might broadly be parts of the same category. As opinion poll clearly reveals, approximately 94% of the people who participated, went for amendment in punishments for rapes and setting of expert committees dealings with such problems. Many of them even felt that punishments for rapes should be decided taking into account the views, knowledge and analytical depth of psychiatrists and medical experts. Infact only 9.3% of the total people voted expressed faith in 10 year punishment for parental rapes, only 16.1% for kid and infant rapes and even in ordinary rape approximately 60% voted for a seven years sentence as not enough. G.S. Josheph, an employee in Centre for Biochemical's research equating rape to murder and Vinod Agarkar's (same institution) proposal to deal through Marshall Law with rapes is indicative of society's growing fury. Polling and deep analysis of rapes, especially parental rapes, suggests review of punishments in the country. More comments on this are included in part 6, as part of the study of the poll.

Another problem arising from rapes is the extreme attitude taking birth in some victims like "all men are bad". But experts and Dr. Lal feel that rape "is a medical emergency. If immediate medical action is taken and girl given proper mental and psychiatric care, such an attitude might not even develop".

However, when the girl is raped, her prestige shattered and is unjustifiably banished from society, she might start feeling this way. And when we men feel bad on hearing from any woman that "all men are sick", "all men are vicious"; we should also realise that this attitude is a gift of the male dominated society and it's cold, egotised and morally wrong handling of a victim.

One more horrifying thing arises when a woman raped and humiliated as Gargi Kaul so rightly points out in her article "From Sita to Phoolan" (HT, Sat. Mag Sec. Feb. 13, 1993) that "if women especially in the rural areas have to demand to get respect then they are likely to emulate Phoolan Devi". Indeed, if women are humiliated and the law passes decisions decreasing rape sentences, because culprits become victims of their own lust, and police instead of saving the victims sometimes choosing to 'enjoy' through custodial rapes and Sivapatis and Bhanwari Devis Publicity raped, is the women to be blamed if she emulates the bandit queen? Like Neena, working in a screen printing firm at Chandni Chowk says, "I will be happy if woman raped becomes a Phoolan and kills such people. Can anybody forget such a crime?" Indeed, nobody knows many Phoolans are in the making and all for the lack of a proper attention by the favours society with its sticky stigmas and egotised individuals.

Rape is a very big menace. And needs proper attention and proper care. Parental rape is so heinous a crime, that it's even difficult to be believed. If the Jeet Singh case is any indication, every parental rape leads to a shattered family. It is the family who is supposed to teach virtues and right conduct making good individuals, good citizens and good society. But when the father, the head of the family is out to cross all limits of vices and villainies and break one of the strongest of all relationships what can be hoped for the society. Every parental rape is grave danger to individual and society and must not be passed off as a bad news but properly thought, analysed and acted upon. What is now needed is a sort of Renaissance where every citizen joins and voices against the menace; cutting the society of its stigmas and the law of its loopholes. Otherwise, we would have to move in the 21st Century with parental rapes as everyday news that has immuned us and culture passed off as a term that used to exist in the century gone by.

It must be understood by one and all; once and for all; that rape is done to satisfy one's beastly desires leading to the break-down of an innocent life. As Neelam Shukrapani of Delhi School of social work puts it, "No one is forced to Rape". One rapes because one wants to rape. While discussing punishments about rape culprits, their psychological and sociological factors must be thought and talked of but in no way should they form an excuse for their crime.

Rape is a great insult. But only for the individual because her 'self prestige' gets shattered. But because her character, her thinking, her being remains exactly the same after she has been raped, her social prestige also remains the same and she must be looked upon as the same social being.

The opinion poll indicates that people have lot of fury in them. But the fury is passive. But one day, I hope, the fury will activate leading to vaporisation of this menace from the face of earth. I am waiting for that hour. But that hour must come soon. Because, after rapes; parental rapes have knocked society's door and become public news. Very soon, the knock of a brother-rape shall be heard. And if that happens, that shall be very late a moment to think and act.

Part Two

IN SEARCH OF A CULPRIT

IN SEARCH OF A CULPRIT

If a culprit is seen as a personification of an emotion, Tihar Jail will assume the form of a vast Kaleidoscope.

Tihar Jail is a encyclopaedia. Sherlock Holmes would have called it one of the greatest criminal laboratories in the world. Each culprit is a book in itself. He is surrounded by a unique complexity, run by the waves of innumerable emotions, behaviourisms and mannerisms. His crime and the incidents that moulded it, his psyche and the people that contributed to the making of it, his parameters and the things metered, together form the basis of a deep study. He has a definite aim, yet his being behind the bars talks of its aimlessness. A culprit thus offers scope of a study of varied complex problems of psychology and sociology, psychiatry and ethics and all the two thousand or more culprits housed in the mega structure is the key to understanding the entire humanity at large. Tihar is an institution of observation, deduction and comment.

Each culprit is there for a crime. Each crime has copulated with a chain of issues. Some are moving on their coach of time. Behind the bars, for causing secular unrest. A community problem related to culture and society, to the constitution and law, and to religion and human understanding. A young man waits amidst shadows of terror to be taken to the gallows. He forms a part of the love triangle in which he became the usual hero turned villain and killed his competitor - A stormy individual question versus society. A competition of two phrases - all is right in love and war and to kill is only god's right. Thus this structure is a structure of issues of debates, of conflicts. We research for truths in the free world. I sometimes feel that in the free world all lies chained in the cover of vanity and hypocrisy decorated by the cherry of practicality. In this chain world, all issues assume a free form welcoming the ardent seeker to search and discover truth.

As I sit in my room and write these lines that have moved from the eyes of the editors and publishers and the vast arms of the printing press to lie decorated before you, my mind has gone some forty kilometres from my residence to the great crime lab. I can see the vast door, the guards and the long walls. As my mind ushers itself in, it moves through the hundreds of cops and the thousands of culprits, frantically searching for those men who lie behind the bars after causing much turmoil and pain - in our hearts, and beneath the undergarments of their daughters .....

I am not searching for the men, labelled as culprits by the society and confirmed to be so by the law. I am searching the culprit in them, beneath their skins.

One of them is gone - Jeet Singh is no longer in prison. He is free. Living once more in the society amidst men, though he is a beast.

As I have mentioned in the preface, this book was completed in May 1994 but was later amended, photographed and as a result doubled in quantity and quality in May 1995. I had investigated the Jeet Singh case as soon as it had happened. When I went there a year after he was free. I kept this fact hidden till now, for I wanted to give you enough time to decide for yourself how you will treat Jeet Singh. Sympathize or ostracize him. I told you the complete facts of the case and after narrating this blackened attitude of incest to you, allowed you to let your grey sense form an opinion about this black form of consciousness. Now when this sad development is shared with you, at this juncture, it allows me to investigate how you feel about the issue in general and the culprit in particular. I can see a sense of terror and grief in most of the faces. You somehow feel your sixth sense rise in your being to inform that it's a wrong development. Things are going to be bad.

And they are. Jeet Singh has again come to his house. He lives in the same four walled structure ...... and sleeps with his daughter. What has the punishment done to him? Has the culprit in him been punished? Has his daughter after all her revolution and revolt seen peace? Has she not been under more complex strain than before? The answers to all these questions is what neither you, nor me wanted. But truth is truth and must be faced as the truth.

When Mrs. Amrita Singh informed the same, I could see the terror in her face,. "He is free and all are afraid of him. He is scot free." To her at least it seems that his few months in jail have been only as good as no day in jail.

The reader might be wondering that in a book that houses so many photographs, why I chose to exclude Mr. Om Prakash Parasher's photo. He simply never wanted it. He even wanted to get his name cut from the book. The man who had spoken so boldly suddenly seemed to be the same common man, whose fear and passiveness causes irritation. "Why do you want to ruin me?", he asked me, on being requested to oblige for a photo, "cut my name from the book. Write the story as your own investigation, not as something I told you. He might kill me. I..... I must save my life......."

This is the culprit and this is the society. This is the culprit generally acknowledged as the human form whose beast within has acquired freedom, and spitted at. But all this happens at his back. At his face, is only a silence. A quiet, tight lipped face. Indifference housing shrieks of cowardice and silent witnessing to a rotting society - a common man's NO to a difference that must occur.

"What can the girl do?", said the DCP Ms. Hazarika when I met her after an year. The girl indeed cant' do any thing. She is raped. She reports. The father is arrested. She is freed. The father is freed. She is re-arrested. Will only this circle go on? Will the girl only get momentary freedom? And if yes, who is responsible? A passive you, or a half-active me? The law or the society where this dirt breeds? We all are to be blamed. But secondarily. The primary responsibility lies where the whole dirt has originated–the culprit. Isn't Jeet Singh an example of a unreformable character?

Think.

Tihar has housed in it another character-Subrata Rai. Arrested for raping his daughter for months. He brought her from boarding school to rape her. He made his daughter his wife, thus breaking a barrier, a bridge, a relation. Will he too like Jeet Singh rape her daughter once he is free?

Think.

I must not disclose the names in a case where a father rapes his daughter whenever he finds the chance. When the mother is sleeping in one room, the other room smells of fires of sex and fumes of hell. The daughter will never complain, the father will never cease. Will the daughter start hating sex? Will a male make a female a male hater? If yes, can we hate the male or should we try to love him?

Think.

It has almost become a fashion now-a-days to sympathize with the culprits, films going steps ahead by making audience shed tears for a hero-villain. Some critic go to the extent of commenting that some films show the triumph of good over evil just for a positive signal from the censor board.

Indignating.

Wilson John, a noted journalist of The Hindustan Times, once while writing "Charles Shobbraj : Death Machine" said quoting a psychologist:

"Deep inside, all of us have a desire to be anti-establishment. That is why we like criminals ...."

Is this the subconscious anti-establishment desire that gets the better of our reason, when we sympathize with criminals? May be we are not siding with their crime but what looks like a dare to be anti. This comment assumes form and meaning when one views comments from the common man where he finds a sympathy for even crimes like rape.

Today some people talk of treating culprits other than punishing them. "Punishment is no solution", they will outrightly say. On being asked what measures, either they will be silent or will give replies superb in theory and senseless in practicality. All because talking of pro-culprit statements has somewhat become a fashion, and fashion has the quality to win your praise by capturing your reason and activating your illusion.

I can never forget Ved Marwah's line when together with Surinder. K. Dutta in the H. T., writing on crime, he said that we always try to find the man in the culprit and never the culprit in the man.

Greek philosophy has always believed that man is basically an animal - barbaric and uncivilized, who tried hard to enter the corridors of civilization but his animalhood comes to the fore now and then. The great American writer, D. H. Lawrence stressed the same and highlighted it in his poem on a man and the serpent.

Man has in him a serpent craving for crime. This serpent in many, comes to the surface and poisons the social fabric and ethos. By being pseudo-sympathetic to the culprit, we let these serpent exist and make culture perish.

Philosophy and psychology are two great studies - both lead to ultimate truth - the first in the relationship of spirituality and humanity, the second in behaviour and man. Both at the same time share a common danger - that of being too superb in outer look and hollow in the inner structure. Thus both must be used with great caution and concern.

This part is not just a separate section, very essential in itself, but also prepares the reader in itself, but also prepares the reader in a mood where he shall investigate each fact of discussion that follows with the central argument of this part in mind. And with a open, judicious grey sense, succeed in understanding the truth and weight of this book.

If I am understood in this section that I shall be forever butchering the culprits with my pen and will only talk of them with a black tongue, this, I confess, is not the case.

But culprits should by no means be sympathized with. They, in all cases, are aware of their crime as being wrong, unnatural and unethical. Moreover in many cases lies no problem with them. All is hyprocrisy.

We must learn that we should never sympathize with the culprits which has a hidden sense of pity and is very near to being an assent to their behaviour, as a passable action. These assents and sympathies are a mirage. We must learn to see desert where the desert is. Illusive oasis soothes the eye and decays the being. For if many have intense psycho problems, many are totally normal and hypocrite. And even psychologists' who have talked of culprits having possible psycho strains, compelling them to parentally rape, maintain that the factor of immorality is certainly there. Above all, by being pseudo-sympathetic we tend to lesson our attention to the poor victims who are for no fault of theirs raped. Every solution from psycho treatment to execution should be searched for but with reasoning and element of maturity. Otherwise, it might just generate a laugh, which is never desired.

What is required is a judicious eye that gives justice to the culprit issue. Where culprits are not sympathized but understood. Where solutions are stated, may be even the most lenient ones, but because they are substantial and not a fashion of the times. This is what the book exactly does.

We can search for a proper punishment platform for the culprit only when we scan the culprit in him. If we shall start scanning the man, how can we be expected to analyse the culprit?

If anybody needs sympathy it is the victim - the innocent lamb.

True understanding of the culprits is most essential to understand, why, this book appears and is a victim's defence.

> On the social grass,
> And cultural river
> Black serpents swim.
> For victim's preservence,
> For ethics' existence,
> Victims need defence.

Part Three

THE PSYCHIATRIC VIEW

THE PSYCHIATRIC VIEW : EXCLUSIVE INTERVIEW WITH DR. ANANDI LAL EMINENT PSYCHIATRIST

** The Dictionary just defines rape as a "Sexual intercourse without consent". But how is rape defined as problem in psychiatric terms relating to the trauma of the patient and her mental condition and family reactions. How would a psychiatrist deal with rape with respect to its psychological impact?

The definition of the rape shall remain the same. That is, sexual intercourse without consent. That, and with its finer details will remain the legal and valid definition. However, from the psychological point of view the rape as defined legally, attempt to rape, molestation and attempt to defile a woman's modesty will lead to similar sort of psychological impact on the victims and her friends and family members. Though the intensity and duration of psychological consequences will vary in cases of actual rape and attempted rape. In any case, rape both actual and attempted is a very traumatic and stressful event for the victim.

* What are in short, the psychological impacts of the victims that come to you as patients?

The first thing is that many people would go into a state of shock because of what has happened. And that shock can take various forms. It can take the form of depression. That is the person becomes quiet, doesn't want to eat, doesn't want to talk to anybody, doesn't want to communicate at all. Otherwise also the patient becomes sleepless, continues to get the repeated experience of that particular event, in the form of nightmares. She gets up with the same feeling that something will happen to her. There can be hypervigilance and exaggerated startle response. There can be difficulty in concentration and irritability or outburst of anger. There is sense of foreshortened future. She doesn't expect to have a career or marriage or long life. There can be physiological reactivity upon exposure to an event that symbolise or resemble an aspect of the traumatic event e.g.; a woman who was raped in the elevator breaks out in sweat when entering any elevator.

In child victims, it can take the form of loss of recently acquired developmental skills such as toilet training or language skills.

It can also take the form of general paranoia. She becomes suspicious of everything. Even minor things and day to day activities will fill her with fear. She would constantly be filled with the terror that something would happen to her some one is conspiring something against her. Then there is fear of pregnancy as a possible consequence of sexual violation. Fear of possible transmission of dreaded sexually transmitted diseases esp. AIDS continues to haunt the victim.

This is the post traumatic stress disorder. Some victims develop delayed stress disorder may be as late as several years after the event. Some go in to a state of chronic post traumatic stress disorder.

There can also be a complete denial of the event. That is another 'defence' mechanism. The victim gets the shock but denies it completely. Inside the victim feels it but on the surface completely denies it. She leads a normal life but inside feels very much hurt and this denial can take various forms at later stages. The expression of that inward feeling can be very hurtful later on.

**   Can this self denial, to a larger extent, lead to madness?

Yes, self denial can take the form of madness. Even paranoia can lead to madness of the patient.

**   Have you dealt with patients who had fits because of the shock they got from rape?

I have seen patients like this but not too many to make a very valid judgement about it. But patients like this do come.

**   Keeping the name a secret, can you site a example of any of your patients in a little detail, talking about her trauma?

I will tell about a patient of mine who was a working woman, of a senior capacity in a government undertaking. She reported of having been molested by her superior in the office. She was brought by her husband because after that incident she was in a very bad shape, in terms of not being able to join any activity, not being able to do anything and felt sleepless also. Obviously, she was passing through a lot of psychological trauma at that particular juncture. We did try to help her as much as we could. She required some medication also to put her at rest. Talking to her and trying to work in that direction also helped her. But I'm sure the initial trauma she underwent would last for a long time ...

May be for life ....?

Yes, may be for life also. It is very difficult for any patient to forget about that thing. Actually, for the patients who pass through this sort of trauma the progress for good recovery depends on several factors. Some of the indicators of good recovery are symptoms developing shortly after the event, brief duration of symptoms, good premorbid functioning and social support system and absence of other medical and psychiatric problems.

** **In general what are the parents' reactions to the daughters who are raped?**

One would be a significant rage towards the society in general and the culprit in particular. The stigma is also very much there but the initial rage is towards the person who has committed rape and to the society in general. Because, some of the times, it so happens that the parents are not able to protect the interests of their child because of the circumstances. The daughter is forced to go to work because of the financial difficulties. They hold themselves guilty that since they couldn't provide for the needs of the family, they sent the daughter to work and that resulted in that traumatic and shocking incident. The guilt can be there in them. And it also leads to depression over what has happened. "What shall the society say ...."? The stigma attached to that.

** **You defined rape in great detail talking on those terms how will you define parental rape. Ordinary rape is rape by a stranger or a friend who deceived you. But how about the father who gave birth to the girl, was supposed to take care of her but did this to her. How will the girl feel in such circumstances?**

That will be even more traumatic on the same lines. But the trauma is going to be a very, very severe one. Because the closeness and affection had developed in the two individuals in different dimensions and if that is converted into such a sort of thing, it will have a severe and lasting impact on the individual concerned.

** **Can the mental trauma of the victim lead her to commit suicide?**

O yes, it can. If a person is in that sort of a state and that particular point where she is not able to get emotional help and she is left to feel that she is lonely and helpless and hopeless in that situation, it can lead her to commit suicide. Rape is a very stressful factor and unattended stress can surely lead to such a thing.

** **You talked of unattended stress just now that can lead to suicide. So parental rapes, we all know is such a bad thing. Even talking to somebody that it was your father who raped you, is so shaking and traumatic. The girl can't open her lips, not even to her mother, perhaps. Not to society because social knowledge of such a incident will of course bring a lot of insult to the family. So the trauma remains caged in her and grows with time. So can that mean that suicide factor is more in parental rapes than ordinary rapes?**

I would put it that the trauma in parental rapes would in any case be much more. And so will also be the chances of suicide.

** **As a psychiatrist you have dealt with so many cases. You understand the fury of the victim, her indignation, her mental trauma. To the outward society it is just a fact that she has been raped. But what she feels is open to the psychiatrist only. Suppose today you are made head of a law making body that is making amendments to the punishments in rape cases. As a person who has dealt so closely with the traumas of the victims, what punishment will you give to the culprit?**

As a person, I would certainly be in favour of the stringent possible punishment. If it is proved beyond doubt that it has really happened with a woman and it becomes known who has done it, the stringent most possible punishment in the law should be given. However, taking into consideration that many a times there are cases of false accusations of rape, while making laws one has to keep a fine balance so that the innocent is not penalised for some thing he has not committed.

The Psychiatric View

** **The law gives 7 years punishment for ordinary rapes and 10 years for child rapes, custodial rapes etc. Do you think that such a punishment is enough? Is a 10 years 'strict' rigorous punishment enough?**

As a person, I would say that it is hardly any punishment. The amount of trauma that is given to the victim is much, much more than the trauma that is given to the culprit in 7-10 years. And if we equate the suicidal implications of the victim, even sentence of execution if given to the culprit will appear less. However, my assessment in this regard is probably an emotional outburst of the individual who has been dealing with the traumas of the victims. May be the law making requires much better and finer handling, taking the totality of situation into consideration.

** **There was a case recently in high court involving a four year old girl's rape where punishment was reduced (Pls. refer to part one) what is your reaction to it?**

I don't think that it is proper. As a person, I would certainly not agree to it. If a person becomes the victim of its own lust and if it is confined to him only that is a different thing. If his yearning is affecting others, I don't think that the punishment should be less in any case. As I understand law, the person accused of a crime is not exempt from criminal responsibility merely on grounds of loss of control because of anger, jealousy, revenge or lust. The loss of control has to be attributable to the fact of existing insanity.

** **Do you think while making these laws, the psychiatrists and medical experts should be consulted? Is the consultation of experts necessary as far as law making goes?**

A person who is well versed with the intensity of the trauma the victims go through; whether psychiatrists, medical experts, social scientist or anybody else, they should certainly be taken into confidence and consulted while formulating the laws and policies regarding this problem.

** **Why are men not raped? Why does not a mother rape her son? Why is it always the reverse case?**

Even in the normal sexual relationship the man, over the years, has been the active partner in the relationship and hence the aggressor in the forced sexual relationship. However, with changing gender roles in the recent past and present the reverse situation can very well be obtained and

I think some cases have started and have been reported esp. in the Western Countries where females have been accused of having committed rape esp. in institutions and custodial rapes.

** **Why does the father commit rape even after being fully conscious of the pious relationship that exists with his daughter?**

I think moral degradation to such a level that not being able to see the reasoning behind what he is trying to do.

** **The man rapes and commits the crime. Still banishment, trauma, shock all fall on the lap of woman. So if the mental traumas of the victims come to the surface and the facts they face are exposed to people and the law making bodies, do you think that the society's attitude will change towards the victims? Do you think in this way the stigma might evaporate?**

Certainly. The amount of trauma the victims undergo, if it is really made known to the people in the real terms, it shall certainly make a hell lot of difference.

Part Four

THE PSYCHOLOGICAL VIEW

THE PSYCHOLOGICAL VIEW : BASED ON AN EXCLUSIVE INTERVIEW WITH DR. PROMILLA KAPUR WORLD RENOWNED PSYCHOLOGIST

A psychologist spends all her working years amidst a living laboratory. The psychologist's lab contains several hundred slides of life, frozen in who are millions of threads of human relationships and behaviouristic phenomena. The eyes of her mind view from the microscope of a case study, magnifying the threads that run "from stimulus to response", discovering points which originated them and those which captured them to their end. Thus is answered several mysteries to a individual's behaviour, and from it a society's behaviouristic response. A psychologist is thus a scientist, a seeker, a magician.

A psychologist meets a stranger and soon comes to know about him more than him. The human psyche is the most complex rigmarole of roads and crossings, meetings and accidents, of passion and emotion. But in this knitted up complexity, lies the key to a fundamental question - why do we act the way we shouldn't act? And, why don't we act, the way we should act?

Parental rape is one of the most turbulent progeny of a human psyche. It involves the study of two human forms, where a psychological turbulence in one merges into the other, making a psycho turbulence born in him. So much is broken and so much made, and what's broken was of such a good make and what's made is so broken that it needs a very deep study to extract the pearl of meaning from the waters of this ocean sized menace.

After travelling deeply into this menace and studying it very closely and minutely, I dissected and observed a lot. That raised a lot of fundamental question, invaluable in importance.

Many were answered by me but in many my analysis showed danger signals of lacking in quality, only achieved by a psychologist who has spent years, years and years in dissecting human life histories and collecting relevant material.

So, I stepped into a museum of psychological chemistry and collected various specimens that on being magnified with relevant analysis showed many facts of rape and the element of psyche related to it.

These specimens were answer to the questions asked by me in a most interesting interview with Dr. Promilla Kapur.

I place for your kind inspection some snaps of this illuminating dialogue that helped me develop my psychology on parental rape.

New Delhi
16th May, 1995
Forenoon

* From times immemorial, it was thought natural that the sex desire was absent in father-daughter, mother-son and grandfather-granddaughter relationships. But now the ears have heard and the eyes have seen parental rapes. Cases of a sexual relationship between a mother and her son are also becoming common. So, does an average parent view his progeny sexually? Would it be right to say that the purity in such relationships has only been superficial, caused perhaps by the constraints of civilization and the common sexual attraction between a man and woman, like everywhere exists here too?

** Actually, by and large, in a normal father the sex desire for his daughter wouldn't be present. It might be present in the subconscious but not in the conscious self. Cases of father raping his daughter, have been happening for ages. But it's only now, and something that's very encouraging, that it has come out in the open. Now people have started talking about it. Cases are reported to the police and also to the crime against women cell and action is also taken.

There is a law against rape. But, till recently, there were hardly any reported cases of a father raping his daughter. The victim in many cases doesn't report, which is because of obvious reasons. She is too young and

The Psychological View.................... 41

too traumatised to report. The mother also cannot report. Firstly, because she has to protect her husband who in most of the cases is the only bread winner. If something happens to him and he is taken to the custody, what will happens to the entire family?–this question constantly strikes the mind of the mother. The most important factor is that it is the false prestige of the family, the fear of dishonour that the family would face in the society, if it becomes public that the father has raped or even had sexual relations with his daughter. The other thing is that as far as the relationships are concerned, the relationships between the mother and father are definite to be spoiled if the mother comes to know that her husband had sexual relations with her daughter. So, the daughter is too traumatised to report and the mother even if she comes to know, hides it and tells the daughter that it's okay and nothing has happened. In many cases now, the most tragic thing is that young daughters, even very young ones, as you must have also read in the papers, of two three years are being raped.

But in the beginning you asked whether an average father or what I call a normal father, can do it, I would say that it is not possible for a normal person. By the study of people who rape, who indulge in incest relationships, it has been found that there is something drastically and seriously wrong with them - mentally or psychologically. They are either sex pervert or there is some kind of sex problem from which they suffer.

Now parental rape cases are not just happening but they are also being increasingly reported. But it might be worthwhile to add, that incest has not just been happening between the father and daughter but also between the father and the son. Sons are also sexually abused by the fathers.

***

* While sexually evaluating one's daughter is immoral but still digestible, wish to have a sexual intercourse is quite shocking. What cases such a sex desire? What is so overpowering that one is ready to break all ethical and social norms and have a sexual intercourse, or what normally occurs, rape the progeny, especially when sexual desires can be fulfilled by other means?

** I did a very detailed study on call girls. And in a number of cases I observed that these girls in their childhood were raped by the father and given to the prostitute homes. In many of the cases the father was an alcoholic. Alcohol comes between the reality and you. The man cannot differentiate, whether the fair sex is his daughter or some stranger a young girls or some middle aged woman. Alcoholism happens to be one of the most important reasons. The other is that psychologically the father might have been sexually abused as a child and that might have deeply affected his mind. So, it psychologically makes him oblivious of the reality, oblivious of morals, oblivious of right and wrong, and his sex urge at that time ceases to be under control. It might also be because he is a sexual pervert, and being a sexual pervert, he cannot naturally derive satisfaction from a normal sexual relationship. For such a person, the only pleasure he can derive is to do forced sex with a person with whom it is socially prohibited.

The fathers in parental rape cases just cannot enjoy sex done in a normal course. These fathers have their wives also. If they would have been satisfied with a normal sex, they have their spouse to satisfy their sexual appetite. But that sadly, isn't the case.

The third reason which is not in isolation but acts and interacts with the two reasons given above, is that such a thing happens because our moral values have deteriorated to a limit from where perhaps neither can they redeemed no rejuvenated.

***

* Can the father be exempted of punishment because of any reason? Can the court exempt him of punishment on the ground that he shouldn't be punished because he is a sexual pervert?

** Not at all. A culprit should be punished. Punishment is a must. But not just the punishment where he is put behind the bars and the matter is finished. He should also be made to confront his problem. He should be made to face the victim, which in this case happens to be his daughter, and also others who are deeply and directly affected by his crime - his wife, relatives etc. So, he should be punished by being put behind the bars and by being made to confront the victim. But along with it, the third thing, which is most essential if one wants to prevent him from doing this crime again, is to have him treated psychologically and psychiatrically.

***

* What should be that treatment?

The Psychological View...... 43

** If there is a good psychoanalyst, he or she would be able to find out the whole life history of the culprit. Once the life of the culprit is analysed, especially the childhood experiences, and the psychoanalyst becomes clear in his mind why the culprit committed a crime like that, he can be treated.

If the rapist is put behind the bars, and is not treated when he comes out after two or three years, he is liable to commit the same deed.

The punishment of law should definitely be there so that the rapist realises that it was an anti-social and inhuman act that he did. He should be made to confront the victim and ask for forgiveness. He should also be given the appropriate treatment, depending upon the case.

***

* What causes sexual perversion? Is one born with it or do circumstances mould one to be a sexual pervert?

** It is the whole life history that goes into making a person that he is. Particularly, the childhood experiences and his early sexual experiences have a deep impact on his personality.

The sexual abuse factor in the victim's parental relationship has a very strong and far reaching effect. In the case of call girls, which I have mentioned earlier in this interview, I did a complete scan of their life history from the moment they were born to the time I first met them. In many cases, it was the same strained relationship between the father and the daughter that lead to sexual perversion. The father raped them and turned them out. They now want to defame the family as an act or retaliation. Sexual perversion comes in as a most satisfying solution.

***

* On being raped by her father– at those very moments; and in the post rape situation, what differences will it cause to the daughter's psycho structure? Will she start hating sex?

** Yes, that happens and we have seen this in many cases that comes to us for counselling.

In one case, after marriage, whenever the husband would approach his wife for sex; unknowingly, unconsciously her whole body would shink and shudder with a sort of terror. Consequently, the husband wasn't able to have sex relationship with her.

The couple shared a very nice relationship and the husband was very kind to his wife. The wife also wanted to lead a normal sex life with his spouse but whenever he would touch her, it caused a feeling of aversion in her. It was not that she consciously did it, sub-consciously she thought that sex is a thing which is evil and not only evil, but something which is done for exploitation. And which is not a normal thing to indulge in. This attitude in her subconscious towards sex was caused because of her sexual abuse in childhood by her father.

Victims not just start hating sex, in some cases, they start hating men too.

***

* In some cases, the father is sent to the prison by the daughter. He returns and starts sexually abusing his daughter. What ill effects will it have on the daughter's psychology?

** This is not true. One thing is that if she has the courage to go to the court, she must have become quite conscious that she was misused and a thing which should not have been done was done. She would be completely frustrated and might run away from the house to escape from being sexually abused.

***

* But suppose she is forced to live with the father......? As in the Jeet Singh rape case[1] ...?

** Even then, when she had the courage to report to the police, she definitely will have courage to say "No". It is always done when some sort of opportunity is there.

It is normally considered that the father can never have sexual feelings for his female child. The mother will say - "Sleep with your father. I will sleep with the other Child". There is never even in the subconscious,

---

1. See Jeet Singh case in Chapters 1 and 2 (Ref. in Chapter-3).

The Psychological View.................. 45

that such a thing can happen. But when it happens, this feeling ceases to exist in the mother and the daughter.

***

* Can in any situation, the daughter give consent to the sexual relationship?

** If she starts taking drugs and alcohol overcome the trauma, in some cases I have seen girls doing that, then under that influence the girl might become oblivious of the reality.

* If a daughter is raped, she becomes pregnant and given birth to a child. Then :

    (i) How would the girl react? Will the father remain a father or will he be her husband?

    (ii) How would the father react? Will her daughter remain his daughter or be his wife?

    (iii) How would the child react on growing up? Will her/his grandfather be a grandfather or be his father?

    (iv) How would the society react? How would the child be admitted to the School? How will he be accepted as?

** In most of the cases, the pregnancy is terminated.

And if by chance, she becomes pregnant and the father says okay to it, then neither the mother nor the relatives and society shall accept it.

If the daughter doesn't tell about her pregnancy, and it is only known when it is in an advanced stage, then normally she is taken to a distant place and the child born is delivered for adoption. Therefore, your queries in most of the cases, do not hold much ground.

But birth of a child in such cases can mostly occur when this relationship is accepted. It sometimes happens that the mother dies, leaving behind only a daughter, and she and her father both come too close to each other. The relationship is liable to breed a child. This is nothing but a case of deranged moralities.

* What about the child born....? How will he react on knowing that he is born of parents, whose normal relationship is that of a father and daughter?

** Normally, this would not happen. Because the father cannot pass off the child as his. The daughter on the suggestion of the father or the father on the suggestion of the daughter or both of them with a mutual agreement reach a consensus that the daughter should get married to someone else. The child is then passed off as the one beget by the daughter's husband. The husband does not know that the child is of her wife's father and that is also kept a secret to the child.

***

* If a wife sees her husband raping the daughter, how will she react?

** Two reactions. One is extreme anger accompanied by resentment, both with the father and the daughter. The daughter in many cases is extremely humiliated for seducing the father. So, her reaction is definitely very very furious. And, if she thinks that she can be on her own, she would not like to live with that person.

***

* But that's strange. Would she not think of protecting her daughter?

** In two or three cases, wives have themselves gone to the Police Station or Woman cell complaining that their husband had raped their daughters; pressing for their arrest.

Depends upon whether there is a free communication and understanding between the mother and the daughter. The daughter should feel free to talk on every issue with her mother. The mother will then take up the matter with her husband. If he realises his mistake and doesn't repeat it, the problem is brought to an end. If there is an understanding between the couple and the wife feels that he has a psychological problem, he can be taken for a treatment.

But if he refuses to cooperate, that is, he neither accepts his mistake nor agrees to amend his behaviours, the wife will be compelled to take up the case with the proper authorities.

But by and large, what happens is that the false prestige of the family and for the girl's honour, the matter is not reported to the police.

***

* Will the wife allow her husband to touch her, after seeing him rape his daughter?

** If she sends away the daughter somewhere, so that the husband isn't able to continue with this kind of act, and is prepared to live with him, then she will be having sexual relations with him. The possibility definitely exists.

***

* Brain has a faculty called reason, which is rational and decisive. Sex is impulsive. How do they co-exist in a normal human being? How does impulse go with reasoning? Does rape occur from a disorder between the two?

There is an absolute harmony between the various faculties of the mind and the mind can be very rational. It can think what is right and what is wrong. Impulses are there. Instincts are there. Emotions are there. But they are controlled by the mind.

When there is imbalance and there is disharmony and there is a lack of fit between the various faculties of the mind, then a thing like this happens.

***

* This is a sexual or a mental abnormality?

** Mental and sexual abnormality both. Abnormality is created by the psychological problem. The faculties are imbalanced and a person is not able to control his emotions. The power of reasoning fails. Inhibitions just break down. The person does a thing for which he sometimes himself repents later.

***

> On the lap of my love,
> You shall always find rest,
> The crystals of my caring,
> Shall decorate thy soul's breast.

> My life has given suck to your life,
> My daughter you are my life.

For centuries, fathers have nursed their daughters with songs carrying the touch of their paternity. These songs in turn nursed the view that paternal relationships were necessarily and naturally devoid of sex. However parental rape, brings in the argument that sex is able to make its presence in such relationships too. Thus the fundamental question which begins the psychological argument on the parental rape behaviourism and slides it forward is whether sex can really make a ground in such relationships in an average female progeny - male parent relation? Thus I began the interview with Mrs. Kapur, asking her whether any average father could view his daughter sexually?

Psychological investigations have discovered that normally a father would not sexually evaluate his daughter. So there naturally lies no question of desiring to have a sexual intercourse.

Thus we establish that the father-daughter relationship still exists and normally a father would wish to have her daughter married off and have a peaceful sexual-mental life with her mate, rather than desiring to convert her daughter's bedroom into a wedding room where he would throw off his robes of a father and wearing the suit of the bridegroom, rape her.

But the possibility of a sexual attraction (only attraction) in the father's subconscious exists. The ethical establishment says that the daughter should be seen only as a part of you and not a female to whom you can be attracted. There is the chance of an anti-establishment, which lives in our subconscious and is tempted towards the opposite.

This happens because we are all born with an anti-establishment, which has varied facets, that go totally opposite to the rules and ethics, established and maintained by the nature. In our subconscious lies a creature that supports the qualities, defined as immoral. Like, something in us makes us appreciate criminals and adore the way they brave law and go against it.

But wherever a sexual attraction for the daughter in the father's subconscious exists, we must realise, that it doesn't make him a culprit. Because though we might give assent to criminals in our subconscious, but

The Psychological View.................. 49

in our conscious we might not even commit the crime of killing an ant. So are we criminals? Definitely not.

Moreover while many anti-qualities might be present in many of us, this anti-quality of sexually being attracted towards the daughters exists, among exceptions. Because through discipline and reason, some of us break away from every bit of the antithesis while many others kill some of it and make feeble the rest. Sexual attraction towards the daughter in most of us is the first to become extinct even before we know it is present.

Thus it would be Himalayan Blunder to think that this subconscious existence of progeny - sexuality exists in a normal father. Even the subconscious existence of it survives in the heart of an exceptional paternal psyche.

Thus, happily for us, the psychological structure of the human civilization still breeds this relationship at large.

After establishing the presence and absence of sexuality, let us concentrate on the psychological phenomenon occurring in a father who has in his conscious self a million serpents of sexuality ready to strike their teeth into his daughter's lips.

Among the reasons that awake this sexuality, alcohol is one. Alcohol always comes in as a handy reason for rape. However, I have always wondered whether when psychologists or criminologists cite the reasons for rape, presence of alcoholism in the culprit is defined as an excuse for their crime.

It is said that alcohol comes between the person and reality, and makes him blind of realism. Thus he is not able to realise whether the female is his daughter or not.

This may be so. However I feel, and I have a strong conviction towards the righteousness of my theory, that it is not true that in cases where a father rapes, he would not have done so if he wouldn't have been an alcoholic. I do not agree with the theory that an alcoholic father becomes oblivious of the reality that the female standing before him is his daughter, and rapes him because he takes him to be a female. Then, why don't all alcoholic fathers become parental rapists? For that matter, not even all alcoholics are rapists.

There are people who parentally rape even without alcohol and there are people who would never rape with it.

This gives us scope of bringing in the theory of immorality and through it explain this alcoholism theory.

Once, I still remember, while typing this book, one of my typists, Mr. Navdeep suddenly asked me - "Do you think that a alcoholic is oblivious of reality? I have myself drunk a lot and I feel that the reasoning doesn't completely die".

I had this reply in mind when Mrs. Kapur was giving the reason of alcoholism.

What I believe is that this happens: Alcoholic fathers who rape, and have no other problem, are basically at the core immoral. They nurture their daughters and their heart starts nurturing sexual lust for them. This grows and grows in their hearts. At first, it moves at a slow pace, being pricked by conscience, later the pace speeds up, and finally the lust gets better of their ethics and reasoning. Sexual lust so much overpowers them that the ethical consciousness moves into oblivion, and it just becomes a sexual desire. The daughter on the extinction of their conscience becomes to them a female only. She is not touched only because they feel that there is a chance of it leaking out and then they might be torn apart by relatives and friends.

Normality arouses the sexual desire but is not able to diminish from their minds the danger inherent. Alcohol increases this sexual appetite so much that it gets the better of this danger part and the lust is by rape fulfilled. The theory might be weak but still holds ground.

It also might happen that the father's being an alcoholic might just be a further proof of his immorality. So, of the many instances of immorality one is that he rapes his daughter and second that he is addicted to drinking.

Moreover, a delegation from the Parliament doesn't go to the culprit asking him to drink. He is self responsible that he drinks.

So, even if the alcohol theory of psychologists holds ground, at its best it seems that while citing the reason why a boy severely beat his friend,

The Psychological View

the answer given was that he had a stick in his hand, so was not able to control himself. No culprit can be excused on account of this theory only, in any way.

However, there lies another reason why culprits rape. If they are themselves sexually abused by their parents or strangers in their childhood, their treatment as an instance of the worst disregard of ethics and morals, makes them completely disregard morality. Thus it might make them sexual perverts or people who give regards only to desires and not relationships and morals.

But here also lies a fact - How is a man born at his core as a pure human being expected to react to his sexual abuse. I feel that there is sufficient scope to hope that he would feel that he would grow to ensure that there is benevolence and kindness everywhere and nobody is abused in the manner that he was.

So it gives us a point where we can assume that immorality has also something to do with incest. Our renowned psychologist holds the same ground too. But becoming a parental rapist because of facing, experiencing and quietly enduring sexual abuses in one's childhood, is a viable point and looks strong enough to be accepted.

Fathers rape because of pure sexual perversion. Sexual perversion is a multi-faceted phenomena. Unlike psychologists, who feel that there is always a violable reasons for a culprit being a pervert, a journalist who has witnessed this problem from all views, feels that sexual perversion might also be caused because of pure immorality, (as in Jeet Singh) in addition to reasons like being raped in childhood etcetera.

So, what should be the punishment to the culprits, according to this chargesheet that we have developed?

Mrs. Kapur talks of a three point punishment programme. In the first phase, the culprit is put behind the bars to make him realise his mistake. In the second phase, he is made to confront his crime and ask for forgiveness. In the third phase, he undergoes a psychological treatment to make him rid off the culprit within him.

This is an excellent effort to solve the parental rape imbroglio. However, there lies a very big problem in it.

This three-tier punishment goes well for culprits who have some strong psychological reasons for committing the crime. Like they were themselves sexually abused in their childhood and this has resulted in their abnormal and unethical behaviour.

Here this three tier punishment works. At first the culprit by being put behind the bars, is made to realise that he is not fit to spend his time in the corridors of society. This anti-social awareness imparted to the culprit is increased when he confronts the victim and asks for forgiveness. The word–"Forgive me" resounds in his heart, it in a way bounces from the walls of his heart to grey cell ceilings to strengthen the anti social aspect of his problem. Thus what was known to him but suppressed is activated. Even if all this fails because he has always been aware of the crime but has never cared, then finally, a psychiatrist unlocks his bundle of life, and relaxing the strained parts, mending the broken ones, and making the right permutations and combinations, cures him.

But what about cases where there is no problem at all? When the culprit is totally immoral? There this structure goes in no way whereas the punishment of execution becomes a vast possibility.

It happens that many culprits are totally beasts and do things just to satisfy their appetite. Where all reasons given by them or assigned to them by their sympathizers, whether abnormality or frustration, stand as a heinous hypocrisy. This aspect of the culprits is discussed in "After thought ...... should culprits be thought about". Thus, only in some cases this three tier punishment works and in others, other punishments including execution must be thought about.

Both these facets of the culprits are antonymous and must be read together and compared. Readers might ask that here I have in some way or the other agreed that some viable reasons exist with the culprits and there I have totally branded them as hypocrites. They must understand that while here culprits are also sexual patients making them culprit-patients, there they are just culprits.

However, going in the line of what I said, I still maintain that every culprit is a beast. For he is aware of his crime totally - if he is sexually abused by his parent and himself does so, he knows that he was dealt with wrongly and thus enjoys being a sexual sadist. Immorality indeed goes side by side even in culprit - patients. I do not agree for execution in such cases, only because if they can be treated by something else, why go for an extreme punishment?

Culprit patients are patients who should be treated but not loved. Only those persons stand a chance of being loved who either do not commit a mistake or commit it unknowingly.

Reformatory measures involving moral and spiritual execution and social banishment are possibilities that can deal the situation with culprits of all categories.

Let us now transfer our attention from culprits to victims.

One of the most horrifying conversions that occurs in a parental rape is attraction converted to hatred, for sex and sexual intercourse. In extreme cases the factor who brings about the forced sex relationship, makes the victim hate the entire community of his sex. But, why does the girl hate sex?

This happens because after being continually raped, whenever the girl thinks of sex, she thinks of the beasts who raped her. As she thinks of the beast she is filled at once with a hatred for him. As sex is attached to the beast, it is also hated by her.

This actually is not a true hatred for sex but what I would call as connective-cum-deceptive hatred. She doesn't hate sex as such, but as she can never bifurcate sex from the culprit, sex cannot be loved and understood by her as pure form.

If somehow the wrongdoer is thrown away completely from her - bodily, mentally and imaginatively and the confidence about purity and beauty reinstated, then she would metre things in the same scale as we do.

However, the most terrifying aspect of the whole menace is that in the absence of sympathy from others, the girl might start taking drugs and end up being a sexual pervert.

Sexual perversion occurs when sex becomes a blackened phenomenon for the girl and in the absence of right counselling, she is not backed in her days of trauma. How is she expected to react?

She might be converted into a living worm, become mad or commit suicide as we have seen.

But she might want to take sexual revenge. Now, she cannot rape. So how would she sexually avenge herself?

Some people strangely react to pain. To soothe themselves they would give themselves more pain. So to the girl the most shooting thing to combat forced sexual intercourse and insult to her virginity would be to herself let her virginity be insulted. She would through this find a strange sense of freedom.

And she might enjoy by defaming sex that defames her family, defames the womanhood, defames the homo sapien, defames ethics and values - defames everybody. She can't rest till she defames everything. What you hate, you defame. She hates sex. So she defames it.

One thing that hurts the most is that some women, as we are told, instead of sympathizing with their daughters, accuse them of seducing their fathers.

I have never been able to understand that if a woman does nothing and still the man is seduced, how is the woman accused of seduction? What do you expect? That a woman should cut her body assets and throw them away or blacken her face and then exist?

We have become so overconscious that women seduce and men are seduced that we don't seem to understand that a term called self-seduction also exists.

Overconsciousness of anything to a point of obsession breed a patterns, of wrong understanding and in this case this psychological complexity can only be solved by proper social awareness.

Then, arises another question - how on earth can a woman allow her husband to touch her when she has seen him raping her daughter?

Mrs. Kapur told the same problem that Mrs. Hazarika talks of in her exclusive interview with me for "The Police View". The daughter gets thrown out, every thing forgotten and consequently a reunion. A woman so unwomanish and devoid of understanding for a little girl or a young lady, who in addition was also a tenant for nine months in her womb ......

The Psychological View.................. 55

In our country women adjust with men which is sometimes a quality, sometimes a foolishness, a sin. Here the woman is as much to blame. Women must discover their inner strength, especially if they pray Maa Kali to help find solutions to women problems rather than increasing their complexities.

Parental rape exists as a disorder in the mind of the culprit where sex overpowers the reason, making the grey faculty numb. This disorder creates a vast socio-ethical chaos.

If a father rapes her daughter, he gives her the ability to become pregnant. The father has beget her daughter. Biologically, at least, nobody can break this fact. By raping her, he has made her his mate. By breaking the bridge maintained by nature, the father has made the relationships of parent and husband copulate and join with each other. This is a biological bomb - an unethical catastrophe. A natural gap maintained by nature for centuries has been compressed. Thus a human form that originated from a human form has rejoined into it. The origin was a pattern, synonymous with cosmic order. The destruction is a pattern synonymous with cosmic disorder. A spiritual, moral, ethical anarchy. Another human gluttony, sitting on whom creation cries . . .

What happens if the daughter gives birth to a child and he comes to know the truth ..? Born by a man who his half his father half his grandfather. Just a sexual union, just a sexual birth. A baby whose birth represents a final descent. Whose parents are a ball of confusion. Whose parents' relationship is unacceptable to God, society, law. Whose birth was the breaking of relationship and joining of two oppositely sexed wires resulting in a short circuit, bringing the darkness of hell. Have you realised the confusion amongst which the child will live? Now I hope the dear reader shall realize the ocean deep complexity that is created by a parental rape.

A normal rape has been occurring for centuries. As a contrast there are women who seduce men, change beds every night.

An immoral exception - rather a sort of a antithesis to parental rape exists. Father and daughter with a consent merge into a sexual relationship. Thus a immoral consensus quakes the earth of the moral world.

I have neither mentioned this fact to penetrate into the foul world of depraved mentalities nor do I like to spoil the mood of a mature, ethical reader. This psychological antithesis has a criminological danger attached to it. It might happen that a daughter welcomes her father's sexual move but when all this is discovered, to escape infamy, calls it a parental rape. Law must be beware of such hypocrisy. Society should now become cautious of incest relationships and accepting them as a fact, must see to it that they do not breed.

Ours is the land of The Ramayana, The Mahabharata. We live in country of such pure morality which has breed Swami Ramakrishna Paramhansa who married a five year old girl but never lived with her and seeing her as an image of great Goddess Kali worshipped her. What a divine presence in relationship of marriage. How can we allow a person to make his daughter his wife in country where wives have been worshipped as images of great Goddesses? Lord Shiva has explained to us to purity of marriage by taking the form of Ardhnarisvara. Can you allow sex to be stained with so much dirt in such a country?

Nature shrieks for help on seeing an unnatural show of sexuality. And civilization cries and says this :

> Nature maintained a bridge,
> Between father and daughter,
> Helped them to meet,
> Kept them separated.
>
> Each father, each daughter,
> Had a bridge.
> Many have it preserved,
> Shattered it has been by some.
>
> Where preserved,
> Beauty lies.
> Where broken,
> Terror strikes.

Part Five

THE POLICE VIEW

THE PEOPLE VIEW : EXCLUSIVE INTERVIEW WITH D.C.P. AND EX-CHIEF OF CRIME (WOMEN) CELL, MS. YAMIN HAZARIKA

** How does the Police view rape as a problem related to woman exploitation? What I specifically want to ask is that how is the reaction of a responsible police officer different to such exploitation cases than to others?

Actually, I haven't come across such cases directly in a police station. All woman crimes are considered very serious. Parental rape is a mixture of disbelief as far as the people are concerned. The reaction is of course that of a deep shock and anguish to me.

** For example of a case of dowry is brought out to you as the chief of the woman crime control cell and suppose a rape case is brought out to you. How will your reaction to both the cases be different? Will your worth and anger be more directed towards the latter culprit?

I would react equally to all situations. I feel even beating of a woman is very serious. Even dowry, harassment is very serious. But in police terminology rape is considered a serious offence. For us here is women crime control cell all crimes done to woman are considered equally serious and given equal emphasis and attention. But in a police station rape is considered a serious offence and other crimes like dowry a minor offence.

** Why is that thought the police from the beginning has always tried to curb the rape cases so that these cases become lessor and lessor as the time proceeds, we have been seeing in society that these cases are quite increasing? Infact they have become quite public like the Bhanwari Devi case and the Sivapati case - A lady who had been stripped, dragged and beaten in front of the public. What can be the reason of it?

The rape cases are increasing. Surely they are increasing. All crimes are increasing because of increase in population. It's also that more people are reporting these cases.

** But why have these cases become 'Public? We have heard of so many cases where a woman is stripped in public and beaten. Though the police is there and in every state there is a woman crime control cell. So how are these cases allowed to become public to so large an extent? How is a woman allowed to be raped in front of hundreds of people? This "Public Rape" is altogether a different dimension to the problem. Rape is considered a crime that is done secretly in a room and not publicly .....?

If there was a policeman there, he must have done something about it. I can't believe that there was a policeman there and he didn't do anything. But there were so many people there. Why did they keep quite and not do anything? At least they could have voiced against it and reported to the police. We can't expect them to act there and then at the scene of crime, but they should like responsible citizens report to the police.

** What has been the mental conditions of the victims in such cases and after proper punishment has been given to the culprit, has the victim got the social status she used to enjoy before she was raped?

Rape is not such a dirty word anymore. There was a lot of stigma attached to it before which is not there anymore ....

** That means the people's reaction to it has changed altogether.

It has changed. Quite a lot.

** What do you think is the reason for it? How much is the police responsible for such a good development?

It is general awareness that has been responsible for it. Awareness rising from the operations of the press, the media and .... to a certain extent the police also. Of course, I'll give credit to the police too. The stigma, as existed earlier, has vapoured out. Many people now feel free to report such cases to the police. They don't hide it as they did before. And as far as other women exploitations are concerned, lot of people come to the police to report about beating, dowry deaths etc. Over the years, more and more people have started coming to the police to report woman crimes. If you see the statistics; in 85 only 54 rape cases were reported to the police which have considerably risen to 122 in 1993.

** **That means people now have more courage to report such cases........**

Not courage. That stigma .... Earlier you had that feeling that you shouldn't wash dirty linen in public. If you are raped, you should keep quiet. It's bad to talk about it. Such feelings have gone. Everyone talks about it now. Everyone is much more frank.

Earlier people wanted to hide it. Now they want to talk about it. They want to 'punish' the culprit. They don't want to hide the shame. Earlier the whole mistake was put on the head of the poor girl. I won't call it shame. It's not shame. It's defying the girl. You can't call it shame of the girl. How is she to blame? Now the feeling has come that a rape case must be reported. The culprit must be punished. The whole attitude has changed.

** **Meaning that the situation has altogether taken a new form. The worth and anger is directed towards the culprit and not towards the victim.**

Yes, now people report the crime. Earlier the tendency was hide it due to social reasons. Rape is not a 'self centred' problem now. It's a larger problem. The scenario has become bigger, the canvas of the problem has increased. The problem has, let us say, assumed social dimensions.

** **This particular rape - father raping the minor daughter and four years back the elder had committed suicide, also because of sexual harassment. How would you view this particular problem? Would you view such type of problems under a different light? If yes, would you please elaborate.**

Yes, I think so. I would view them under a different light. It's not just a question of rape. Though rape itself is a very, very horrible thing. It's a question of your whole life, a question of your customs, a question of humanity. Father' is not just a man. He is a very special person. A father-daughter bonding is very strong. They way mother-son's bonding is. One person whom you love completely. By doing so, he breaks the trust. He breaks the love. It's a whole world crashing. It's really the whole world crashing down.

** Can we say that the relationship the girl looked for protection is a protection no more. At least in these exceptional cases.

Yes. Whom can she trust? She can't trust her father through she had looked upto him for protection.

** Do you think that such rapes need different punishments? Much stricter punishments? And if yes, what should these punishments be?

Yes, surely. I think such cases need very, very strict punishments. Because, it's not just a question of sexual lust or yearning. It's something much beyond that. Even raping a child or a kid by anyone is something beyond an ordinary rape. It's very, very villainous. It's really very sick.

** What should that stricter punishment be? How to expose the crime in such a way that the people fear to do it?

For an ordinary rape, the punishment is 7 years. For gang rapes, custodian rapes and minor rapes it is 10 years. I think it should be much more than that. I don't say a death sentence or life imprisonment but it should be much more stricter punishment.

** Talking deeply about crime, we see that crimes other than rapes might have a motive behind them. You might have a motive to kill some one. You needed money or circumstances were against you or you did it in panic. But there is no such thing in rape. Rape only has sexual yearning as a reason for it. So doesn't a seven years sentence for an ordinary rape sound less to you?

Seven years is a good sentence. Because it is a strict punishment. It comes in a major punishment. We can't possibly hang a man for rape. The punishment has to commensurate with the crime. We can't give him a death sentence.

** And why not? Why shouldn't he be hanged?

I don't think it is justified. A person can't be hanged for rape.

** But no matter how much the society develops, the girl can't enjoy the same position as she did before she was raped. She has to live in a stigma, altogether for a whole life.

No, I don't think that the stigma attaches to it so much. It has a lot to do with her emotions, mental state. And if the victim is a kid, to her future mental and psychological development.

** You have said repeatedly during the course of this interview that the stigma is not so much there now. May be it is not so in big cities. But what about the villages where time is still in the primitive ages. So talking of rape cases there, the question of rape assumes different proportions.

If you look at it in the way that rape means the woman is in a way sentenced for life. May be .... you can say that. But I still feel that the punishments given by police (other than for parental rapes) are enough.

** We just talked that now the girl can't even feel safe in the custody of her parents. So talking of such a worsening position in society now. How would you advise women to be aware and to make themselves able to protect their prestige by themselves.

That way, the society would become a paranoia. But, I think the girl can know if a particular man is making advances towards her. You can make out if a woman is trying to seduce you. I can make out if a man is making advances towards me. As far as a stranger is there, one should be cautious and if she is; can be easily aware of the stranger's attitude towards him. But as far as a father goes, I won't advise the girl to suspect or inspect the father unless the situation really worsens or the actions of the father themselves become proof enough of his presence being an insecurity. As a mother, I would advise my daughter to be careful to men in general but I wouldn't tell my daughter - "Be careful of your father".

** May be because the father-daughter relationship is a golden relationship .... you would want that relationship to exist.

It's not fair. The existence of the father-daughter relationship has to be there. You just can't break it by telling your daughter to be cautious of her own father.

** **May be also because such cases are exceptional.**

Exceptional and also it's not fair. As a mother I might cautiously view the situation at home but I really can't advise my daughter as such.

** **You just now said that if the girl feels that she is in danger because of any man, she should be cautious. But there are certain societies where the girl feels a danger to her chastity but still is forced to live there.**

If such a case is there, she should report to the police.

** **But would the police believe it if the girl just says she suspects somebody?**

Why not? The police will call the man, talk to him and review the whole situation.

We have people coming to us. By talking to people.

We can make out if the girl, her complaint is genuine or not. If the case is genuine of course the police shall see to it that everything remains all right. But even if the case is a paranoia, we do look into it. We just don't leave it. There was a girl who ranged me up from Faridabad saying that her parents want to poison her. Obviously, we could make out that it was a paranoia. Still I got the whole thing checked. So we do look into everything that's brought to us.

** **In this particular case, that I had mentioned earlier, (Jeet Singh Chauhan) both the sisters were raped by their father. While the younger had the courage to come and report the matter to the police, why do you think the elder sister didn't have the courage to talk to the police. When the law was there to save her, protect her and give justice to her?**

Lot of people won't come and report to the police in 'such' cases.

** **That is we can say because of the bonding in the family......?**

Yes....... who would want to see her own father behind the bars. And with such a heinous reason for his imprisonment.

The Police View

** **So we can say that the stigma is there, at least, in these exceptional cases.**

In this case or cases like these the stigma would be with the family. Because the 'father' did something wrong. The whole family would be cracked if the father is caught and the fact that he raped his daughter becomes known. In the general rape cases, such stigma can't attach.

** **If the father gets out by bail, in such cases how would the police protect the girl?**

The father would get out on bail. Obviously, the mother and the daughter get thrown out; even in the cases of child rapes. And what happens very sadly is that in the man's family his parents will support him through all his wrong doings. Isn't the grand child weeping to death? It's amazing! They should be concerned about their grand child who has been raped by the father and her whole trauma and mental horror, but they will just stand solidly behind their son who has done something wrong, which is very, very unfortunate. But it happens .... !

** **Isn't it male domination to a villainous extent?**

It's not male domination. I don't know what it is. But it's very, very funny. Not to stand behind the grand child–the victim and the suffer; but to throw her out!

** **Now-a-days we see that rape cases pass out as a matter of fact with public. If not everyday, every week there is a rape case and there is not much of an analysis. Why do you think that the society has become so indifferent or immuned to such cases?**

The people, society does react to a rape case. It is not immuned.... I don't think so.

** **In a police station if a rape case is brought out. Or if such a case is brought out to you, do you get calls from the general public requesting you to give much stricter punishments? Or is the general public not connected with the police? Only the victim and victim's relations are connected to the police.**

The public does not meet us. But people are talking about it. - the woman organisations are always active. Ordinary rape, I don't think people take as such a horrifying thing now, as child rape is coming up. People have got used to rape. Because there are worse things happening now like child rape and parental rapes. Rape is something that has been happening. But child rape, parental rape is a new phenomenon. So, people are more concerned about it. People are scared of child rapes. The fear that it might happen to their kids always hovers on their mind.

** We have seen in films and stories girls going in for self protection. Would you think it would be an exaggeration if an advice is given or an order passed to every school to train girls to protect themselves?

Yes, I think girls should learn self protection. I would advocate this idea. We are propagating this theory of self protection in a very big way.

We think that rapes, molestation, dowry deaths, eve teasing and beating of wives is because the girl is physically weaker. So you've got to counter that vile by learning protection techniques like marshall arts. We are taking this particular subject in a very big way.

** Is the police trying to take this idea to every school?

O Yes! Last year we had an ad. on T. V. on this. We trained upto 700 girls last year. This year we are approaching schools and colleges and asking them to take up this self protection training programme. We're trying personally and through the media to extend this theory as much to the public as is possible.

** In the end, what would you like to add about rape as a major problem?

Rape is a very big problem. The trauma, the terror, the mental torture is very large with the victim. I strongly feel special rape cases. Workshops are now being opened where the victims are told how to cope up with their mental trauma and make life better for themselves. Though Rape is the worst thing that can happen to the girl but still the expert treatment she gets at such institutes adds a lot to her relief.

The D.C.P. says that the stigma is not so much attached to rape now. I confess, that this is not really the case. Though if it would have been so, it would be the biggest joy to any feminist or woman activist in India.

The fact that the stigma is still attached to a very large extent with rape must have been clear through *The psychiatric view*. The respected D.C.P., a very concerned police officer, may be feels that because she deals only with those people who come to her office and report. Further, the rape report graph constantly increases in her office charts much to her relief, making her conclude that the stigma with rapes is by and large gone. But while dealing with rapes, we must take into account not only those cases which are reported but those hundred times more which are not. We must also think of the cases where the rape is not reported to the police and the victim mentally tortured by her family members. If the stigma is not attached to rape; why then so much mental trauma, that we discovered while viewing this menace psychiatrically?

(Ms. Yamin Hazarika is at present the Deputy Commissioner of Delhi Police, 7th Battalion.)

CRIME AGAINST WOMEN IN U. T. DELHI

Reported cases under the head crime against women for the year 1986, 1987, 1988, 1989, 1990, 1991, 1992, 1993 and 1994

S. No.	Head	1985	1986	1987	1988	1989	1990	1991	1992	1993	1994 (Till Jan. 31)
1.	DOWRY DEATH	54	79	79	103	109	117	125	126	122	07
2.	RAPE	88	97	104	127	161	96	214	276	306	16
3.	EVE TEASING	756	2021	1777	2941	2414	2061	2376	2301	2108	142
4.	M. O. WOMEN	94	112	95	130	159	177	203	226	160	23
5.	DOWRY PROHIBI-TION ACT	10	10	12	10	10	06	06	05	04	02
6.	406 I.P.C.	71	141	210	390	268	198	137	238	308	41
7.	498-A I.P.C.	222	266	344	349	336	369	431	598	792	61

Source : Crime (Women) Cell.
Courtesy : D. C. P. and Ex. Chief of the Cell.

Part Six

THE SOCIOLOGICAL VIEW

THE SOCIOLOGICAL VIEW*

It is a play, four lakh years old. Millions and millions of artists have participated in it. Once making an exit, they have never re-entered. All the world's greatest civilizations have been the glorious stages of its multi-stage structure. The unfolding of its curtains has been the unfolding of histories. The changing of its acts has been the changing of cultures, replacement of dynasties and changing of civilizations. The world's greatest heroes-Lord Rama and Jesus Christ have participated in it. The world's greatest villains-Adolf Hitler and Mussolini have played their parts and gone. The world's greatest wars have added to its turbulence. The world's greatest acts of peace have added to its magnificence. The Ramayana has been its story, the Bible its screenplay and the Quran its dialogue. The Vedas have been its lyrics and the flute of Lord Krishna its music. The play began in prehistory, continued in history and now merges to meet the satellite future. Being played every where, by everyone, every time, on the directions of the Almighty Father, this play tells the story of Man.

Lakhs and lakhs of years back, man kept his foot on earth. The imprint of his foot was the seal of his supreme authority on the planet. Man has ruled the soil, the water and the sky, with his grey sense penetrating and conquering every zone of consciousness.

The first act and first scene of this vast play, records man as a nomad, hunting animals and eating their raw flesh. His bows and arrows and the blood they tore out of the skins, has been lost somewhere among the layers of soil.

Thousands of years ago, the first civilization started taking its roots and soon gave way to mammoth examples of architectural and artistic magnificence and splendour.

---

* *Based on an exclusive interview with Prof. (Dr.) M.Z. Khan, Head of the Department, Social Work, Jamia Milia Islamia; and Eminent Writer.*

As you move through the widespread ruins of the great city of Persepolis, with the wind howling and shrieking through the large walls and pillars, it seems that the wind has brought with it all the noise that was in this city of Ancient Persia. As you fold your hands in respect of the great God, The Ahura Mazda built on a cracking grey wall, you can hear the creaking of history that is all left of a great civilization. As you see King Darius the great's audience hall, and if you are a good dreamer, you would soon hear the whispering of a thousand men.......

The ruins of civilizations are in fact finely built proofs of the man's achievement, through the ages.

Civilization represents society. Man for years has lived in society, as is natural for his, he being a social animal.

Society has bred many goods and many evils. It has represented the highest and bred the lowest. And through the walls of society, a stone has been thrown on the innocent babe of morality.

How did this stone fall from the great social wall? What damage has it caused to the wall? To investigate this stone of parental rape, I was sitting on the seventeenth of May 1995, in the office of Prof. M.Z. Khan. As the fans slowly moved and filled the air with their half cool breeze and the curtains made a low noise as they slide against the creamy walls, I looked around the whole room. It seemed as if the Professor's Office was a massive laboratory wherein was stored all the turbulence and storm of the complete social action of the human existence.

Before I could being my interview, the Professor looked at me and stared with his wisdom filled eyes. Then leaning back in his chair, he questioned–"Mr. Sharma, what do you think is parental rape?"

"A great moral breakdown", came my one sentence reply.

"Moral breakdown....?", the Professor said as if I had passed a wrong statement. "As a sociologist, I feel you require a second thought to your assertion...."

"But I am sure of myself", I defended.

"Let me explain", he said, and that began a most interesting, thought provoking and what's more important, an interview full of constructive argument.

THE MORALITY ISSUE

"Morality to me is a very confusing term", said Prof. Khan, thus beginning his long lecture on the subject, "What has been moral and what immoral has always been a subject of argument.

Though he was tricked, Prophet Abraham, who is common to Christians and Muslims, happened to have sexual relations with his own daughter. When I say Prophet Abraham, I am referring to a role model. He was certainly a role model in his times.... I agree that this is mythology and not history. But ultimately Rama must have been there, otherwise there would have been no epic. So, what do you say?

Rape is happening, rape has been happening and perhaps it will happen. If we use this angle of morality and immorality to explain this phenomenon, I feel confused. Perhaps this would deserve a second thought. The definition of what is moral and what is immoral differs from person to person, from publishing group to publishing group. And what is moral in India, may not be moral in the United States.

If you ask what is my approach to parental rape problem as a person, I would call it break down of social norms, social morales and social values. Norm, as you know, is a behaviour that is adhered to the largest number of people. The accepted code of no sex relations between father and daughter, uncle and niece, brother and sister, is cracking down. That may lead to different problems.

Can we make this kind of assertion that people during Ram raaj were highly moral and people during Narasimha raaj highly immoral? Because human problems during the reign of Lord Rama and that during 1995 remain practically same. And we can find examples where breakdown of norms are taking place in Kal Yug and were taking place in Sat Yug. So, I would call it breakdown of social values and norms, rather than moral norms....."

I do not at all agree with the illustrated Professor's view and anybody else who might be taking the same view.

I agree that morality is a very confusing term. What is moral in one country, may not be moral in the other. And even in one country, at different regions, the same subject may be viewed with a different moral parameter. As time takes a turn, many-a-times moral issues also take a somersault.

But that doesn't mean that we shall stop making assertions about a thing as moral or immoral. An age old proverb says that "Truth remains a truth even if no one says it and lie remains a lie even if all say it". The question is to believe in yourself and through a right judgement make a moral assertion.

The more important observation, however, that I shall like to make, is that there are some issues that even with the debates and conflicts, have, with absolute majority, been viewed as moral or immoral, and the majority has never been questioned by a no confidence motion. Will anybody call it moral to crush a new born babe's head under a grinding machine? Or cut his legs and laugh while he shrieks?

Rape has also by and large been viewed as an immoral phenomenon. To date I have never met any spiritual teacher who has written a book asking the reader to rape, as it does a great service to man and humanity. The absolute majority goes with my view in calling rape immoral. Thus my argument certainly holds strength.

Parental rape is immoral as it breaks the bridge that has been maintained by nature for millenniums. As it forcibly snatches sexual privacy, the most delicate fundamental right.

The Professor himself, in the end of this interview, says that rape violates fundamental rights. A fundamental right is a basic right that 'must' be granted. And one is born with the fundamental right of respect to sexual privacy. If this is violated, immorality is definitely done. And if the Professor has the same view, how can he contradict himself and say that it's a confusing issue whether parental rape is immoral or moral?

If something is a complex issue or a confused one, it never mean that it cannot be defined. Besides, which subject in the world is agreed upon by every person, everytime and everywhere? The Professor calls rape a breaking of social norms. I am sure that there must be someone who would challenge it. Not one. But thousands. So, will sociologists leave this view.....? Both you and me know the answer.

Consider the danger involved in calling the morality issue related to parental rape a confused one. If it is undecidable, even one percent, whether rape is oral or immoral, then the probability of calling rape moral is also there. Thus it means that it might be ethical to tear a daughter's clothes, it might be ethical to touch her naked body, it might be ethical to have an intercourse with her, it might be ethical to donate her for the sexual pleasure of her father's friends, it might be ethical to give her deep traumas, it might be ethical to sell her to a whorehouse.... Yes, I can hear you say– "STOP THIS NONSENSE".

It is beyond doubt that we can in no way allow anybody to call rape as moral. Where does our culture go then? If we say rape might be moral then Lord Ram might have been wrong to kill Ravana for abducting Mother Sita, it might have been the right action to insult Draupadi in the court and then Lord Krishna might have done a needless action to save her.... Gandhiji might have been wrong in calling rape the greatest crime to humanity, Law books might have made a mistake in punishing rapists.... In turn our whole heritage stands on one single question- "Is rape moral or immoral?" I, at least, would rely on my sensitivity and maturity and what's more on the greatest knowledge and teachings of The Mahabharata, The Geeta, The Quran and The Ramayana, then on what might be a sociological passion....

It must be understood that it is most important to be clear; whether we are looking at this menace sociologically or psychologically, whether we are spiritualists or industrialists; that rape decidedly is immoral. It's a wave of unethical temperament, cutting the social fabric from within. And if by any chance, we would call rape moral or even make a probability assertion to the same, we could in our lifetime, see a culture and heritage, amassed in thousands of years time, by the collective greatness of God's incarnations and human's spiritual escalations, melt away. Our culture cannot be allowed to be mislead with issues that govern the Parliament of a fool's paradise.

THE EXECUTION DEBATE

Professor Khan asked me, how I felt that culprits should be punished in parental rape cases.

When I named execution as one of the possible punishments in mind, he looked at me with a very amazed expression. I was totally taken aback!

Dr. Khan totally dismisses execution as a possible punishment and I am bound to dismiss his view. It is because of this and several other reasons that this argument holds considerable importance to the issue in general, and to the sociological perspective in particular:

"Sex has more to do with human psyche than with law. And if you look into the history of olden times, then you shall see that laws governing sex relations came much, much later. I am thus trying to pinpoint at a question–If we have parental rape, is it a legal problem or is it a social problem? And my assertion is that it is much more a social problem, a psycho social problem. So, we should talk of psycho social intervention rather than law. IPC is there, provisions are there in it and may be some indirect reference is there in CRPC also. Now if you feel that since law doesn't have sharp teeth and we further make more stringent provisions or we make new provisions in the law books in the hope that we would be able to combat with the problem, my feeling is that we would be living in fool's paradise. Because, if this symbolises a breakdown of social norms, 'morales'(?) and values, then probably we need to initiate socio intervention, rather than rely on law. Now, let us be rather mundane. Suppose we start enforcing IPC more vigorously. Then what is going to happen? A policeman would we peeping through every window, so as to see what kind of possible relationship is going on between parents and children. It is possible? And will it go with the constitution of India and fundamental rights.....?

So I am not saying that law should be down away with or disposed off. That is not my point. What I am saying is that it is essentially a psycho-social problem. Law should be there. But over reliance on law could be meaningless. Probably, we need to mobilise public opinion, we need to have more citizens intervention, probably we need to have more NGO intervention, more family rights, to promote more relationships in the family, to strengthen the institution of the family. Through that we could be having a substainable intervention. And probably not only we would be in a position to curb borderline cases but we would also be plugging in the catchment area. Probably we sometimes feel that law is the answer to all human social problems, that is rather a very tricky thing and it has its own faults.

An outside example which is not in the line of your thinking but still is worth mentioning. This law, the Dowry Prohibition Act, was brought in the law books in the early 1960's. Do you know how many cases thus far have resulted in conviction? Well, up North, down South, everywhere dowry is being demanded and given. Muslims, Hindus or Sikhs–all people no matter of whatsoever religion, caste or creed, but especially in the middle class, they demand and they receive dowry.

Only 3 cases so far–2 in Goa and one in Kerala have resulted in conviction. I am not referring to cases reported, I am not referring to cases tried in the court. I am talking of cases where punishment has been awarded by the court. And in those 3 cases, what had happened? Those foolish people had accepted dowry as an immovable property. In case it is immovable property there is a document. So, in these 3 cases some document was there or what we call, documentary evidence. Consequently, they were apprehended. Otherwise, in every marriage you will see dowry being given, demands also being made and nobody being booked by the law. That is why I say, that over reliance on law to curb and control this kind of incestual behaviour in the part of father, is not going to lead us anywhere.

There is a philosophical and operational difference when we talk of capital punishment.

Perhaps we think that we are still living in medieval times or ancient times where harsh punishment is able to deter certain forms of behaviour. It is not even deterring murder. 39-40 thousand cases of murder are registered by the police of this country every year and most of the people who are apprehended by the police are rather poor, simpleton people. Some of them are from rural tribal areas, some of them are from slum areas, and from unplanned colonies that you have in Delhi and Bombay and other metropolitan cities. These are the people who have had no education, who are engaged in no paid occupation, who are not very knowledgeable and who are of course not very influential and so are not able to go out from the clutches of the law or legal procedures. Patently, believe me Manish, patently, they are from this class. Because those who are educated, those who are influential, those who are moneyed, they always manage to come out of the law. They are able to have the best possible legal counsel if you are still not convinced, I would also like to site the example that in the nineteenth century England, they thought that to tackle social problems effectively they had to scale up the punishment structure. Many crimes were penalised be execution. They did so for a large number of cases, even for pickpocketing. Outstanding writer Charles Dickens, has written that those were the times when hanging was done publicly. Even as pickpockets were being hanged, publicly, pockets of the onlookers were being picked.

So, capital punishment deterring whom? That is why I say that it is a hangover of medieval and ancient barbarism. And so you see that most of the countries have done away with it. Britishers gave us this " death by hanging" punishment. Now in their own country in 1969, capital punishment was abolished. And I believe that they are happier than Indians without capital punishment. So is the case with France....lot many countries.

I would like to repeat myself that it is a psycho-social problem and can best be fought by psycho-social measures."

I shall now, step by step, prove that execution stands as a very viable punishment and it is wrong for a social scientist in particular and social science in general to advocate the contrary.

I feel that Professor Khan has very severely detached law from the society. Also, social scientists, it seems, become so conscious of social relationships and their invaluability in tackling any problem that they seem to add no value to other systems in operation.

At the first it seems that law's power has rather been misunderstood. Nowhere, do we mean to make law an instrument of paranoia, by making policeman peep through every window. At the first, we are not even suspecting the father-daughter relationship. So, there's no question of any public censoring. (See the section "Dissecting the Poll"). In this way, I myself feel, relationships shall be broken, rather than being preserved or strengthened.

Secondly, it seems that Professor Khan's negativistic attitude towards rape, arises not from the fact that execution is not a fit punishment, but that there is corruption in the law. This is more than evident through his statements like–"Only three cases have resulted in conviction in the Dowry Prohibition Act" or "39-40,000 cases are registered by the Police of the country every year and people who are arrested are rather simpleton people".

If law has not been effective because of such reasons, it clearly throws light on the shortcomings in the implementation structure. But the viability of the punishment remains, that cannot die because it has not been executed properly.

The Sociological View

Professor Khan feels that instead of strengthening law, we need to mobilise public opinion. So, I mention here, that in the opinion poll that I took, 58.5% Voters of all categories combined, have gone for execution or open execution in parental rapes.

The illustrated Professor says that "There is a 'philosophical' and operational difference when we talk of capital punishment". When the Professor is confused whether rape is moral or immoral, why talk of it in philosophical terms? Philosophy of rape is essentially a moral discussion on rape. Above all, even the greatest philosophers and spiritualists have said that in certain cases, execution, serves as the "greatest office of charity".

The whole problem arises because Mr. Khan feels confused on the morality issue, whereas it is a decided surety to me (and I am sure to most of my readers) that rape is immoral. Once we start talking of rape as an immoral phenomenon, and further realize after a deep study, that with some culprits there is no psycho problem, the punishment of execution becomes a high example of benevolence and charity. Because then while the culprit sways to and from on the gallows, dead and cold, we think of the poor, innocent victims who had to become the lust of the barbarian's beastly appetite and would have now dried up their tears on the legal avenge for their insult.

I read a few months ago in the papers that a saint used to lure barren, infertile woman that he will bless them with a boon to have children and in the process raped them. Is he not fit to be killed? What philosophical argument can say the opposite? In this case, instead of a "philosophical and Operational difference", I rather see a philosophical and operational similarity.

Or, what was philosophically wrong in the court's death sentence to a culprit who had killed tens of virgins after raping them? (And yes, he was normal!). I, at least, bow my head in esteem of the court.

The Professor also contradicts himself. He says:

"Perhaps we think that we are living in medieval or ancient times, where harsh punishment is able to deter certain forms of behaviour".

But, he had said earlier:

"Can we make this kind of assertion that people during Ram Raaj were highly moral and people during Narasimha raaj highly immoral? Because human problems during the reign of Lord Rama or during 1995 remain practically same. And we can find examples where breaking of norms are taking place in Kal Yug and were taking place in Sat Yug..."

If human problems remain same, and same breaking of norms are taking place in two eras separated by thousands of years, then why can't harsh punishment "deter a certain form of behaviour" now, as it did in medieval or ancient times?

Though I myself feel that things are not same in Sat Yug and Kal Yug. In no way can Sat (Truth) and Kal (Black) match each other. And it is because time has so blackened, that the past appears spotless, shining and faultless when compared to the present. Harsh punishments seem inevitable today, if they were necessary yesterday.

The other argument against execution is that in a country where 39-40,000 murders are registered every year, most of the people apprehended are simpletons.

At first, I feel that the illustrated social scientist has been rather too softened for these simpleton folk.

But, let us leave murder. That is not my issue of discussion. My subject is rape. And in rape, these simpleton people coming from the slums are not really that simple. Slums in themselves are matchboxes that breed rape (Read "Dissecting the Poll"). Incestual behaviour is also a problem mostly attributed to the slums.

This also lends us another useful argument that execution in rape is formed of completely different dimensions. Execution for murder and for rape is vastly different from the ethical parameter, moral perspective and criminological implications. As I have already stated in Part One, there may be a reason to murder but there is no reason to rape. Even if one is psychologically affected, he is not forced to rape. And let us, as I have rather pleaded, search for the culprit in the man than the contrary.

The Sociological View

The second last point made was a leaf from one of Charles Dickens' books—While a pickpocket was being publicly hanged, pockets of the onlookers were being picked.

Let me at first investigate the validity of this. Being a student of literature, a writer, and a journalist, I know that being one of the greatest journalists and social commentators of all times, Charles Dickens was bound to use the tool of exaggeration in his writings. So it rather seems that Charles Dickens wanted to criticize the punishment of execution in pickpockets, may be it being his personal opinion that it was not a right punishment. We can speculate the same to a very high level of probable surety, as Dickens was as a writer and a person on the side of the poor pickpocketers and petty thieves. His writings symbolise a concern for them and their problems. Thus he might have been too emotionally overcharged while thinking of execution for pickpocketing, as he only thought of pickpocketers, by and large, with pity. This is the background from which this scene might have originated. Dickens I am sure is not referring to an actual incident.

So, what do we believe in? A caricature of a particular politician, drawn as a monster by someone who might be hating him. Or the pinging of the same politician as a saintly, devout human? Exaggeration is never the reality, but a magnification of the reality in the way we want it to be.

It is, in any way, just an incident. I might tomorrow cite an incident where a social scientist talks of strengthening the family relationship and rapes his daughter. How will Professor Khan react to it?

If cases of such punishment failure are there, then there are such cases of failure in every profession or line of action.

Let us, for one moment, believe that Charles Dickens is absolutely correct. But is this still a complete picture?

Dickens has shown that while a pickpocket is publicly being hanged, onlookers' pockets are being picked. But what about the many among the audience who must have become cold with terror and gone home with a vow that they would not commit even a slight social or legal misbehaviour. This must have happened. But this argument has totally been missed.

In today's lenient atmosphere, if public hanging is introduced, I am sure people will be filled with terror for a crime.

Last and most important argument is that here execution is being talked of for pickpocketing, while we are talking of execution for parental rape.

It would be wrong to say that pickpocketing and parental rape are miles apart. No, they are totally different. There is absolutely no comparison between them.

If Britishers have abolished the capital punishment, I feel the need to ask them whether they abolished it with parental rape in mind?

Let us remember that for every daughter raped, there is a Christ crucified on the cross. The crime is so immoral, that, perhaps, God, in the form of Jesus Christ, taking man's sins on his shoulders, will have to take another incarnation and reascend on the Cross.

I sometimes think that if the great Almighty Father in the form of Lord Christ–one of the most holy beings and a pure personification of piety can allow himself to be crucified for man's sins[1], why can't a man be given simple hanging for such an immoral sin? But if you want to send an invitation for the rebirth of Christ to die on the cross, then the case is different.

I have felt that sociologists tend to become too conscious of social power to the extent that they ignore the power of other institutions. I remember meeting during the opinion poll, two students from the Delhi School of Social Work who said that punishment is no solution and that

---

1. Persons not having the knowledge of Bible, that records the life of Jesus Christ, generally feel that Lord Jesus was captured and put to death on the Cross and He could not have escaped, even if He had wanted to. Superficially, it does seem that Christ, the great messiah, was captured, tortured and killed. But, infact, had He wanted, Christ would have easily escaped His death. Could anybody have stopped Him had Jesus so desired to escape? But He was born as a messiah, He had to suffer for the complete sorrow of mankind, and it's sins. Robert Reid, translator-commentator of "The Gospel of the Kingdom: according to St. Mathew", says–"Jesus was held to the nails by the will of God. Little did the religious scoffers realise the divine intent being fulfilled at the cavalry".

culprits are abnormal. By making such general arguments aren't we abnormally dealing with this menace?

This year my house was illuminated on Diwali, in celebration of Kind Rama's victory over Ravana, for abducting his wife. But Jeet Singh's daughter celebrated no Diwali. Her heart was all dark. When I think of how her life can be illuminated, I at once start seeing Jeet Singh on the gallows.

STRENGTHENING THE FAMILY STRIDE

Wise men, after collecting a lot many pearls of experience, and with it eminence, gave us a very invaluable teaching, whose validity is too high to be crossed by time. It was the golden truth that the best way to treat a disease is to prevent it.

When we talk of dealing with the effects of a mega problem, we should also involve, as a parallel discussion, measures that would not allow the menace to take place at all.

Sociology offers us a very valuable source for the same.

The most important institution that affects an individual is the family. Family is the synthesis of many human relationships and is the widest road which runs from the womb to the grave. The institution of the family influences the constitution of a man's psychology, and is very deeply responsible for the making of an individual. The harmony or disharmony, harmonizes or disharmonizes a man's behaviour structure. Though a million factors inside and outside an individual contribute to the making of him, the family is one of the biggest stones that hits the waters of a human's consciousness, and it's waves thus carry a lot of effect.

Social science has always studied deeply the relationship of the family and the individual, and research has shown that many a time, the input of force that a family injects into the individual, effects the output of force, that a individual outpours on the society.

Professor Khan gave a very meaningful lecture on family and individual in parental rape, which offers a great scope of research, analysis and thought, for the prevention of parental rape:

"The structure of the family has come in under heavy pressure. And this post 1991 economic globalisation is adding to the problems of family structure and family function. Cities, lack the desired quantity of healthy intervention from NGO's and government agencies. And in slum areas or in urban areas we do not have any institutional arrangement at all to interact with the family.

The effects of a family are very deep and far reaching. The negative side is a very tragic story. People take to gambling because of unhealthy family environment. People take to drugs because of unhealthy family environment. Though everywhere we talk of the family, family's effectiveness and family's role in prevention; what have we done to strengthen this institution? Particularly with the fact that in the recent decades it has come under a lot of pressure. Practically, we are not doing anything. We have programmes for aged people, we even have programmes for the prostitutes. But are there programmes that come to your mind for strengthening the family or what you call family life? If we try to provide support, if we have schemes to strengthen the family, then probably we will be doing so many things into one, including delineating this kind of parental behaviour. I personally feel that if we really mean business, in dealing with this problem, then there should be a two way attack-curing the effect, reading the effect, and curing the cause that leads to this effect. Curing and dealing would be to lay focus on people, who deal in this kind of behaviour".

One of the gravest tragedies is that we tend to view a family as a personal institution, affecting only the persons that make it.

Nobody doubts that family is a private structure. Where individuals live together and enjoy life without inviting interference, except needed.

But society is a group of individuals. As individuals group themselves into a family, a society thus becomes a group of families. Thus when we talk of a social problem, families as small power units of the great social powerhouse, assume a very important form. Studying any social problem without studying the family, is more or less equal to the desire of reading a book without reading its pages.

Family thus is both a social institution and a private institution. Family life demands a great deal of study when searching for perspectives in a social build up.

The Sociological View

Let us further analytically examine this fact.

We live in a family and take many important decisions. Many of them are exclusively personal, with the law detaching itself from any interference. But a little observation brings out the fact that how deeply they leave an imprint on the society, as a collective force.

Marriage is a personal decision affected by the family and ones own psyche. Whether I am open minded and will marry and girl of any religion or I shall be very particular about the religion, sub caste, caste, of my bride; is my own wish and my own right. Nobody can interfere.

But ask this question to a thousand individuals and make a poll. The answers will throw light on whether the society allows interreligion marriages or not.

Thus if we desire to bring a society where the social structure allows religions to tie nuptial knots and Vedas coexist with Quran, a personal counselling to every male is required. We are thus interfering into an individual's personal decision. But it is necessary because each individual decision shapes up the marital attitude of the society and gives it a secular or a theocratic form.

Each family has its own problems. It's a couple's personal life whether they have love for each other and time for their children or not. Can we interfere?

We cannot. But at the same time, we realise how deeply the parents' relationship affects the psychology of a child. And, many a times the dark, dingy atmosphere of the family makes the youth end up for the poisonous glow of the opium den. A thousand such cases have given rise to the terrifying social problem of drug abuse.

Though drug abuse and marital attitude are more common examples, sometimes family atmosphere shapes a sex criminal, even though other factors like immorality, are there.

Thus, family life affects social life. So the roads of social service will have to enter the family. But it requires that the family members do not feel personally robbed, otherwise they will never interact.

One of the solutions is may be a two way programme by NGO's. In the first phase, the representatives distribute literature and message on many important family issues as a general counselling, not questioning the personal lives of the members.

In the second phase, they work so well that they win the confidence of the people and thus people themselves come to their counselling centres with their exclusive family problems and they are solved.

Magazines like Sarita and Women's Era have carried for years, help columns, where a distinguished psychologist solves the family problems of the readers. Problems are solved, families are affected by the peace and thus many waves of the society's undesired turbulence brought to rest.

If the emotional tensions and misunderstandings within a family are given a chord of peace, they might contribute to preventing the rape imbroglio. What's needed is a hand which can enter the main door, and travelling through the rooms of the house and corridors of the inmates' hearts, collects the dirt that has collected and throws it away.

If families are brushed clean, the hope looms large, that the society will see the horizon of perfection, which is very ideal, very pretty, very calm, but.... a dream.

SEX PERMISSIVENESS AND RAPE

If any of my readers has taken an outlook that family's effect on rape means that this menace occurs in India because our society is not permissive towards sex, it is a complete reversal of truth.

Dr. Khan says that "You have rape in India. But you also have rape, even parental rape, in such permissive societies like Sweden and Denmark. They are highly permissive societies where very young people start living together and things like dating and mating, are institutions that are rather commonly accepted. But where we have this kind of permissiveness, even there cases of rape take place and quite a few are also of the category of parental rape".

Permissiveness can never stop rape. Sex is not a desire that can be fulfilled if given in plenty. I have found highly immoral, such so called saintly statements like "salvation through sex".

In western countries people openly kiss each other on the roadsides. But in USA, a woman is raped every two seconds[1].

If a person every night has an intercourse in bed, that doesn't mean that he will tolerate his sex desire towards a woman who would not want to have sex with him.

Sex permissiveness only means that sexual desires are freely allowed to go beyond that of a single woman. A man and a woman will feel free to satisfy their sex desire.

But it certainly has no authority towards a sex desire being produced. It only gives a free scope for sex desires to be satisfied.

Then if one desires to make love to a woman, who shows indifference to him, he might rape her, if his sexuality superimposes over his conscience.

Even sex permissive societies construct rooms where women are tied to the bed, and by the sexual spark of the culprit, clouded in the doom of insult and trauma.

HAS THE FATHER-DAUGHTER RELATIONSHIP BROKEN APART?

Dr. Khan feels that the father-daughter relationship is not breaking down. We find that even sociologically, the relationship still is in existence, though it is the attitude of its inevitable intactness which has been shattered because of the coming of parental rapes.

"I do not entirely agree that they are facing breakdown. I would adhere to the idea of family breakdown. Earlier we had large families, now we have joint family.

This inter-generation relationship within the family is undergoing a phase of transition. Earlier there was military obedience. Whatever was said by the eldest member of the family was the word of law. Military obedience is getting replaced by what we call intelligent corporation. And

---

1. Such statistics are always subject to change.

that has to be. Ultimately literacy level is going up, media level is going up, global change is taking place, so it is obvious that the transition from military obedience to intelligent corporation would be there. So that is the kind of change that I see rather than father-daughter breakdown.

A parent daughter relationship is there even in societies where there is one parent family. Where the daughter doesn't have to worry that she will have to fill some name in the father's column. Even there the relationship between father and daughter, mother and son is there. So if we have relationship even in one parent families what to say of families where the family structure is intact."

SUPERSTITIONS AND RAPE

Dr. Anandi Lal told me of a superstition where virgins are raped with the belief that an intercourse with a virgin can cure one of a sexual disease.

Dr. Khan adds that in the Yellow River Civilization was a belief that having intercourse with a thousand virgins will make one immortal.

He however feels that examples of rape occurring because of superstition are very scanty.

But even if one in a thousand cases this occurs, it is horrible to think that a woman is robbed of her sexual respect because of a ugly superstition. Literacy and education must spread to every corner of the world, as only literary fragrance can kill the poisonous smell of the flower bed of superstition.

But the above superstition also hints at a culprit's immorality. Nobody moral would rape a woman for immortality or for curing oneself from a sexual disease, that is again achieved through an unethical copulation.

SOCIAL IMPLICATIONS OF RAPE

Dr. Khan says that there are vast social implications of rape and parental rape. It is "patently a threat to social structure and social functioning. It contravenes the entire legal structure, violating the fundamental rights. And people not only physically, but also psychologically and emotionally enforce themselves upon others".

Parental rape is the harbinger of cultural doom. It violates the daughter's fundamental right to sexual privacy and is also a naked violation of the father's duty to sexually protect his female progeny. The foundations of society are broken when the structures of parental rapes are erected.

When we are talking of such a vast catastrophe, we cannot risk to divert an inch from the valid path. A slight deviation might take us miles away from the solution.

Thus, in no way, could one risk the wrong highlighting of the morality and execution issues to parental rape.

It is in this spirit of duty that I had to go against Professor Khan and sociology, while maintaining deep respect for both.

Sociology tends to become, at times, too scientific. And in this cold atmosphere of logic, fails to admit inside, the warmth of ethics and morals, thus bringing to life a wrong approach to this issue.

Immorality has existed because of its hypocrisy. If you are confused whether parental rape is immoral or moral, you admit the probability of its being a moral form. At once, this devil, clothed in the guise of a saint, shall capture the crown of morality. And where immorality rules on the chair of ethics, the country exists in the deepest, the darkest and the ugliest zone of doom.

Part Seven

THE SEXOLOGICAL VIEW

THE SEXOLOGICAL VIEW*

Nobody knows whether Paradise still has "that forbidden tree whose mortal taste brought death into the world, and all our woe". But our common ancestors, Adam and Eve have died and perished, a several million years ago.

But they have left before them, their large family, which lives on all the lands between the seven seas, and grows and grows bigger with the relation of sex and procreation.

Life is a charge produced when the Ova and the Sperm meet. Sex ignites the capsule of life and thus is the most fundamental relation to a man.

Sex is a universal phenomenon. It sustains a million species around the globe. A simple three tier system of attraction, copulation and reproduction creates the phenomenon of life and is responsible for the vast turbulence on earth or the ocean of consciousness.

Sex is a phenomenon, not only because it charges the phenomenon of life, but because from womb to the tomb, sex is the most fundamental and important meaning behind relation, psyche and emotion.

The aim of sex is procreation. Procreation requires a complete merge of male and female forms which is brought into force and effect by the revolutionarily powerful pull of attraction. The power of attraction gives birth to a million sexual relationships and thus, in the process of bringing the male and female together to produce the circuit of life, sex has bred the complex structure of several male-female permutations and combinations.

---

* Based on an exclusive interview with Dr. L.K. Bhutani, Professor and Head of the Department of Dermatology and Venerology, All India Institute of Medical Sciences.

Sexual behaviourisms have been studied, researched and analysed for centuries in every civilization, country and continent. Vatsyayan scanned across all sex perspectives and penned the sex serman of India - Kama Sutra. Sophocles highlighted great sexological complexity and psycho-social confusion when he immortalised with his pen the Theban Legend of a king marrying his mother in ignorance of her identity and the catastrophe caused by the knowledge that he had inflated the womb of a woman, he had come out from, some years ago.[1] Sexual studies and sexology has been an obsession for search, research and deduction.

Every sexual relationship seems a transparent light emitted when two sexes meet to form a unisex. But when this light touches the prism of sexology, it emits various colours and shades of human sexual behaviour and throws light on the several questions that have been gripped by the dark.

I made the transparent light fuelled by a parental rape sexuality, touch the prism of sexology. The colours and shades of meaning emitted by the sex prism are shared with the ardent seeker, who seeks for solution to this abnormal sexual phenomenon. And thus, has entered the laboratory of a sex scientist.

WHY AREN'T MEN RAPED?

The roots of rape are even older than the roots of civilization. It has always been, like sex, a universal phenomenon. When civilization became the thesis of man's existence, rape assumed the form of an antithesis. Civilization always tried to root out rape but rape succeeded in becoming a universal postulate of the constitution of civilization.

But why has rape been largely a man-crime, with women rape cases being exceptions? Most of the law books of the countries, do not contain any punishment for a woman who rapes - for we by and large cannot even imagine a woman raping a man !

The question is indeed very complex. Women and Men both have sexual desires, and if there are beastly men, many women too can be equated to beasts. Why then, do women not rape and men go to such a large

---

1. Read "The Theban plays" by Sophocles; Penguin Books.

extent, that they do not just rape but force sexual intercourse with their own daughter......?

Dr. Bhutani says that "if you look at this question from the biological sense, man is the more active partner of the two and his sexual desires are aroused more easily than a woman's sexual desires. While it may be biological it may also be partly social. Society feels that women, sexually speaking, ought to behave in a more restrained manner, rather in an aggressive manner.

Man is more aggressive in his sexual urges, sexual desires and sexual behaviour. There is not so much restrain. A man can go without a shirt but a woman without a blouse and a bare chest would evoke large scale criticism. Even if you'll find women permissive societies, it is more as a revolt.

But women do rape. And some cases have been reported in western countries".

The social stigma related to women, indeed, has a lot to do with this argument. Where women are expected to protect their virginity and are abused, spitted, starved, stripped and killed when they are raped, how can they even imagine to rape .....? If they are hanged on being raped, one cannot imagine a treatment, which at least the Indian society will impart to a woman who shall rape.

Males are by nature more aggressive, this aggressive consciousness is increased when they are allowed to go half bare, if their wish to go bare is related with a desire to sexually expose and sexually attract.

Male's biological aggressiveness, which is a natural inheritance of a male species and the sociological aggressiveness which is a social inheritance, cloud together into his psychology. If he is moral he shall control his aggressiveness and limit it, if not, it might lead to making him enjoy from a forced intercourse.

Let us investigate this activation cum aggressiveness factor keeping the entire male species in mind. This aggressiveness is common to the entire male species. Why then do some men rape and most of them not? The answer lies in morality and consciousness of morals.

Thus active sexuality of the male only provides a reason, why females do not rape. If somebody would make it an excuse of siding with culprits, at the best, he would be trying to sell ice to an eskimo.

THE SEXOLOGICAL DIFFERENCE BETWEEN SPOUSE AND FATHER DAUGHTER SEXUALITY

There are varied sexual relationships that are present between humans. But obviously there must be some sexological difference between relationships like that of a husband and wife and that between a daughter and her father.

However, purely sexually there lies no difference. "Nature", the illustrated professor comments, "must have made the function of sex, as a means of procreation. So, species would have been extinct if there would have been no sex.

If you look at the animal kingdom, I don't think they differentiate between son - daughter or father. So, to an extent, this difference seems social. For example, if the father and daughter did not know that they were blood relations, they would fall in love with each other.

But I think it is a very sensible social restrain. Suppose, there is a consignment of marriage or it is not even consignment but an incestual relationship, then you shall see that the genes inherited in the father and the genes which the daughter has inherited from the father, those of which that are abnormal, would get together, and if there is an offspring, he would be more abnormal. Any child born of an incestual relationship, is more likely to be imbalanced, having greater problems because of genetic inheritances.

Again, whoever made the institution of marriage had a lot of basis for the same.

In the first case it assumes that you have a monogamous relationship, as long as you stay with the institution of wedlock.

The second part that it does is that it provides security for the progeny. So you grow up in a secure environment. If parental rape occurs. That is broken".

The Sexological View

Thus trying to estimate the damage done by the menace of parental rape, we gather a lot of material, when we study the issue from the eyes of a sexologist.

The doubling of abnormal genes in a daughter - father born progeny is a great biological danger. It also gives a signal that even biology and nature does not permit blood relations to enter the relationship of sex.

However, I have felt that sexually there lies no difference between a man and woman going in for sex, no matter what relationship they have, only because it is beyond the powers of sex to attach a limit.

Take any father and daughter for instance. They are both human beings. Each human has an entrusted duty to take part in the process of reproduction. Thus he has in him a sexual consciousness. As human beings can only copulate when they are attracted towards the opposite sex, the opposite sex attraction is also present in every human of the species.

These two functions shall also be present in the father and daughter. Now it is for them to inactivate these powers when they react to each other. Sex cannot make in the body a system where one is averted towards his blood relations and relatives and attracted towards others. Thus sex will become activated whenever and wherever we see opposite sex charge. It is our duty to use the power of the rational as regards our sexuality, and thus confine it to the wise limit.

Because we know that whether ethically or morally, biologically or socially, it is wrong to enter an incestual relationship, we must keep ourselves away from it.

If we still do that, we shall activate the sex circuit and it shall ignite. But being abnormal, its effects shall very soon be seen and the activation of such a sex, will charge to effect a catastrophe and something, somewhere shall be torn apart.

When somebody ravishes, somebody perishes.

THE MAN IN THE CAVE : AN IDEA TO ESTIMATE THE POWER OF SEX

In order to make an estimation of the power of sex inherent in a homo sapien, I put up a question involving a man in a cave.

Let us think of an impossible situation. A man is confined to a hut and is given food and water every day but is not allowed to see anybody. He survives and sees the day of youth. Will he have sexual desires?

The Professor said that the desires would in all probability be aroused. "You have just confined him to a cave or a corner - But biologically his senses would be roused. Many times, we find that people have had no contact with a woman but the moment they touch a woman's hand, there is a peculiar type of sensation that flows through. So, he would be sexually roused. It might take a little time because he is not conditioned to it. But he would definitely be roused".

This gives an indication of the power of sex. It can become conscious by its own. Even if a person doesn't see a fellow being of the opposite sex, his powers would be awaken in all their force and form.

More than that, Dr. M. Z. Khan informs that man is much more sexually powerful than other living beings. He is always sexually activated unlike most of the animals, who have a mating period. Man's sexuality can also be roused in a sexual situations.

Man has inherent in him an infinitely powerful granule of sexuality, containing a vast reservoir of power. If used constructively it become a beautiful facet of creation and construction and a couple might as well say:

> We joined by sex,
> And solved the most complex
> riddle of life.

But if used wrongly, it leads to molestation and rape and vomits barbarism.

> Man rapes,
> And destroys the myth
> that he is man.

DOES RAPE OCCUR IN ANIMALS?

While studying an issue, you come across many questions that do not offer any solution to it. But they are important for they not only enhance but complete the knowledge, information and learning of the whole

The Sexological View

perspective in question. They are invaluable in their insight and penetration and every research scholar praises them for their depth. One such question, which is common to all categories of rape, and opens up a new section of study on the subject, is that whether animals rape?

Sexuality is a very complex area of study. Animal sexuality is all the more difficult, as it as such difficult to study and animal behaviourism.

We are studying this question decide whether :

(i) Brain and Intelligence has anything to do with rape. Is rape a product of high profile human intelligence? If it is established that animals do not rape, it might be probable that man's intelligence led him to think that even sexual pleasure can be stolen or snatched. On the other hand, if it is established that even animals rape, it would mean that sexuality produces in all beasts an enjoyment and a sense of pleasure and the more wicked ones choose to seek sexual gratification by force.

(ii) Rape has something to do with high sexual levels in homo sapiens or even animals in their mating periods are capable to the decline of rape.

(iii) If animals do rape, is it there too a basically male crime or a crime done by both the sexes equally. Thus, studying sexual behavior distribution in the sexes of animals.

However, to the best of my knowledge and belief, to date no study on this topic has been done. When I put this question to our illustrated sexologist, he very modestly admitted that this topic was his limit in particular and of sexology in general. He could only hint that rape might occur in animals :

"Rape basically means forced. We sometimes observe that a dog is running after a bitch and the bitch is resenting. The females seem to be genuine in their resentment. The possibility of defining that as rape definitely exists. But the other possibility is that the bitch is running to make it all the more attractive".

This is a new area of study, but as my three points propose we must arrive at an authority on this, to make our knowledge on rape complete.

One thing strikes me : if animals do rape and even in this animal kingdom virginity is lost and traumas imported to the victim, it means that the psychology and behaviourism and emotional complexities of the animal kingdom is very deep and animals are not just creatures that sleep, eat and die. There is much that lies within ....

The haunting fact is that if rape does occur in animals, how can we end it? Can anybody give me the answer? I am searching for it ....

HORRIFYING EXTENSION OF PARENTAL RAPE : CAN A WIFE BE RAPED BY HER HUSBAND?

The central incident of the Ramayana is the abduction of Maa Sita by the demon king Ravana. The Central incident of Mahabharata is the attempt to rape Draupadi and her protection by Lord Krishna. As the Ramayana and the Mahabharata are the most important writings of India, or in other words, the centre of gravity in the cosmos of art and literature, and are works of spiritual and ethical establishment; it establishes the fact that rape is to the core an argument of ethics. Rape, basically, is an ethical problem.

Throughout scanning this menace sexologically, I realised, that neither me nor my illustrious doctor, whom I had chosen for this deepest argument on parental rape menace could alienate human sexuality with ethical laws and social norms.

Thus, it gives rise to a fact that sex is not just a question that involves two bodies that meet, that ignite, that discharge and that produce. Their meeting, their ignition and their discharge involves a million perspectives and issues. Sex might be an individual's personal issue but it is at the same time a social - psychological - ethical issue. Infact the sociological aspect or sexuality superimposes over the personal, and a sexual issue must be studies from various angles and only when these angles are brought to a synthesis that the door of solution should be believed to have allowed us inside.

The most important parameter to weigh sex is ethicality. Ethical laws have always supervised sexuality and we saw in the last chapter in "The Morality Issue" how sensitive all this is.

The Ethical and social norm is so imminent to sex study, that no sexologist can deal with deep sexual problems without bringing it into account.

As far as ethics are concerned, they are the harbingers of renaissance. They offer new perspectives to the discussion on sexuality, revolutionizing our study, insight and thought.

To see the truth and weight in my matter, investigate this statement "Rape is forced sexual intercourse "from an ethical microscope.

The institution of marriage is such a great social bond, that nobody feels the need to scan the sexual relationship of a husband and wife. It is felt that marriage permits co-existence; and interexistence undoubtedly permits intercourse. But have we ever tried to think of a situation when a husband forces the wife to have an intercourse with him, when not even the infinitesimal part of her permits that. Isn't that rape ....?

I know that my reader would be staring at this page with shock and disbelief. I can understand that you have realised how hollow our sexual passions are, allowing the worm of rape to enter any institution of human relation.

If this thing happens in thousands of couples, in every direction, imagine how many rapes we give consent to each day. Thus the seemingly okay sexual relationship of a husband and wife, that has enjoyed perpetual consent is not so innocent as it looks.

But why have I included it here? What importance does it have an a parental rape discussion?

The importance is infinite. If the relationship of marriage, which society and law has never challenged and can perhaps never challenge on grounds of rape, breeds such dirt when placed aside the white cloth of ethics, just meditate for a moment and realise how ethically, spiritually and morally relationships that have been named "RAPE" stand? When ethics challenge the seven rounds around the golden fire amidst the holy chanting of the Vedas, where shall you place the forced sexuality of a father with his daughter. If the ethical perspective is alive not extinct in you, can you even for a moment stand beside the Church and look into the Cross with your eyes, if you are thinking of a report of parental rape in the papers.
I cannot .

I have, in every page of the book perhaps, tried to bring this shame in you, because only this can make you criticize this menace. When you shall learn that ethically even spouse relations can bring rape into effect only then would you realise that parental rape is totally unpassable. This shall feel you with shame and when you shall remember rape, while reading the holy sermons of the Quran, Bible or Geeta, the ethic power shall activate your shame into a positive desire to alienate it. This desire must come in every reader that reads this book. The book, otherwise, is a failure.

I had always believed that even a husband can rape a wife, but was half sure of ever penning it. But one line of Dr. Bhutani that "ethically, writers say, even a wife can be raped", activated the dormant confidence. I found that this postulate had to be developed as a section, in the Sexological View.

Somewhere a priest ties a couple in a nuptial knot. I want to say:

> Undrape her,
> But do not rape her.

Because somewhere a husband rapes.

A father swings her daughter to her bed and closes the light. He takes her in his arms.

Where are we swinging our culture to? Where shall this bounce take her?

I can see Satan laugh.

MAN'S SEXUAL FANTASY

The brain weighs 1.4 Kilograms but the real weight that it carries is infinite. Flowing on the floors of the brain is the spirit of intelligence.

This spirit of intelligence is the spirit of civilization. It has created a magnificent combination of fact and fiction, myth and reality; where trains of the theory of relativity travel at a speed of one hundred and eighty lakh kilometres per hour and reach the hundreds of feet long Pyramids that rule Egypt. The theory of evolution is able to see on its large screen the

The Sexological View

story of the complete chain of organisms, a million year long; and breaking the rules of nature, man and dinosaurs meet at a Park in the modern era. Galaxies million light years long are studied as if they are next door neighbours and satellites disrespect the code of privacy, photographing other planets without their will. Paradises are lost and regained. Sherlock Holmes and Poirot. The Sun Temple and The Light House of Alexandria, Illiad and Odyssey, Darwin and Einstein ..... the list is endless !

This superhuman intelligence of the human world is a vast reservoir. It is like a river, that when stopped is a dam which irrigates life and flourishment; when made to run, races civilization to ruins.

The DNA or the deoxyribonucleic acid is the code of life. It has in it, a million combinations, which travel into all directions; intersect, dissect, deviate and meet; thus constructing he individual's profile. The profile combined with the power punch of the outer environment, determines a direction called the human deviation. It determines a human's preferences, likes and dislikes.

The senses feed on this genetic structure, suck this deviation and make it to reach the heart–the master activator of emotions and preferences of the body. The preferences of a human, produced by DNA, are activated by the heart. The heart produces the wave of desire. The waves of desires reach the depth of the brain - the headquarters of body control and coordination. This desire here makes the complete blueprint of the action which it aims. Once the blueprint is made, the brain gives the final command. And, the blueprint is transformed into reality.

If there had been a museum which had a collection of human brains, you could have, perhaps, been able to scan the entire blueprint of some of the greatest actions of the world. And amongst it's ruins, you could have found freezed in the dead grey sense, along with the world's greatest acts, the complex structures of the world's greatest crimes, black threads of preference, desire and fantasy interwoven into spine chilling murders and .... parental rape.

Yes, parental rape is perhaps a sexual fantasy. Immoral expectations converted into horrible actions by the grey sense. The work of a genius. But a genius filled with boiling immorality and frozen evil. The same cold and sharp intelligence of Professor Moriarity, the master genius of crime, controlling the entire London Mafia, in the chronicles written by a retired army surgeon, about his genius friend of 221 B Baker Street in the grand, old days of Queen Victoria.

This is my entire theory, which I have held, from the days I first understood the ravishing hunger of rape and the fluid of intelligence in the brain.

I put this theory of mine to test. So, while me and Dr. Bhutani were sitting in his nice, quiet study, with my questions and his answers trying to figure meaning out of the sexology of forced sex, that make virgin's shrieks, the history and truth of human civilization, I asked him whether he considered sex a sexual fantasy? Are all these abnormalities - rapes, incestual rape, parental rape .... even homosexuality and bestiality, the sexual fantasies of a human brain that first weaves strange illusions and then brings them into action?

"To say what is abnormal is very difficult", he said, dwelling into the fantasy perspective, "If you can arouse discharge by masturbation, somebody picks up an animate and inanimate object and arouses discharge by it.

Where do you put a line between normal and abnormal? Normal and abnormal is mostly defined on the basis of social sanction. Normal is done by the majority and abnormal by the minority. But Masturbation is what a vast majority of individuals do, but which is the most discredited form of sexual arousing. I often quote it that it is the most condemned and the most widely practised form of sexual gratification. Any average Indian will define masturbation as bad, though knowing fully well, that majority of his countrymen do it".

"But", I reminded him, "Nature conceived of sex just as an attraction between individuals of the opposite sex." So how can homosexuality and bestiality be normal? Isn't this the parameter of defining abnormality?

"You are quite right in saying that Nature conceived of sex as a means of procreation. But nature also attached the tag of pleasurable sensation to it. And when the pleasurable sensation got an upper hand, sex assumed the function beyond procreation, in the human civilization. This is the reason why people go to more than one partner and do not stick to one mate. They do not find adequate satisfaction with one sexual partner.

The Sexological View

As much as the restrain limits you to having relationship outside certain things, the intelligence that you have makes you go ahead and do any type of pleasurable things. Animals do not have intelligence, so you won't find such a behaviour in them.

After all, a husband and wife just do not have sex twice or thrice a lifetime because it is two or three children that they want. They have sex sometimes two to three times a day, a week, a month, a year".

So here lies the answer. Sex has the function of procreation but comes with the flavour of sensual pleasure and carnial enjoyment. Perhaps, because it was very necessary for a species to engage in sex in order to sustain and maintain itself and thus life in general, nature turned sex into a pleasure so that possibly no living being could stay away from it.

As human's sexuality is always aroused, thus he is always attracted towards the taste of sexual pleasure. This is so strong that he manages to sexually activate himself even in a sexual situations. And, as according to Dr. Khan, "a lady totally clothed in a burka also might sexually allure a male".

With a desire to have more and more pleasure, immorality unrestraining the restrain to stay in limits, guided by intelligence, the fantasy is created, and once its blue print is formed, the senses join to bring it to action.

Pleasure is not just responsible for fantasy but also for what is a sexual behaviour outside allowed limits, like adultery, pre marital sex and sex mania. Normal rape also comes in this category.

While we, Dr. Bhutani and myself, almost perfectly arrived at a consensus that homosexuality and bestiality is a fantasy, created by the couple of pleasure and intelligence, the doctor felt that to "say that incest is abnormal is sexologically very difficult". But he throws light on the genetic disaster of the same and I have pointed that this is proof enough. Through genetic disorder, Biology perhaps says - "stop here. This is the limit".

More than that, Dr. Bhutani agrees, that socially incestual relationship is a catastrophe. And as human sexology cannot be allowed to be alienated from sociology, it is a further proof that parental rape is not a normal occurrence.

So, aided with viable proof, I request my reader to allow me to exercise my right of opinion in my book and term incest as an abnormality, rising out of an immoral desire and a genius but evil deviated brain.

A fantasy rapist sits like Professor Moriarity, "a spider in his web". He weaves the threads of his fantasies into a cage. As a victim enters, the silent threads "radiate" and she is trapped ....

One of the theories of AIDS is that man had an intercourse with a monkey. Monkey's body system transferred the HIV Virus and gifted the disease of AIDS to us. So immoral are we and so high is our sex mania, that one AIDS patient through a chain of sexual intercourse has brought AIDS to a point of epidemic. If it bursts, life blasts ....

Will anybody inject the vaccine of ethical control in the human body system so that monkeys, daughters and life may be allowed to be conceived and not killed, by sex.

THE INFANT DEATH

Whether by incestual rape or by other forms of child abuse, whenever infants are raped, they die.

Dr. Bhutani says that "they do not die because they are raped. They die because of the injury done to them, when they are raped. When such an organ is inserted into an infant, there is severe injury and bleeding, resulting into death".

Forget for once, what occurred in the father's mind when he killed his own daughter, when he had himself made to be born.

Think for a moment the shrieks, the tears, the agony of an innocent babe, when her delicate body is made to endure an intercourse. Think where you shall place a picture of an infant butchered more severely than if all his fingers were cut one by one or he was put in a can of boiling oil.

Infants demand protection, more because they cannot demand it. I submit for the Supreme Court's inspection a infant bled to death, with her short petition told by each drop of her blood :

> I had broken off from a penetration,
> To see the world,
> And not to be penetrated,
> To blood, to tears, to death ....

Hon'ble Mr. Chief Justice of India, every silent infant waits for your decision. And hops, when her case comes for hearing, the court shall not be adjourned sine die ......

THE GLIMMER OF HOPE

The infant death is a scar on the face of love. Everywhere a human lives, a shriek can be heard. Everything which is human shivers. Civilization trembles with aversion when it sees its face in the mirror.

So, is all gone? Have we nothing left?

It was in this frame of mind that I asked my last question : Can a raped daughter ever be fully cured?

The answer was like a bowl of hot soup to a naked body shivering in the severe, biting winds of Autumn.

"In medicine or biology", the doctor began, and his face at that moment reflected the glow of a bishop, "you should never ask questions whether something can ever happen or can something never happen. If corrective measures are taken, why not? If a child had been maltreated by her parents, not sexually, but otherwise, can he not grow to be a healthy individual? He surely can be. There are several insecure homes where children have turned to be secure adults".

Yes, hope lives. Hope never dies. Satan made man loose paradise but Lord Jesus Christ regained it for us. Where our Lord is ready to be or crucified for our sake, there surely lies hope.

But we must act. We must become symbols of mercy, and like a million candles of warmth, convert a raped daughter's autumn into spring.

Agreed that today when I say "Good Morning" my lip quivers. The morning isn't good. But I can make it to be. For hope is immortal.

Some saints attain enlightenment on a cremation ground's ashes of death. If some of us will spare a moment of our selfish lives and meditate for a poor victim, her happiness shall take rebirth, like Phoenix, from her own ashes.

Part Eight

THE OPINION POLL

THE OPINION POLL

Place	:	In and around the Mall Road Crossing.
Date	:	16th of March 1994
Time	:	1.00 p.m. to 7.00 p.m.
Total No. of People involved	:	118
Sum total Categories	:	05

A NOTE ON THE POLL

The existing punishments written for the three rape categories in this poll are :

Ordinary (12 & above)	-	7-10	Years
Kid & Infant	-	10	Years
Parental	-	10	Years

These are not 'orthodox' punishments for the above category rapes; in the sense that even life imprisonment for a rape has been given. Again, imprisonments are even reduced. However, in most of the cases the above punishments are given.

The opinion poll asks a particular voter that whether the existing punishment for an XY category rape is okay or whether life imprisonment or execution should be given. The meaning of the question is, that whether for an XY category ape the 'generally given punishment' is right or should 'always' life imprisonment or execution be given.

ABBREVIATIONS USED

EP   Existing Punishment
LI   Life Imprisonment
EX   Execution
OE   Open Execution

OPINION POLL - (ONE)

VOTING CATEGORY		VOTER CATEGORY	
		Students	Men Professionals
Number		37	28
Ordinary			
7-10	EP	18 (48.6%)	08 (28.6%)
	L. I.	12 (32.5%)	10 (35.7%)
	EX	07 (18.9%)	10 (35.7%)
Kid and Infants			
10	EP	05 (13.6%)	03 (10.7%)
	LI	15 (40.5%)	07 (25.0%)
	EX	17 (46.0%)	18 (64.3%)
Parental			
10	EP	03 (08.1%)	02 (07.1%)
	LI	11 (29.8%)	06 (21.4%)
	EX	18 (48.6%)	12 (42.4%)
	OE	05 (13.5%)	08 (28.5%)
Is there any need to set up new committees to decide punishments for parental rapes		34 (92.0%)	27 (96.5%)

OPINION POLL - (TWO)

VOTING CATEGORY		VOTER CATEGORY		
		Women Professionals	Housewives	Total of all Categories
Number		34	19	118
Ordinary				
7-10	EP	12 (35.2%)	9 (47.3%)	47 (39.8%)
	LI	17 (50.0%)	7 (36.8%)	46 (38.9%)
	EX	05 (14.8%)	3 (15.7%)	25 (21.1%)
Kid and Infant				
10	EP	05 (14.8%)	6 (31.5%)	19 (16.1%)
	LI	05 (14.8%)	6 (31.5%)	48 (40.7%)
	EX	11 (32.2%)	5 (26.3%)	51 (43.2%)
Parental				
10	EP	03 (08.9%)	3 (15.7%)	11 (09.3%)
	LI	12 (35.3%)	9 (47.3%)	38 (32.2%)
	EX	16 (47.0%)	7 (37.0%)	53 (45.0%)
	OE	03 (08.9%)	0 (00.0%)	16 (13.5%)
Is there any need to set up new committees to decide punishments for parental rapes		33 (97.5%)	16 (84.21%)	110 (93.2%)

POLL CONCLUDED

Part Nine

DISSECTING THE POLL

DISSECTING THE POLL

Having seen what the poll delivers, let us now deeply study the opinion poll. The poll in which different sections of society participated is a representative super minimodel of India. The basic thought, the basic orientation of this opinion poll is the movement of India at large. The poll answers many of the questions, the answers of whom we have been searching for throughout this study and thus demands deep examination and critical analysis.

One thing about the poll that immediately strikes the mind and that has been talked in some details towards the end of the first part is the no. of persons going in for execution. In the final section of the poll, where all the different categories are joined, an amazingly high 58.5% of the voters go in for execution in parental rapes. And, it must be noticed that out of this 58.5%; 13.5% are those that go for open execution. In kid and infant rapes also a quite high ratio of 43.2% go in for execution.

In the beginning one feels that the voters were off-their heads while they were participating in the poll. Otherwise, how, in a society where rape is obsessively a woman-crime and the victim is defined as a woman with a black womb can suddenly all turn into feminists and suggest execution as a punishment.

But, just a little insight is needed to reveal the simple facts hidden in this opinion taken by the majority of the voters, or in general, Indians. The answer revolves around what I call the Pregnancy Theory.

Rape is considered a crime from woman's point of view and the man left to roam about free not because the man is considered pious and pure. No, definitely not. Majority of God fearing Indians cannot have this belief. It is because the fact that in the post-rape situation, it is the woman who becomes pregnant and brings this black relationship to light. Thus the womb of the woman to the Indians becomes a black womb and the woman impure and impious. The poor victim with her 'inflated womb' with the impious child is unacceptable to society and is totally ostracized. Thus beating of a daughter when she is raped or killing of a sexually assaulted sister is basically frustration thinking about the implications of the incident in a narrow minded social infrastructure and cultural background. The mistake, of course, is the inability to understand that the girl is not at fault because she struggled to protect her virginity and because she struggled to save her chastity her, womb is also pious and pure. The deeply rooted thinking that the woman in all situations has to protect her womb because she is born with the boon to bear the offspring can perhaps never die - at least, it has remained till now. So, it doesn't matter if the victim was one and the rapists ten. Because the crucial and the single decision maker in the rape incident is the womb. The woman becomes pregnant thus she is the culprit.

It must also be noted that in kid and infant rapes where the victim is sexually immature and the pregnancy factory doesn't exist, the girl is given a better treatment. She in most cases is not beaten up.

The worth of the people with rapists is definitely there but they can not with the deeply affixed, centuries old values side with the victim. But they at the same time, do not definitely side with the rapist. He is the culprit and is the target of worth and fury. But this worth doesn't activate because majority of people believe that they can not gain anything by voicing against rape. This factor deepens when society offers examples of a poor father's failure who struggles to death and infamy trying to get justice for her raped daughter. Also with the orthodox social jungle with fierce beasts around, the poor girl's parents prefer to keep quiet, than to voice and be eaten up.

But, in a opinion poll which doesn't offer individual names, till the voters choose to comment, the voter feels free to loosen his collected fury against rapists at large and thus is easily able to say — 'He should be executed'.

For parental rapes, the reason for people going in for execution is very simple to understand. With the Ramayana as a cultural guiding light with its values of ideal human relationships; the breaking of a father-daughter relationship can not be digested. So, the reason, I fear, that parental rapes can increase is not because people justify parental rape but because with the existing social infrastructure people don't feel free to define rapes as unjustified.

So, this is the reason for this fury and it's being passive in nature. But with my favourite moralist Henry Fielding, I say, that passive goodness serves no sense. It's indeed good for nothing.

We shall discuss the question of execution as a punishment, being right or wrong afterwards, but for the present let us look at an important implication of this decision.

As discussed before, approximately 60% go in for execution in parental rapes and 44% for minor rapes. This stands totally opposed to the existing punishments in law books. Infact 60% of the people in ordinary, 84% in minor and 90% in parental rapes have not expressed faith in existing punishments. This inharmony between law and people opinion is very crucial and of high consequence in a democracy because every democratic structure stands on the words - "by the people, for the people, of the people". So the law makers and law commentators should do a lot deal of hard work studying this inharmony and trying to sort things out.

Let us now ask freely - should constitution be changed? Should execution be allowed? But for this we need to study the problem with the culprits in view. So, let's wait till part 10.

Though only three-four, but there were voices favouring reformatory measures for rapes. If these reformatory measures are applied to the culprits and they sexually educated, it might serve but little purpose. Would you educate a rapist father-'look, what you did was wrong. She was your daughter'. Such a thing, at least, would be an education that would invite laughs and jokes. Because at this end, we journalists might ask - "Didn't the father know that always? He definitely did. He knew that while he was raping his daughter. So, what purpose does it serve?" I don't think that there is so great a spiritual teacher today who can convert a father - rapist to a feminist-saint. Because the father who has the courage to rape her daughter and villainy to digest his immorality is definitely an incurable monster. Declining morals might be uplifted but extinct morals certainly cannot be rejuvenated.

But there is one thing where reformatory measures and sex education can definitely help. This is in preventing rape. Because rape is a disease that cannot be cured, but the vaccine of sex education can definitely go a great way in preventing it.

In the Republic, while discussing his cave simile, Plato had given a comment too valuable to be missed. Consider this para out of the Philosophical dialogue :

"But suppose", I said, "That such natures were cut loose when they were still children, from all the dead weights natural too this world of change and fastened on them by sensual indulgences like gluttony, which twist their minds' vision to lower things, and suppose that when they were to freed turned towards the truth ....

The real meaning of this dialogue by narrator socrates is philosophical and unconnected with our thought. But the crux of this dialogue is that bad passions can be weeded out, if right education from the beginning works against them. This is what even Fielding believed when he showed the education of Amelia's children in AMELIA.

If sex education is given from the beginning from the least possible age and fear inculcated in the young minds towards breaking the codes of right sexual conduct, rape at large can be prevented. Sex education should aim at controlling sexual instincts and inserting to the blood a hatred for rape. Because rape many a time occurs due to wrong sexual information gathered at a young age which leads to youngsters crossing limits and engaging in crimes. Where sexual knowledge is the combination of vulgar books, wrong films and information by half matured and misdirected friends; rape is very much possible.

While writing this piece, I am reminded of the Article "THE GROWING CANCER", by Suneet Vir Singh in the Hindustan Times Saturday magazine some time back. Suneet writes that "the maximum number of cases involving the "disappearance" of minor girls are reported from the slums and unauthorised colonies of east Delhi". She feels that this is because ten to twelve people are packed in one room which creates problems. For understanding what Mrs. Vir Singh exactly means, consider her description of a typical single room in a place like the suburban areas of Seelampur in Delhi and what happens there :

"On winter nights the unmarried son, the adolescent daughter and the tense nephew are all huddled up together, right next to the newly wed Bhaiya and Bhabhi. While the old grandfather is too deaf and the parents are full of fatigue by the end of the day, what goes

Dissecting the Poll

through the mind of that 20 years old younger son, or the daughter, who has just arrived at puberty or the teenage nephew, when the roomless bhaiya and bhabhi use the quilt for privacy?"

Thus when the "20 year old younger son" and "the puberty reached daughter" whose sexual instincts have arisen witness night after night a sexual intercourse what will happen? Naturally, as Mrs. Vir Singh says, "The little match box of a house" will create conditions "in which a sexually deprived youth shall loose his head" and this loss of wisdom might end in rape.

What can be done? Surely, we can't start talking of providing persons of such economic classes a four room flat where the 'Bhaiya" and 'Bhabhi' can satisfy themselves in a private chamber. But, sex education might prevent the 20 year old son to satisfy himself through rape. If there is someone to whom the 20 year old can talk to regarding his sexual hunger that rises every night, who can somehow keep him in safe limits, a rape case shall be prevented.

It surely is not easy. I am not a day dreamer to say that. But it isn't impossible. If a head gets loose on witnessing right under his eyes an intercourse every night; it can also be in safe limits, if it hears everyday- "Gandhi Ji said the biggest crime is rape".

We also need to keep a check on what youngsters read and what youngsters see. As a collegiate, I've never gone dozen blues. While they are banned at halls (thankfully) they creep to the video set from the video libraries. While it's pretty difficult to check each and every library in town, it is surely possible for every parent to check what his son is seeing at the video. A blue film with all the black it exposes, definitely can ruin a mind and while many would satisfy themselves through a two sided accepted intercourse some might go for rape. Thus education and check is necessary and can surely prevent rape.

But, you might say that while all this is okay for rapes, what about parental rapes. To an extent, reformatory measures can prevent parental rapes also. Because again quoting Nihar Ranjan Senapati; making a person conscious about the duties of a father might make him conscious enough to realise what a father-daughter relationship means and prevent him from turning into a father-rapist.

But, this preventive education in case of parental rapes is a very risky factor. Parental rape is still a new phenomenon. So, you surely can't include in the school curriculum a sex - education period where boys are taught - "It's wrong to rape your daughter". Because though the present has broken the staunch faith in a father-daughter relationship it hasn't broken the relationship as such. In a time, when parental rapes take you by a shock you can't include it as a normal phenomenon. Further, in most young minds, parental rape possibility does not exist. Such education might make them realise that a parental rape is also possible. This realisation can be very risky also.

Again, girls can and should be made aware of rapes but would it really help if they are told to be aware of their fathers? It might turn out to be a catastrophe. Because not two fathers in every hundred think like that for their daughter. It would be totally unjustified to them if their daughter suddenly starts suspecting them or if a paternal kiss meets with aversion. And, if all daughters will this awareness created by such a sex-education, start suspecting their fathers, the father-daughter relationship from one angle breaks off. Where does our culture go them?

It's risky to make young minds aware of parental rapes. But, if not this, what then? Even if for exceptions, parental rapes still stand as a danger. So either we throw parental rape awareness idea out of our minds or mould it in a safe way. I take the latter path.

First of all, let us start this education as an experiment - on a selected group of individuals. In this education, girls should be told of existence of parental rapes but just as an information or maybe as a general comment on the declining standards of morality in a moral science lecture. But at the same time girls should be told that this is an exception and it's wrong to suspect fathers. This, can be done artfully with lines like :

"It's a relief such a thing is an exception ! After all, how can such a pious relationship break. And it's foolish and bad on the daughter's part to suspect her father. Because not all, infact, exceptional fathers are bad. Above all, we all know that all daughters can know if their fathers cross the limits. But we know, it shall never happen. Man fears god to this extent at least".

In this way, the information is also passed and the fear also not created. In a similar artful manner, the problem of parental rape victims coming to the police can also be solved. For, it can be said :

'Every girl should feel free to report to the police. I even say that those girls who stay away from the law when they are raped by their fathers are fools. If they come ahead, there shall be some to stop them but there shall be more to guide them.

This line given above, as readers must have realised by now, holds importance when thought in relation to Jeet Singh Case. The younger daughter would not have reported to the police after such a long time had she been properly guided.

Thus, in this manner, sex education and reformatory measures can both educate and eradicate the menace of rape. They can also create bolder victims who feels free to come to the police, as already discussed in the above para.

When we have opened this question of closeness, let us deal with it closely. It is very important for the menace of rape to end that the victim feels free to report to the police. Because the wrong social attitude which if hasn't accused the girl as a culprit then surely has treated the girl as a culprit; has survived because the victim has chosen a corner to weep and not a crossing to protest. She must throw the cover of darkness now and come out under the sun and boldly tell every body that she has been raped and demands justice as a right and not as an obligation. If the victims shall stop accepting rape as a individual fault but as a big injustice directed towards the ruin of their chastity the problem shall fade away.

But, the beginning of every such protest, normally begins at the Police Station. The police, sadly, for the general public is a source of terror and not composure. The common man feels very nervous in going to a police station. He somehow feels that going to the police to end his problems is the beginning of bigger problems. A woman without, chastity is a living being without life. She, with the attack of rape is insulted, insecured shocked and depressed. When she thinks about the Police Station a fear that's synonymous with the average Indian grips her too. But more importantly and very tragically, one thing is out to shake off her faith in Police almost as soon as the thinks of going to the Police–and this is nothing else but Custodial Rapes.

Custodial rapes are the biggest bridge between rape victims and law. Can a raped woman think of justice in high optimistic terms, if the police that has been set up to prevent rapes, rapes women and that too right in the police station.

The existing general punishment of 10 years for custodial rapes is at least to me, highly unsatisfactory. Because the custodial rapes are done by law implementors who are supposed to preserve the legal and basic moral position of the society. Custodial rapes, need the severemost treatment. Law implementors can never be excused to break law. I am reminded of the Maurayan administration where severemost punishments had been matted out for the law body officials. Democracy is the political system that should least excuse any loopholes or moral breakdown in the law. Because democracy runs on the closeness between law and society. Any deviation takes it close to dictatorship.

Lastly, a question arises - why such a big ratio for confidence in existing punishments for ordinary (teenage & above) rapes? In the final category almost 40% have expressed faith in a 7 years punishment as against 16% in minor and 9.3% in parental . This is because we have got immuned to ordinary rapes. Getting immuned to ordinary rapes, is all right. After all they have punctured out heart for centuries. But at the same time what is required is the right social attitude to combat and eradicate these 'ordinary' rapes. Even though a very low percentage has gone for execution 60% have expressed faith in extreme punishments. This fury needs to be activated. This only shall prevent us from being immuned to minor and parental rapes. Because may be if we end 'Ordinary' rapes their terrifying cousins shall also ultimately fade away, leaving way for a healthy, open minded society where culture moves on the right track watered by morality, humanity and clear vision.

Part Ten

AFTER THOUGHT : DO CULPRITS NEED TO BE THOUGHT ABOUT

AFTER THOUGHT : DO CULPRITS NEED TO BE THOUGHT ABOUT

Reading this analytical research till this stage, readers might brand me as an over obsessed feminist or a pseudo moralist taking into account a burning social problem from only the fair sex in view. Sociologists and law commentators might attack me for not even once commenting on culprits or saying a warm word to them. Not wanting to be defined a sentimental fool or an excessively emotional feminist, I now devote my attention entirely to the culprits.

The first thing that is a hot favourite with sociologists and all those who study this problem from the 'culprit-angle' is that those committing rapes, are mostly abnormal-especially in kid and infant rapes and essentially in parental rapes. I agree. Definitely the abnormality is there. But what does this 'abnormality' mean?

Most people take this abnormality to hint at insanity or an off-tracked mind; which is not the case. The culprit who molests a three year old kid or a 10 month baby or a father who sexually assaults his daughter are not normal. But the abnormality means that their sexual instincts are highly out of control. Their hunger is so vast that it demands constant satisfaction, diversifying satisfaction and indiscriminating satisfaction. Meaning that they need to satisfy their hunger at regular intervals. This hunger needs a companion change constantly. One wife or one lover can not satisfy the appetite. And; this sexual passion doesn't discriminate between persons–they can be of any age groups and at worst can even be nieces or daughters.

But, surely, the culprits are aware that what they are doing is wrong. We can not expect a father to think that molesting his daughter or a four year old neighbour is normal or pious. So, when these people are aware that what they do is wrong, why don't they go to a sexologist and keep their appetite in control through proper medication? They can take ten rounds of a sex specialist everyday when they are trapped with a sexual disease but don't feel the need to take medicines to control their instincts. And why don't they do that? The reason is simple. They don't feel the need. Their 'abnormality' is a boon to them. They want to enjoy through it. So why control it?

That is why I can not, at least, whether you brand me as a sentimental fool or a cyclic, sympathize with such abnormalities. Such an abnormality to me is a criminal instinct. If the person concerned doesn't control it through medicines it must be severely controlled through law.

Second factor that leads to minor rapes and even to parental rapes is frustration. Not really sexual but social in nature. Unemployed youths with heavy burdens on their shoulders, people totally frustrated with their jobs or existing lifestyles tend to pacify their heat of frustration through forced sexual intercourse which is very easily obtained through helpless and innocent kids and infants. While talking of rapes, many people shout— End this frustration; give jobs, create proper living conditions. Rapes will stop! While I was taking this opinion poll, one person Anil K. Sharma, a scientist in Road Research at Mall Road while siding out parental rapes said that punishments are no solution to the problem but foolishness. And the frustration which is the root cause should be weeded out.

When I listen to such comments I sometimes go off my head. It's difficult to keep cool at such moments. You are frustrated with the social degradation that has left you unemployed while the less capable are roaming in cars. Or even worse, a dedicated and hard working official of high calibre, you see the useless being promoted to high positions. This rotten system frustrates you. And your answer is your moral degradation that allows you to sexually molest innocent kids and women who haven't contributed to your mental disturbance. While you yourself are frustrated at a degradation and abuse it a thousand and one times every day, you degrade yourself a million times more to cut this frustration. How very ironical! And more so, if the whole thing is viewed with respect to parental rapes. If a father tells me that he raped his daughter because being unemployed he was frustrated, I might be tempted to give him a ferocious slap. Your answer for not being able to provide for your daughter's food and clothing is to unclothe her of her chastity. Very hypocritical indeed.

You marry. To end your frustration of the day you have sex with your wife. Even marriage in terms of sexual appetite looses its moral as

After Thought : Do Culprits Need..............

well as original meaning, but till this stage, it can be digested. But the situation becomes out of control when you try to search for answers to your frustration through your daughter's lips or the neighbour's cheeks. Moreover, such culprits will shriek in courts before the judge that their rapes were results of frustration and they deserve no punishment. What do we say to such immorality?

Let us look at this frustration from another angle to completely view this point in true light. There are many, many people who fact such social frustrations in terms of unemployment and rotten official life. Then why do some shriek against them through their writings or demonstrations and some through rapes? The heat of frustration through unemployment and related causes is so great that no one can bear it and all want it to end. If it can be cooled by sexual satisfaction why don't all go for it? Why some? The answer is–Morality or a complete absence of conscience and ethical control. Those who are moral and people with a living conscience can never ever think of rapes in any situation. They might end their frustration by drowning themselves in the Yamuna than to drown somebody's virginity. Only those whose morality has become extinct and the right code of conduct broken loose, can think of rape as any answer to their frustrations and mental suffocations.

I never mean to say that frustration resulting from social causes should not be a cause of sympathy or concern. Sociologists should speak of it, social workers try to eradicate it, journalists comment on it and mass media focus it. But please don't side with frustration as a disturbance that leads to rape. It is not frustration but immorality that drives one to rapes. The rapist is never socially frustrated–he is sexually frustrated. And no one can be excused for making a poor woman, poor kid and more tragically a poor daughter, the object of his sexual passion. Social frustration as a reasoning behind rape is a mask to hide your yearnings, passions and immoralities.

Third reason behind rapes, which doesn't go with parental rapes is rape as a punishment. In conflicts between two social groups or two communities, the means of attack include attacks on the chastities of fair sex of both sides. Socially and economically high landlords punish poor tribal girls who voice against them by "fixing them". Such punishments are most common with social workers in villages who open their mouths against the autocratic landlords or existing social backwardness. (No one, at least I, hasn't forgotten the Bhanwari Devi Case). The landlords feel that the only way to close their mouth is to make it 'impious' through a forced sexual intercourse.

I am sure that no sociologist or a research scholar on the menace of rape shall appreciate this reason for rapes. This is one reason, at least, which has met with total criticism as one of the blackest immoralities existing in our society.

We have now talked of all the reasons that make culprits rape-abnormality or psychic-disturbance; frustration and rape as a punishment. In all the three reasons, we saw, while dissecting them in the minutest manner that it is the culprits who are at fault. In the first case which is abnormality or psychic-disturbance; no matter how much inharmonious their mind and heart are; the culprits are fully aware of rape as an immoral–intercourse. Frustration is the worst example of a hypocritic reasoning where culprits very slyly pass of their immorality as morality and throw all their blame on the social order. The third reasoning doesn't need to be talked of at a round table conference or a women's seminar; to be labelled as immoral. It's to the core a barbaric and unethical attitude of person or groups. So, do we really need to think about culprits or would it serve any purpose if we do? That was the reason why I always looked at this problem from a feminist angle because I knew it would lead us nowhere to talk about culprits.

Should culprits be executed in rape cases, more so in kid-infant and parental rapes? Should execution be made a necessary punishment?

I can't outrightly given an answer to this question. For execution is a punishment that's ultimate in nature. When we talk of a punishment that means an exit from the world, it's unjustified for anyone to come at once with a positive answer. But, I would surely say, that while at every Diwali we illuminate our houses celebrating Lord Rama's victory over Ravana who had kidnapped his wife never harming her chastity, execution at least seems a point to be thought upon when we talk of people making women naked on streets before hundreds of people and spitting on them.

Let us, just assume, that an amendment has been made and execution made a necessary punishment for all rapes. Now, let us analyse how effective this punishment is and what purposes it serves. What are the positive aspects it kisses and what are the negative aspects it shakes hands with. We might, like this, end at our destination that has been playing hide and seek with us for long. Being optimistic in nature, I start with positive aspects.

We start with open execution. Consider the scene: A busy crossing. A man tied with ropes. Hundreds of people around. The police. And, the victim.

The man's sentence is read by the police, accompanied with sounds of abuses and sighs over the incident. The man is then shot in front of the public and sounds of a thousand claps match the sounds of bullets.

What happens? This open execution inculcates fear in the minds of all onlookers. And those with sexual instincts big enough to lead to rape leave the scene with frozen hands and beating hearts. The victim amidst the claps and abuses has achieved her zenith–she can move with her head high and prestige unshaken.

Let us look at ordinary execution now. We look at it from three different angles: the people executed, the people for whom they are executed and the society as affected by the execution.

We have seen before, that in all factors leading to rape, the culprits are at fault. Moreover, we have also discussed that while reformatory measures and sex education can prevent young minds from becoming rapist, it can do little to prevent people who rape to turn into saints. For while young minds are easily "impressionable", matured minds are not. People who have polluted the moral atmosphere of the country; the wheels of a nation that move it to the heights of glory or depths of infamy and who cannot be cured have been executed. At this juncture, it seems well. Execution seems a glorious punishment when we think of the sex racket in Ajmer that had rocked the headlines of the newspapers a little time back where young girls were first raped and then photographed naked. We must also remember that rape can also make the victim a victim of AIDS.

Martin C. Battestin, a noted literary scholar while exploring moral depths of Henry Fielding in his book "The Moral Basis of Fielding's art : A Study of Joseph Andrews" said that while Fielding believed in the high notions of charity; preaching his readers to forgive people of all their mistakes; even he felt that where forgiving someone would just mean letting an incurable disease stay in society; extreme punishments should be given. He believed that "in special cases even the hangman's office would be the highest example of charity in the Kingdom".

The treatment given to victims in rape cases is extremely unsatisfactory. When we think of the severe mental traumas victims undergo in terms of fits, suicidal chances, nightmares, foreshortened future, low chances of marriage and extreme depression and view all this with the fact that the people doing it are largely at fault; execution as a punishment seems not bad. For the severemost punishment might win the woman inflicted with the severemost injury peace of mind and may be prestige too.

Lastly, this execution would be for the society. After all, culprits are punished not so much cure them of their faults than to insure that their corrupted minds do not infect the society. Execution might be the best means to see that this sexual infection does not spread.

Throughout this study, while viewing rape as a means of extreme traumas for the victim and the ultimate fault committed by the culprit, we have again and again thought of death sentence as a possible solution to it. This was deepened when the largest percentage of voters in the opinion poll in parental and kid rapes went for capital punishment. So by making execution as a punishment; all bodies would be converting the hopes of the majority of the populace to reality. Such a punishment definitely goes on the guidelines of democracy which runs on the wishes of the people. It can also serve to put an effective check to parental rapes, which as we have discussed, stand to-day as a danger to cultural unity and the nation's existence in moral and ethical sphere.

Execution is a possibility and perhaps a good one too–it cannot be denied. However, I would again say that I have talked of execution just as a good possibility and am not in any way writing this book with its motto as—Make execution the only punishment for all rapes.

For even if execution which stands as a possibility is included then it should be of course deeply studied for years first. After all, the question in mind is that of life and death, so what if the persons concerned are culprits. When we hold them as members of the society and not out-casts, it becomes an essential duty and not obligation that we speak of any statement connected to their life and death only after studying all its aspects and impacts.

After Thought : Do Culprits Need............... 133

While execution stands as a possibility, some factors that stand in its way should also be examined. Rape in 100% cases is done with the knowledge of it's being the most immoral human action. However, even if in exceptions, rape sometimes occurs as an impulsive action. The culprit is not basically immoral who now and then plans to molest women. He is suddenly attracted towards a particular woman. He tries to win her; fails. But is never filled with an intention to rape. But, suddenly, at the spur of the moment, he is filled with the uncontrollable passion to have an intercourse with her. His sexual appetite increases in the form of an outburst to such heights that reason is unable to keep him in control. As a result, the never intended rape occurs. But such exceptional culprits repent highly afterwards. And to a person who is repenting of his fault it's unjustified if he is executed. I am writing this piece of thought with Balwant Gargi's T.V. Serial-"Sanja Chula" in mind. Pankaj Berry, played exactly the character I talked of above.

This was the reason (and there might be more) which compelled me not to say at any point in the research about exception being made a necessary punishment.

But then such reasons are exceptions and anyway don't go in parental and kid rapes and so exception still at large stands as a good possibility.

But then, with execution there are many more solutions to the problem. The first and the foremost is that if society's attitude towards rape changes, then may be the need to even discuss execution as a possible solution to the problem would not arise.

Today's way of talking about victims is that because the woman has the boon to give birth to the offspring, she in all situations should preserve her chastity. We should take it in this way that because the woman has been given the blessing, by God to give birth; it is the society's duty to protect her virginity and if anyone attempts of forcibly break it, he should be ostracized as culprit guilty of blackening the choicest and the most divine blessing by God.

Rape has always been viewed in moral and ethical terms but with wrong moral and ethical standards. So what are immoral and unethical, have for centuries been passed off as ethnically right. This has resulted in pain and agony for the victim and in some way or the other, escape for the culprit. If the society develops an attitude, that understands the total innocence of the victim and given her the same importance and same social position that she enjoyed in the pre-rape period, no punishment would be needed, leave aside execution.

This is because when rape would not socially effect a woman's prestige her personal pain would also be minimized to a very great extent. Because loss of virginity and sexual insult indeed pains the victim but what pains her more and what infact, is the real pain is that she is not accepted into society and that nobody is ready to marry her. But, if our society is converted to such a social infrastructure which by no means blames a raped woman but continues to love her as if nothing has happened, for the woman much dread and terror in the word rape would vanish off. Also, if, in such a society the culprit is totally ostracized, he would live a living death, ten times more horrible than execution. Because, one reasons for punishments not being able to work out is that the culprit is not ashamed of his imprisonment because he knows that he shall be accepted in the society as soon as he goes out. Nothing hurts a man more than social ostracization; he being a social animal and thus social ban of the culprit in a rape case shall prevent hundreds; even thousands from trying to commit it. Rape is a dreaded word for the girl's parents. They live with the fear that there are chances for their daughter to be raped. This makes them preventing the girl to remain outdoors after the sun sets or not to allow her to visit criminally sensitive places. But in the boys' parents' heart the fear does not stay that chances of their son committing the blackest villainy are there. This is because society is moulded like that. I am sure if society is constructed on the terms I mentioned above; rape would not remain a dreaded word for the girl's family though of course they might still try to keep her virginity safe with the same concern. At the same time, rape would become a dreaded word for the boy's parents because of the social infamy it would bring to them. This would go a long way in combating rape. Because while people with evil passions in their hearts would themselves fear to commit such a crime, parents would also keep a check on their son's activities and his moral growth with age.

Such a society, I fully realise, is very difficult to be obtained. It's not easy to change a social infrastructure constructed centuries ago and renovated by each generation. But if 'Sati Pratha' can go, which had once looked as an incurable evil, the social narrowmindedness towards rapes can also vanish. This can be brought about firstly by extensive media coverage. Ms. Jayanti Patnaik's wish about each newspaper devoting one of its page everyday or once a week to women's problems is a good suggestion. Day after day or week after week media coverage of woman exploitation can surely shake the society. In framing the society on the above mentioned lines, the law can also contribute a great deal. For example, harassing of a rape victim by relatives or friends in any way should be completely banned. Usually the law only deals with giving the culprit the punishment. It isn't connected with the victim. Once the punishment is passed to the culprit, the thing is forgotten off. This is where the real problem lies. There should be special cells made by government that should deal with the victim—in seeing that she is not harassed and is completely accepted in society. These cells should extend emotional help to the victim, so that the confidence in her that's completely shaken by rape is reconstructed in her being and rape doesn't leave her a creeping worm but a living lady. Then, as Mr. Vishwa B., whom I've already quoted before said, every rape case should come in the headlines. Moreover, it should be very severely criticized and the culprit pinched with pointed words and extreme criticism. Such front page in-famy would create terror in society towards rape.

We have talked earlier in part 9 and partly in this section also that reformatory measures for rape culprits are very difficult to work. Surely, they are. But this thing must be given a try. Because, if one in a million chances it works out it would go a very long way in dealing with the rape menace.

How the culprits should be educated and how morality and ethical values inserted in them should be decided by a panel of the country's most eminent spiritual leaders, moral preachers, doctors and legal commentators. The recommendations of such a study should be worked out in experiments. It might work as a wonder with the rape culprits.

But, in solutions other than execution, social banishment is the most hopeful thesis. Social Banishment, if not in ordinary and kid-infant rapes, can surely work very easily in parental rapes as it has worked in the Jeet Singh case, where under the guidance of Mr. Om Prakash Parashar, people have decided not to have any contacts with Jeet Singh Chauhan.

Having devoted a great deal of attention on punishments regarding rapes we must now turn to a result that has come out of this long study, and that is, that rapes demand a great deal of study and setting of different panels for framing decisions on its legal aspects and making long needed and necessary amendments. Where things are vastly changing with respect to the jurisdictive dections to social problems in society, rape also demands a change in the legal machinery's handling it and combating it as a socials and cultural menace. We must never forget that 94% of our society wants this to be done.

The Supreme Court has given the freedom to commit suicide.

SC's decision to let a man decide himself the limits of life needs to be applauded at, as it serves to eradicate many problems connected with suicide as a legal ban.

But, as some-body asked–when will Supreme Court grant the freedom to live?

In the social infrastructure that exists today, rape is a means of great emotional breakdown. Where every increasing second of life is an addition to the intolerable emotional pain, the chances of suicide are very large. As Dr. Anandi Lal said–"If the victim is left to feel that she is alone, she might commit suicide".

Supreme Court has granted the right to commit suicide. The citizens have a right to dig if life becomes a hell. But can they never hope to life again if life at one stage becomes a death each day? When will the country's judicial panel grant the right to live? Where you are not tortured, blamed and ostracized for something you don't have a share in.

The daughters of Jeet Singh Chauhan and their hundreds of fellow citizens are waiting to see the final down–When their country shall grant them the right to live and not the obligation to exist.

Part Eleven

THE HOMOSEXUAL ELEMENT

THE HOMOSEXUAL ELEMENT

It is debatable whether it is a true sin or a true boon that normal very easily becomes monotonous for a human being. He tries to break this monotony by inventing and dwelling in abnormal forms, prohibited by nature, thus making a new but a strange world governed by the element of obscure and the grotesque.

This abnormality has made its way into each face of society and civilisation and has made strange homes. However, the most antonymous forms to the normal are seen in the examples of sex.

Sex is the symbol of life, maintenance sustenance and perseverance. A homo sapien acquires the tag of Man only when he merges with his mate in the relationship of sex. Before that, he is merely a male or a female. Individual represents in himself a half and thus incomplete form of life and it is only when two opposite sexes copulate that a unisex, neutral in form, is formed and a great merge portraying completeness of life occurs.

Sex in humans has a very simple rule attached to it. Simple and fundamental, elementary and natural, only opposite sexes attract each other and only they are filled with a desire to sexually interact–this is what the rule of nature says. However the mind is a combination of a million nerves. And in each nerve a granule of intelligence breathes. Such infinitely powerful intelligence is indeed a phenomenon. When this phenomenon is deviated to the positive, masterpieces are created and maestros are born. But when this same phenomenon is deviated towards the negative, powerful but abnormal forms are reproduced. In sex, man has ceased to follow the simple rule of opposite sex attraction. He is also attracted and copulates with a being of the same sex. And this is, as is very well known, defined as homosexuality.

Homosexuality has always been in existence. The Kama Sutra devotes a full chapter to explaining homosexuality.

Homosexuality has always been an issue of controversy. It has always been defined as a immoral and unethical form, a complete antithesis to the laws of nature and a perfect antonym to normality. It has also been considered a taboo to talk about it.

But slowly and slowly the society has begun to accept homosexuality as a part of human existence. But, it still remains an issue of fire and storm.

Homosexuality has never been an integral part of culture and being an antithesis to normal sexual behaviourism has always been isolated, practised by a minority of individuals, of deranged mental structure.

It is thus, not always easy to get a homo mate. Scandals of sex slaves for the satisfaction of homosexual hunger is not a new news.

But again getting a sexual slave, is not easy, excluding one case when this slavery can be very easily obtained. In the case of a father-son relationship where a father can easily rape his kid son. The high probability is that the son might not even understand what goes between him and his father each night, even after having a hint that these bed scenes are not a normal part of one's life. He can also be easily threatened to keep quiet.

Dr. Kapur hints that homosexual parental rapes have also been happening. Immorality has increased to such an extent, that houses are governed by fathers who are governed by a sexually dismantled brain and thus do not only breed rape of a daughter but that also of a son. The abnormal phenomenon of homosexuality has thus taken a spine chilling form and aspect in the dirty world of parental rape.

In our society homosexuality is a taboo. One shivers even before he can utter a syllable in connection with it. In such a society homosexual parental rapes can never came to the light. Our society needs to understand that even if immoral, unethical, unnatural; homosexuality is a fact and thus needs to be studied and understood to create an atmosphere where homosexual abuse is openly reported. Being quiet to it; can only let the menace of sexual abuse grow, destroying lives and society, souls and civilisation.

In the Indian culture and ethos lies one of the biggest problems, bred by lack of understanding, which is nothing short of a social menace and cultural catastrophe. We have added respect, importance and value to some relationships and social behaviourisms. But when they are broken we tend not to speak against them. What a paradox indeed; This occurs because the heart of the society is afflicted by the worm of narrowmindedness and blind understanding posing as bright knowledge.

We have always respected the family as an individual existence and further as a block, millions of whom booming to form the social structure. Individual is supposed to impart great respect to the family and fulfil his duty towards it. Each family is also supposed to breed values and ethics. Families are expected to interact with their neighbours in a harmonious way, thus resulting in a society where the rights and duties are perfectly distributed and morals slide it to spiritual harmony. I have always respected this facet of our society and I am glad to have come from such a family. But this consciousness to respect family relationships and preserve the family to preserve society has bred many illusive and oblivious forms in our structures of understanding. We have become too conscious of the fact that it is essential to respect and preserve the family and family relationship that we forget that where a member of a family breaks all codes of conduct, he should immediately be disowned to save the family and thus also the society. Instead, when a member of the family crosses his rights and projects his duties we shield him thinking that it is saving our family.

Thus the worm is allowed to exist and he eats the palace from within, preserving its outer beauty and making everything hollow from within. On the surface of its such a society will look preserved and beautiful, in reality it will be all hollow and worm eaten, decaying and foul smelling and will soon end into oblivion. Such pseudo preserved society will someday or the other crumble into ashes and die. An illusive understanding of a great fact allows poison to breed, which gives suck to death. All because we have become so conscious of our duty towards the family that we forget that always sustenance is not the only act of perseverance, destruction also leads to perseverance.

Same is the fact with homosexuality and rape. Because, these issues are a sign of abnormality and immorality, we think that is immoral even to talk about them.

I wanted to photograph a young lady of a good family with the caption "Whom can she Trust?" For this book, signifying an atmosphere where immorality has led to total lack of trust on a female's part and gives terrifying indications that the 'burqa' and the "purdah" might be back if all this continues for a substantial time period. I talked to young ladies on the road but nobody obliged me with one, as soon as they heard that the subject of the book is rape. They thought that such a photograph in such a book will be the key to a storm in their house and might obstruct chances of their getting married. Now very disgusting. Have our schools and colleges parents and guardians, saints and preachers bred this light of knowledge into our fair sex which is even danger than ignorance?

When shall we be able to understand that to talk on bad issues with an aim to criticize them is a very holy action, since it activates the atmosphere of good, thus declining the strength of the evil. This illusive and blind understanding of rape, homosexuality and family pride has been such a terrible trio that homosexual parental rapes are not allowed by it to come to the police station or be falshed on the screens of the multimedia. All this, when the trauma in it is phenomenally catastrophic.

A homosexual rape effects very deeply the faculties of body, mind and soul, shattering the blocks of a human existence. Examining parental rapes, we have seen how deeply a parental rape cuts across a human being because of being a forced sexual intercourse brought about by a relation that was expected to protect the victim's sexual freedom. Homosexual abuse is all the more shocking since those who are not attracted homosexually view this sort of intercourse with a shudder; repulsion and aversion. For them to dream of having a homo intercourse is enough to send tremors through every bit of their body. Thus being raped homosexually makes them hate sex and might well bring perpetual aversion to it. The chances of suicide and hypersensitive mental disorders multiplies a million fold in a homosexual rape.

Viewing the whole problem from the fact, that no such case is in public, but is happening amidst many a four walled structure, one is really emotionally moved and terrified imaging the terrifying reality of a repeated homosexual rape and the victim made to suffer this hyperturbulent trauma, and decay and waste away from within because he cannot tell it to anybody who can lock things out.

But the question is that how many such sex slaves would we allow to be born? How long would we allow the beautiful relationship of nature to be torn apart, from whatsoever reason the destructive process have been born? How long would we allow the presence of such terrifying snapshots of reality in the album of civilization? How long would we allow our fundamental rights to be blasted apart? So, how long would society wait till we openmindedly view homosexual abuse and make it public? After all forced sex ceases to be a private affair. It assumes a form of public importance which should be globally condemned.

This book remains a woman oriented book where parental rape is studied as a problem of a woman and girl child. However, as parental rape is a vast issue combining varied aspects, a book of the title "When Fathers Rape" is incomplete till a mention of those sex maniac fathers, who rape sons, is included. So this piece assumes, perhaps, an invaluably important form.

Problems of incest are very complex and therefore their solutions lie very far away.... Perhaps they lie locked amidst a swamp of narrowmindedness and illusions and thus can be captured only when we learn to catch reality and not shadows.

Part Twelve

CRITICAL ISSUES

CRITICAL ISSUES

I

THE PUNISHMENT CONSENSUS

In this book, we have discussed varied punishments for the culprits in parental rape cases. The punishment question thus lays scattered throughout the book, questioning every possible punishment, stating its pro's and con's and including it as a possibility.

Readers might have felt that I am merely acting as a commentator-journalist just describing the possibility, and not formulating form the varied possibilities, the principle.

However this is not so. I have written this book to arrive at a consensus to the complexities related to the parental rape menace and even in what I have called "a mega introduction", prepare a piece worthy enough to look like a file of solutions.

The problem with parental rape is that culprits in it cannot be given any one punishment. It cannot be said that this particular punishment should be given to all culprits.

This happens because of varied reasons that we have seen. In addition to it, there are many punishments offering equal scope for a favourable solution. The victims are also a part of the menace and their post-rape traumas must be studied and taken into account, to calculate the damage done by the culprit. This again might vary from case to case.

Thus what should be formed to deal with the menace is a multipunishment structure where the whole situation after a rape case should be studied, especially a detailed scan of the culprit and on the basis of it, the most suitable punishment should be given.

The formation of this multipunishment structure requires extensive study and a very diverse and representative participation, including people from all facets of the society.

II

THE VICTIM'S DEFENCE

Dark, dingy, dusty room. Everything still and motionless. Faint rays of the moon fall on a pale, horrifying face which sits on the window. The window overlooks a terrifying barren tree. The barren tree reflects its barren branches on the woman's face. The lips of the woman tremble, her heart beats, her hands are cold. Maddening nervousness.

Depression.
First snap from the victim file.
Gift for being raped.
Satanic copulation, Horror's insertion.

She has locked herself in a room. As the fan slowly and slowly moves, tears slowly and slowly come down on her face. She cries–"All is destroyed. Nobody loves me. I will have no husband, no career, no children. Why did this happen to me.....?"

Sense of foreshortened future.
Second snap from the victim file.
Gift for being raped.
Satanic copulation, Horror's insertion.

Rita was getting late for her office. She never took the lift, but that day in hurry rushed inside it. As she moved in and the lift started moving, she suddenly started trembling. Her body was in seconds soaked in sweat. She remembered that day.... The life. The man. The Rape.....

Physiological reactivity upon exposure.
Third snap from the victim file.
Gift for being raped.
Satanic copulation, Horror's insertion.

Everybody who comes to this mental Retardation Cure Institute observes Snehlata, the sixteen year old girl. A one in thousand only would have watched a more spine chilling case of mental retardation. She is so horribly mentally retarded that she seems to have been born without a brain and has somehow managed to exist for sixteen long years. But who knows that when she was four years old, she was the most cute and intelligent kid ever seen. One full year in bed with her father, a hundred forced doses of sex and all her mental strength was squeezed from her. She is now a shrinked, ugly, pulp like form of a human being.

Mental retardation.
Fourth snap from the victim file.
Gift for being raped.
Satanic copulation, Horror's insertion.

> She was sleeping peacefully in her room. Then she saw a horrible dream.... She is sleeping. Suddenly her father enters. He ties her to the bed and.....

> She woke with a horrible shriek. Every day, every second, every breath of her life she thought the same thing.... It is over now. But it will start again. Her naked body shall again be butchered....

Paranoia.
Fifth snap from the victim file.
Gift for being raped.
Satanic copulation, Horror's insertion.

> Room No. 5, Bed No. 1. A girl lies on a bed. As you watch her, you start trembling. Is she really human? Flesh soaked completely, all bones visible. Eyes have moved deep inside and every nerve can be seen. When you shall sleep in the night, she will be visible in your imagination.

> But do you know that she horrifies you but you horrify her more. You, me, us. The whole society. She hates us all.

> Her father raped her and give her AIDS.

AIDS through a forced sexual intercourse.
Sixth snap from the victim file.
Gift for being raped.
Satanic copulation, Horror's insertion.

"Mad ! Mad !", said the street boys and threw stones at her. The stones hit her and even as the blood oozed from her body, she was laughing. Laughing with her eyes sparkling like fire and hair giving the horror on her face a Midas Touch.

Madness.
Seventh snap from the victim file.
Gift for being raped.
Satanic copulation, Horror's insertion.

"Rupa, open the room", the inmates of the remand home knocked the door. While everybody was enjoying the festival function, Rupa had locked herself inside.

No reply.... The door was forced open. Rupa's corpse was swinging to and fro, tied to the fan by a chunni. Her eyes had moved out. She looked horrible.

Yes, her death was horrible. But wasn't her life more horrible than this death....?

Suicide.
Eighth snap from the victim file.
Gift for being raped.
Satanic copulation, Horror's insertion.

Once again she got that horrible convulsion. The paper trembles as I move my pen on it and write about that convulsion.

Fits.
Ninth snap from the victim file.
Gift for being raped.
Satanic copulation, Horror's insertion.

"Why do you sell your body?", I asked that prostitute.

"My father bought my body for his pleasure. It has been sold for ever. What's the harm in using it now to earn money?", she replied, laughing loudly.

Critical Issues

Sexual perversion leading to prostitution.
Tenth snap from the victim file.
Gift for being raped.
Satanic copulation, Horror's insertion.

"I hate all men", she cried and banged her head against the mango tree, in a desolate area. She shrieked this line a thousand times.

Male hatred.
Eleventh snap from the victim file.
Gift for being raped.
Satanic copulation, Horror's insertion.

The daughter's innocent cries filled the room. But why is her mother crying?

Pregnancy.
Twelfth snap from the victim file.
Gift for being raped.
Satanic copulation, Horror's insertion.

The hero gently kissed the heroine's lips. But why did Geeta tremble....?

Fear of sex.
Thirteenth snap from the victim file.
Gift for being raped.
Satanic copulation, Horror's insertion.

The ten month old baby's clothes were all soaked in blood. She could not withstand the sexual contact.

Infant death due to force sex.
Fourteenth snap from the victim file.
Gift for being raped.
Satanic copulation, Horror's insertion.

Snapshots of a terrible reality. Is truth so terrible? Is fact so turbulent? Is reality so violent?

Yes, it is. These are the pictures of victims, driven to death by the culprit.

Rape in any way, but most especially parental rape, effects the victim in a multimillion ways, and each way is capable of taking her infinite miles away from normality.

Right to sexual privacy is the most exclusive, most delicate and the most cared for, among all rights of a human being. When this right is forcibly snatched away, when one's sexuality hidden in the cloth of privacy is made forcibly public, what remains....? When she is auctioned in the market of barbarism, she is treated as an animal. Consequently, she becomes an animal.

What asset of a human being remains in a victim? If somewhere her intelligence is snatched away, somewhere she is killed by a paranoia. She looks like a living form made of biological, physical and chemical substances but what makes one human–that mental and intelligible form– that withers, fades, dies.

The most affected part of rape is the victim. The culprit whatever may be the reason, enjoys to his full. Thus he satisfies his thirst. But in doing so, he squeezes to death the victim. She lives for the name of it. But what was known as her, dies for ever. If she looks in the mirror, she knows it is not her reflection.

And all this for what reason? What crime?

She asks a thousand questions: I was raped, then why am I blamed? Why did my papa beget me and then make love to me? But she finds no answer.

Every day, when she takes out her clothes, she realises that they were forcibly torn off. When she sees her body assets, she realises that they were misused. When she covers herself, she realises that she has for ever been uncovered. She always feels that no matter what she does, she is naked....

What a terrible picture! That is why my book is the Victim's Defence. She is innocent and she suffers the most, so she should be all means be defended.

Critical Issues

I have tried in this book, as hard as I could perhaps, to bring out a complete picture of the victim and highlight her traumas, so as to make you understand her innocence and her decay. I hope that if the victim is understood and properly treated by the society and given proper counselling; her traumas might fade away with time. At least, such a situation would be right and judicious and would be on the lines of morality, righteousness and truth. And that would satisfy moralists and feminists like me.

THE 17 POINT PROGRAMME

The Law can do a lot of things in bringing the right situation for the victim. Infact the law on rape should develop a full section on victim treatment.

Law must understand that when the victim is as innocent as the white light, any outer factor coming from the Society and contributing to her trauma is a crime. And crime, as law understands better than me, should be punished.

I myself have developed a 17 point programme which law can implement:

1. Use of obscene languages in the court for deciding rape cases should be banned. Lawyers sometimes use vulgar lines like– "Where did the rapist touch you? On what part of the leg? Did he penetrate something inside? If yes, what?"

   Is this language fit to suit the decorum of the court and what goes inside it? And when the SC granted right to commit suicide, amongst the very many reasons one was that it gives further harassment to a rape victim. Shouldn't the court ban such lines, that can be easily avoided and that openly insult the victim?

2. In cases where the daughter complains against her father that she was raped by him and the father is arrested, it should be insured that the father will not live with the daughter. Because if that happens, it might lead to forced sexual intercourse again.

3. Victim in every rape case should be sent by the government to a counselling centre where her complete psychology, emotional behaviourism and mental position after rape should be determined. She should be properly treated to wipe off each bit of trauma.

4. Mental harassment of rape victim by society should be banned.

5. Expulsion of any girl from her school on account that she was raped and parents of other students object to it, should also be banned.

6. Teaching of self protection techniques for girls from eight years onwards should be made compulsory. This would make them able to save themselves from rapists.

7. Minor girls should be imparted freedom to live in a new place on viable account of being in danger from the father.

8. Any one of the parent/guardian's name should be made compulsory for child's registration in various institutions than just the male parent's name. This would ease situation for a mother who given birth to her baby after being sexually violated and doesn't want to tell the father's name.

9. Victim should be given the right to decline to comment on any question in the court that violates her sexual respect and can be done without.

10. Culprit father's right to call himself her girl's guardian should be detached on the plea of his daughter, on grounds, that he was violated the code of being a father and played the role of the husband.

11. Child born to a pregnant victim raped by the father should be officially accepted as the father's child, if point 8 is not accepted. A child has a right to come to this world and be accepted as an integral part.

12. Right to abortion should be made an exclusive woman right in cases of rape, so that she conceives or aborts on her wish. No man, confirmed of raping a woman, should be allowed to move court challenging the child's birth.

13. Women should be locked in only all–women police stations to avoid custodial rapes.

Critical Issues

14. Time for justice in rape cases should be minimised as far as possible as "justice delayed" appears to the victim as "justice denied", adding to her trauma.

15. A case where a victim is regularly raped should not be seen as a single rape case but multiple rape cases of the quantity 'n', n equalling the number of times the victim is raped.

16. If a victim gets AIDS through the culprit, the case should be viewed as rape and murder.

17. Only crime (women) cell should be given the charge to deal on behalf of police in rape cases.

All this can go a long way in dealing with the rape menace and in forming a judicious atmosphere for the victim.

Otherwise with a dual culprit atmosphere–the culprit who rapes the female and the society who treats her as guilty, we seem to look like mere two legged animals, roaming on the Earth for thousands of years.

III

THE PREVENTION CLAUSE

Had there been no sorrow, the earth would have been paradise. However, the irony is that paradise would not have appeared so pretty had there been no sorrow!

Sorrow is inescapable. And this is a universal truth. Happiness may be the majestic Sun but Sun has to bow before night. Every granule of light breeds a granule of shadow.

If man would not have learnt to fight against sorrow, he would long have perished and only his fossils would have remained, buried beneath thousands of layers of soil. But man was born to rule, so he learnt the art of survival. He fought and fought with his axe of hope and knife of strength cutting the chilly wind of grief. Learning the art of survival, he shrieked aloud the ultimate rule of Mother Earth.

"SURVIVAL OF THE FITTEST"

Survival is a multi-faceted phenomena. We do a million things to survive. And one of the phenomenon is Immunization. Immunization dwells in two distinct forms: endurance and indifference, both helping us to live by defeating the sorrow virus.

Rape is also a form of great agony and the last step of the ladder of human decline. Rape is a collective mixture of dirt, barbarism and brings man a step below his mid way position in the three step ladder of God, Man and Beast.

Most of us fight the frustration that this menace of rape breeds in us by being indifferent to it. Once this spirit of indifference is mixed in the solution of our consciousness, our senses become numb to rape. We assume an expressionless gesture towards every sight of this catastrophic phenomenon. Thus we bow our heads before an injustice and as Gandhiji said—"To be a silent witness to injustice is worse than doing injustice".

But some of us learn to endure rape. Endurance gives us the strength of bear this menace and strengthens the desire to fight it. So no sight of rape dashes out a tear from our eye but boosts a dose of strength and will into our heart against it.

Those of us who have taken a pledge to speak against this menace, either by words or sword or pen are sometimes filled with a strange but divine desire. When trying to eradicate this menace, we sometimes feel how good it would have been, had it never existed.

The best thing to make a poison die is to never let it take birth. There is not better destruction than to stop germination. And in support of it goes the age old majestic adage—"Prevention is better than cure!"

But can rape be prevented? Does the dark cloud of rape have this silver lining?

Yes, the silver lining exists. Rape is a disease and can be vaccinated to death. When there would be no rape there would be no multi-million forms of traumas that victims face. So before we think of executing the culprits, why not think of giving an injection of prevention to the animal of rape breeding in society and kill it?

Critical Issues

I have discussed in detail some clauses of prevention as it was very necessary to do that while I was developing an analytical study on the opinion poll. But the subject needs to be framed up now, separately, as an issue. I have introduced it earlier and am now developing it to its full strength.

The first clause of the prevention programme is Sex Education.

Our contracted culture has compressed and preserved a great heritage. But while contraction puts a lot many good things behind its bars, it also sometimes inhibits the fresh breeze, breeding a lot of suffocation within.

And one of the things is that sex has become a taboo. Even to talk of sex, with a desire to root out the poisonous streams that merge from it, is not just forbidden but banned.

With the banning of Sex Education, is banned all doors of a normal sex atmosphere. Our society by and large reacts abnormally to it. And this abnormality copulates with immorality to breed the beast of a multi-facted sexual menace.

Our deep cultural and ethical decline should be enough to warn us. "Better late than never" should now be our sole aim, my dear countrymen. We are today late, but can still sum up things. But if never, everything shall for ever, fly into oblivion. And nothing can be redeemed or rejuvenated from the layers of oblivion.

Time is the most supreme judge of all and its judgement should be respected. Time now talks of sex education being made compulsory for all schools and colleges. It benefits us in many ways:

The first benefit is awareness. By being totally aware of sex, a person shall not wander in the unhealthy realm of video libraries and hypocritical sex education books. These films and books wearing the mask of sex–education are in actuality horrifying mega phonographs. They activate the desire of sex to make it cross the healthy border. Sex education makes us aware of sex and beware of its ills. It knocks at our wisdom with information and injects our spirit with endurance.

The second benefit is the birth of naturalism and inhibition of abnormality.

Most of us are abnormal towards the way we react to sex. For example, kiss is a natural sexual pehenomena. However an average Indian shall react in three ways to it–He shall blush or he shall laugh or he shall be unduly activated. Blushing indicates a complex and inability to adjust to a natural sexual intimacy. This breeds suffocation, which can take varied harmful forms. Laugh is again abnormal and indicates that somewhere within, the heart that laughs, takes kiss to be beyond a natural occurrence. If this theory of unnaturalism in him takes the form of adventure or daring, there is no need to explain the danger hidden. Activation on seeing kiss scenes also indicates a reaction beyond necessary control to sex which can be inhibited, if sex being natural occurrence is somehow inserted into a child.

Third factor is personalised and private counselling.
While a boy or girl might feel shy to talk about his sexual problems to parents, he might do so to his sex education teacher.

Fourth factor is anti menace prevention.
Whereby, talking about how unhealthy and uncontrolled sexual life breeds horrible problems, a fear for unhealthy sex might inserted.

Fifth is anti menace feelings activation.
While discussing of sex, it is more than natural that the mention of sex crimes like rape shall arise. These can develop into large discussions, where the teacher can activate the positive minds and calmly inhibit the negative outlook that might be present in some students.

Sixth is anti-menace force organisation.
While activating the positive attitude against sex crimes, the teacher might breed a very healthy situation. Students might themselves talk of forming a force against crime. Helped by police, this can go a long way in solving the menace.

Seventh is anti-blue file campaign.
The teacher can through a very psychologically prepared lecture stop students from seeing unhealthy stuff.

Eighth is positive law participation.
Teachers can form student courts where students take up an old rape case and play the roles of the judges, lawyers, victims, culprit and onlookers. This would breed healthy arguments and counter arguments.

Ninth is real life witnessing.
Students should be allowed to watch culprits and victims in rape cases. Talking to them and seeing their condition, would break the culprit in them if any.

Tenth is stress on a family based society.
Sex education should involve stress on a family based society, thus making passive a behaviours that's anti to it. Such things go a long way in promoting healthy atmosphere.

Eleventh is active participation in sex related punishments in schools and colleges.
Students should choose punishments for boys doing eve teasing.

Twelfth is media defence.
Good media films should be shown. The mass communication effect can be magical.

Thirteenth is good literature.
Sex period should also be theoretical, involving a curriculum and examination.

Fourteenth is encouragement on a co-male-female behaviour.
Males and females as friends interact with each other, making an integral and not dipolar society.

Fifteenth is teentalks and related discussions on dating and mating.
This goes a long way in being a positive mediator in teenage sexual relationships.

Sixteenth is general sexual knowledge.
This imparts knowledge of usage of condoms and other related facets. This should be done to prevent students from going to wrong into centres like bad books and films for the same.

These are the various factor and benefits of sex education. There can be many more. What is required is a positive development of the same.

Sex Education can thus be divided into varied, separate action granules.

I. Sex awareness and full knowledge programme.
   - Complete knowledge on sex, in stages.
   - Theory of naturalism.

II. Private Counselling Centre and Personal Help Programme.
   - Facility for a separate centre for private discussion between student and teacher.

III. Debate and Discussion Programme.
   - Anti sex crime debates.
   - Debates on all modes of sexual behaviour.
   - Openness on sexual issues through open discussion.

IV. Anti Sex Crime Force Programme.
   - Formation of anti sex crime forces at school levels as student subsidiaries of the police.

V. Action through Fiction Programme.
   - Anti blue film campaigns.
   - Burning of pornographic literature and cassettes.
   - Award for discovery of video liberties and book shops selling pornographic literature.
   - Formation of student courts where healthy discussion of old cases takes place, just as in court.

VI. Real Life Project Programme.
   - Visits to Jail, Rape Trauma Prevention and Cure Institutions and Remand Homes to meet culprits and victims.

VII. Spiritualism, Morality and Cultural Stress Participation.
   - Stress of unregulated sex behaviour as immoral.
   - Stress on rape as "the last infirmity" of a human mind.
   - Stress on family life and family codes and norms.

VIII. Punishment Power Programme.
   - Student participation in sex crime cases in schools and colleges which can be dealt without legal interference.

Critical Issues

IX. Curriculum Access Programme.
- Theoretical curriculum, followed by examination.
- Good literature and films shown to students and also learning from such things encouraged.

X. Co-behaviour Programme.
- Co-existence of male and female students, breeding the spiritual positive in them.
- Stress that male-female co-existence is inevitable. But positive co-existence is creation and negative destruction.

XI. Information Package.
- Information on condoms, dating and mating.

This is the complete schedule of sex education with its benefits and various granules through which it can be implemented.

As my dear readers must have seen by now, development of sex education involves help from Government and NGO's. It will be taught in schools but this multi-package cannot be handled by the school alone. Government and NGO's will have to intervene and advise, fund and support, this powerful package.

***

The second clause in our prevention package is Moral Education.

When I was kid, studying in the fourth-fifth standard, I still remember that we used to have Moral Science periods, one of the greatest things that ever happened in schooling. Very sadly, and that reflects too much on our schooling's loopholes in decision making, this period has been scrapped to give way to more science and mathematics periods. Now this period is present in a very few schools only.

I understand, infact, no logical mind can under-estimate the importance of career building in schools. Colleges can only give a finishing touch to a student's mental structure, the muscles of career building are developed in schools only.

But does that mean that schools shall nullify the time for building a moral, ethical and fundamentally good student? We can renovate a house, beautify it with millions, but for that the house must be there. Similarly, engineering and medicine, business and administration makes and country move but the country remains only if morality and ethics live. These are the walls of the country.

Schools must keep a period for moral education. It is a sincere request of a writer who has heard the slight but steady movement of the cracking force amidst nation's walls and thus feels the need to re-strengthen it by the mortar of morality.

***

Third clause in our prevention package is the Government's intervention.

It would be foolish to think that such a massive, and what's more, such a massively important, prevention programme can run without a nation's government. After all the body that governs the nation must play an active role in the governance of prevention measures, to slide this programme of prevention to perfection. This perfection can then be made to lead to extinction; all forms of sexual menace.

The government can help in varied ways:

(i) Assisting and Funding.

Sex Education programme, as we have above discussed, can be adequately funded and assisted by the Government.

(ii) Trauma eradication.

As we discussed, law should see to it that the victim's trauma is gone by proper counselling. A victim's trauma gone, means, in many cases, death of a culprit, that might have been born from this trauma. This is a very powerful prevention.

(iii) Separate Department.

If a separate department is opened, say, in the Ministry of Human Resource Development, for sex prevention, the profit from it is unimaginably big in quantity and quality.

(iv) Stricter Censor.

Our censor has began to see sexuality in films with a bull's eye, but still many of our A films that make it to the morning shows should be banned, on account that their sole aim is to activate the barbaric. This can only be done by the censor, on the directions of the Ministry of Information and Broadcasting.

(v) Formation of Programme Project Team.

Sex education can be implemented in school. But, perhaps, government is the right thing to fund and form a high profile team to formulate a package compulsory for schools and colleges. It can also be an all level meet, where including top profile people, citizens' views are invited and incorporated.

***

The fourth and the last clause in NGO intervention. NGO's can penetrate where government fails, and combined GO's and NGO's can spread their network across the country, making this prevention programme a national achievement.

***

One needs a person with the strength, talent, diligence and dedication of Mr. T.N. Seshan, to unlock this menace of rape that has gripped the society and throw it to merge with oblivion.

The prevention package is a very delicate and sensitive issue and any work done in hurry can further complicate things than easing them. What is required is a dedicated team effort to evolve such an effective programme that Goethe is again able to speak his internationally acclaimed dictum:

"How great is it all planned!"

Part Thirteen

THE INTERNATIONAL PERSPECTIVE

THE INTERNATIONAL PERSPECTIVE

SECTION-I

INTRODUCTION

> I sent my soul through the invisible,
> Some letter of that after-life to spell:
> And after many days my soul returned,
> And said, 'Behold, Myself am Haven't & Hell'[1]

This philosophical verse is the mother of law. It was the womb of this verse that was impregnated by the human civilization and gave birth to the babe of legal consciousness. Thus, the origins of law can be traced only in the soul of this verse.

The passion to understand heaven and hell has been the ultimate endeavour of man for centuries. Heaven is the zenith of ascent; it is the horizon of horizons. Hell is the ultimate in descent; it is the ugliest zone of cosmic realism and the biggest chaos in the cosmic web.

The endeavour to understand heaven, led us to a knowledge that heaven and hell remains in us. We have in us the ultimate calm of Paradise or the ultimate disturbance of Satan's Kingdom. We have in us the structures of spirituality or the majestic splendour of the evil Pandemonium[2], where the Seven Deadly Sins[3] "sit in council[4]".

---

1. From Rubaiyat of Omar Khayyam, Verse 71, The Second Edition of 1868.

   This verse translated from Persian to English by Edward Fitzgerald (1809 - 1883), poet and translator.

2. Pandemonium - The Palace of Satan

3. Seven Deadly Sins : From "The tragical history of the life and death of Dr. John Faustus "by Christopher Marlowe. The Seven Deadly Sins are Pride, Covetousness, Envy, Wrath, Gluttony, Sloth, Lechery (See Act - II, Sc-III, line 112-171).

4. These three quoted words are the last three words from the argument to the first book of Paradise Lost, by Milton.

We create in ourselves a hell and heaven, out of our own action and desires. All that matters is whether our face glows with spirituality or wastes away with material decay, whether we are benevolent or enjoy by imparting sorrow and suffering to our fellow humans, whether we are devout or saintly or selfish and beastly. Inside an ethical, moral and mature individual lies an infinite ocean of calm. Inside a satanic individual, lies a vast turbulence of evil and destruction.

Those who like to live in hell and whose souls are merged in that acid, impart the same to society. Their endeavour is to make the eyes of civilization dream of heaven and see hell.

But our Mother Earth is the creation of Almighty Father. Adam once lived in Paradise. He sinned and was turned out. Man can at least try to convert his material abode on the lines of the eternal and spiritual. For this, the devotees of Satan must be stopped by a code, a norm, a penalty. This is law.

This is the universal reason, why law emerged throughout the world. Laws of every country are brothers, born from the same womb.

There are many problems that are common to all countries. Every country has a law to deal with it. The penal code of that nation, establishes a list of punishments for the crime, thus bringing the particular criminal problem to the zone of solution.

However, the law of every country has it's shortcomings, pointed out by the nation's citizens.

One of the solutions to overcome this is to study the issue is great depth and as a consequence of the knowledge that the study imparts, amend the legal structure.

The second solution, very powerful in itself, is to study laws of several countries on a particular crime, and after studying their punishments, compare them to find a consensus that suits one's own nation and if possible all nations at large. In studying laws on an international scale, the study of the issue deepens and many of its aspects can reach new avenues, greater horizons, open up new perspectives for discussion, strengthen an existing line of thought or change it to a better thinking and action. It can also lend the observation about things not mentioned in one's own criminal

The International Perspective

code for a particular crime but reasoned in the other, or perspectives relating to a particular issue, not commented by any nation. It can also offer general suggestions on issues within an issue, to all nations.

This part serves the same purpose to our issue in question. However, here the whole menace of rape has been deal, because, I observed that writing this issue just on parental rape could be of use but would also be wasting of lot of its inherent potential. Moreover, it is not always so easy to bifurcate parental rape from rape.

This part introduces the complete punishment structure on rape in India, and then does so for a lot many countries. These countries have been chosen through a very viable selection process and are markedly different not only in dealing with rape but in their political, religious and social ideologies.

Because the law of any country is deeply related to its social, cultural and political psyche, proper introduction has been attached with every country, that have been divided in groups. Specific issues of the country have been introduced wherever needed. Laws of each country have been critically surveyed.

Issues common to all countries in rape menace, have been discussed in a separate section.

The list of some cases in foreign countries gives base for argumenting from new angle, issues already evaluated, thus opening new lines of study. This has been included.

This section serves as a powerful comparative study. It also provides information on rape laws in other countries, which are very difficult to be obtained, and thus provides as a powerful information capsule on rape. As rape laws in other nations, worldwide, have been separately stated and further it has been kept in mind that the countries chosen are markedly diverse, it opens infinite horizons of search on rape through an international study.

This part is thus invaluable and interesting. Study of this capsule will enlighten the reader; the information will stimulate his creative powers and open the very, many closed doors of his mind.

SECTION-II

INDIA

THE INTRODUCTION FILE

Profile

• Official name	:	Bharat (Union of India)
• Capital	:	New Delhi
• Continental Location	:	Asia (exists as a subcontinent)
• Neighbouring countries	:	Nepal, China, Bangladesh, Pakistan, Sri Lanka and Maldives.
• Religion Status	:	Secular State
• Economic Status	:	Developing Nation
• Total Population	:	1981 Census - 696,832832. 1996 estimate - 965,515,000, Density 260 persons per Km^2 Distribution - 72% rural, 28% Urban
• Official Language	:	Hindi is the principle official language. 14 other languages with official status, major of whom are Urdu, Marathi, Malayalam, Gujarati and Bengali. English enjoys status of "associate official language".
• Political Status	:	Parliamentary Democracy.
• Feminine Status	:	Woman on the move.
• Area	:	3,287,263 Km^2 Greatest Distance-North-South: 3,200 Km. and East-West-1,700 Km.
• Currency	:	Basic Unit - Rupee Exchange Rate - .05 U.S. $[1]
• National Flag	:	Three Horizontal stripes of Orange - Yellow of Saffron (top), white

---

1. Exchange Rate of any nation is always subject to change.

(centre) and green (below). In the centre of the white stripe is a blue wheel. It is an ancient symbol, also called "Dharma Chakra" or "Wheel of Law".

- National Emblem : Adapted from a pillar that was built at Sarnath by Ashoka, the great. It has three lions and words below are "Satyamev Jayate", meaning "Truth alone triumphs".
- National Anthem : "Jana-Gana"Mana" meaning "Thou Art the Ruler of All Minds of People".

The History and Times of India

B. C.
- 3500 - Beginnings of the Indus Valley Civilization.
- 1700 - Decline and fall of the Indus Valley Civilization, followed by the coming of the Aryans and writing of the Rig Veda.
- 530 - Cyrus the great, invades India.
- 326 - Alexander the great, invades India.
- 321 - Chandragupta Maurya becomes king and lays foundation of the Mauryan empire.
- 297 - Bindusara, son of Chandragupta ascends the throne.
- 272 - Ashoka the great, ascends the throne.
- 261 - The historical conversion of Ashoka to Buddhist and Ahimsa.

A. D.
- 100's - Kushans invade India
- 300-500 - The golden age of the Guptas
- 320 - Chandragupta I ascends throne.
- 375 - Chandragupta-II ascends throne.
- 454 - Death of Kumaragupta, slowly leading to weakening and decline of Gupta empire.

- 606 -647 - Reign of Harshavardhana
- 712 - Coming of Islam.
- 1000 - 1030 - Raids of Mahmud of Ghazni.
- 1398 - Attack of Tamurlane
- 1498 - Vasco-Da-Gama reaches India.
- 1526 - Invasion of Babar and birth of the Mughal empire.
- 1539 - Sher Shah drives Humayun to exile.
- 1555 - Humayun reclaims the Delhi throne.
- 1556 - Akbar the great ascends throne.
- 1600 - Foundation of the East India Company
- 1605 - Jahangir succeeds Akbar.
- 1628 - Shah Jahan succeeds Jahangir.
- 1658 - Aurangzeb succeeds Shah Jahan, killing elder brother Dara Shukoh.
- 1707 - Fall of the Mughal empire.
- 1757 - Foundation of the British empire
- 1857 - The Great Rebellion.
- 1869 - Mahatama Gandhi is born
- 1873 - Queen Victoria takes the title of the "empress of India".
- 1885 - Burma becomes a province of India.
  - Indian National Congress is formed.
- 1914 - Rise of Indian Nationalism.
- 1919 - The Jalianwala Tragedy.
- 1920 - Non-Violence Campaigns by Gandhiji.
- 1947 - India gains Independence
  - Partition of India into Pakistan.
- 1948 - Assassination of Mahatama Gandhi by Nathu Ram Godse.
- 1950 - The Indian Constitution goes into effect.
- 1961 - India retakes Goa, Daman and Diu from the Portuguese.
- 1965 - Indo - Pak War (II).

- 1971 - Indo - Pak War (III).
- 1975 - Indira Gandhi declares emergency.
- 1984 - Assassination of Indira Gandhi.
- 1991 - Assassination of Rajiv Gandhi at Sriperumbadur.
- 1994 - Rupee made fully convertible by the Finance Minister.

Looking back
Looking beyond.

My country is my mother. It is a bed of soil out of which I was born. It is in this bed of soil that I will go, after life shall leave my body, and it shall be left all alone. My nation is the womb that nursed me before my life and a cradle that prepared me for this life. My nation is the grave where I shall sleep for my eternal rest. And from my womb to my grave, this is the soil that shall nurse my life with its golden grains of food and sweet droplets of water.

India has been a land of great depth and has imparted a lot of meaning to the word civilization. Whether in the spiritual mysticism of philosophy or eternal calm of religion, the music of lyrics or the rhythm of music, the extraordinary creations in ink or the majestic creations in stone .... India has been the world's guide in culture and creativity.

India has been distinct in every form of its existence. Its geographical existence has been that of a majestic queen of Asia. If you will look at the geographic position of Asia you shall realise that it is a continent within a continent. That is why my nation is sometimes called a subcontinent.

Indian language family is a vast reservoir of human communicative behaviourism. All dialects combined, 1500 languages decorate the culture of the country. 15 of these languages have certified their authority by being accepted all over the world. These languages in turn have had an intercourse with creativity, giving birth to the progeny of literature. Indian literature houses the complete knowledge of all the world literature combined. Sanskrit, one of the oldest languages of the world has an equally old heritage in literature where manuscripts have churned the gold of sensitivity, meaning and talent. Kalidasa is one of the world's literary gems. Bengali boasts of the noble leaurate Rabindranath Tagore who was in himself an incarnation of genius - musician, poet, writer, artist, essayist, dramatist.......

and a phenomenon! Hindi has rocked in its cradle Tulsidasa who immortalised spiritualism with his Ramcharitmanas.

India is a nation where God himself as Lord Krishna explained the divine meaning, and his words have remained for ever, penned in "The Bhagvad Geeta" - a book read and respected across the seas. We gave the world two epics that were deep enough to become the world's guide in morality and truth - The Ramayana and the Mahabharatha.

India's architectural supremacy has been proved by the iron pillar of Ashoka, which could not be rusted by the wave of time and the wave of envy. Taj Mahal is the architectural personification of an emperor's love, freezed and immortalised by marble and mortar.

The Vedas and The Upanishads are texts that contain an infinite weight of knowledge. They are some of the very few texts, that on every reading, impart to the reader a new sense of maturity and divine realisation.

India houses such a great diversity - thousands of varieties of flora and fauna, all the four seasons, thousand dialects, literature and philosophy of all shades of meaning and description, oceans to deserts and marshy stretches to glacier sheets, a thousand varieties of foods and cuisines ..... the description is endless. All the ink of this globe will lack of authority to write on my country.

But, is all so good ....? Certainly not. India has been a great culture. Today, even though a million positive facets survive, the culture looks threatened. And the reason is that the country that bred the highest achievements of women and still breeds so, also breeds the seeds of incestual rape ....

THE LAW FILE

THE INDIAN PENAL CODE

Section 375-377

Section 375
 A man is said to commit "rape" who, except in the case hereinafter excepted, has sexual intercourse with a woman under circumstances falling under any of the six following descriptions :

First   - Against her will.
Second - Without her consent
Third   - With her consent, when her consent has been obtained by putting her or any person in whom she is interested in fear of death or of hurt.
Fourth   - With her consent, when the man knows that he is not her husband, and that the consent is given because she believes that he is another man to whom she is or believes herself to be lawfully married.
Fifth   - With her consent, when, at the time of giving such consent, by reason of unsoundness of mind or intoxication or the administration by him personally or through another of any stupefying or unwholesome substance, she is unable to understand the nature and consequences of that to which she gives consent.
Sixth   - With or without her consent, when she is under sixteen years of age.

EXPLANATION
Penetration is sufficient to constitute the sexual intercourse necessary to the offence of rape.

EXCEPTION
Sexual intercourse by a man with his own wife, the wife not being under fifteen years of age, is not rape.

Section 376 (1)
Whoever, except in the cases provided for by subsection (2) [follows], commits rape shall be punished with imprisonment of either description for a term which shall not be less than seven years but which may be for life or for a term which may extend to 10 years and shall also be liable to fine unless the woman raped is his own wife and is not under twelve years of age, in which case, he shall be punished with imprisonment of either description for a term which may extend to two years or with fine or with both.

Provided that the court may, for adequate and special reasons to be mentioned in the judgement, impose a sentence of imprisonment for a term of less than seven years.

Section 376(2)

Whoever -

(a) Being a police officer commits rape -
   (i) Within the limits of the police station to which he is appointed ; or
   (ii) In the premises of any station house whether or not situated in the police station to which he is appointed ; or
   (iii) On a woman in his custody of a police officer subordinate to him; or

(b) Being a public servant, takes advantage of his official position and commits rape on a woman in his custody as such public servant or in the custody of a public servant subordinate to him; or

(c) Being in the management or on the staff of a jail, remand home or other place of custody established by or under any law for the time being in force or of a women's or children's institution takes advantage of his official position and commits rape on any inmate of such jail, remand home, place or institution; or

(d) Being on the management or on the staff of a hospital takes advantage of his official position and commits rape on a woman in that hospital; or

(e) Commits rape on a woman knowing her to be pregnant; or

(f) Commits rape on a woman when she is under twelve years of age; or

(g) Commits gang rape,

Shall be punished with rigorous punishment which shall not be less than 10 years but which may be for life and shall also be liable to fine :

Provided that the court may, for adequate and special reasons to be mentioned in the judgement, impose a sentence of imprisonment of either description for a term less than 10 years.

EXPLANATION-1

Where a woman is raped by one or more in a group of persons acting in furtherance of their common intention, each of the persons shall be deemed to have committed gang rape within the meaning of this sub section.

EXPLANATION-2
"Women's or children's institution" means an institution, whether called an orphanage, or a home for neglected women or children or a widow 's home or by any other name, which is established and maintained for the reception and care of women or children.

EXPLANATION-3
"Hospital" means the precincts of the hospital and includes the precincts of any institution for the reception and treatment of persons during convalescence or of persons requiring medical attention or rehabilitation.

Section 376-A
Whoever had sexual intercourse with his own wife, who is living separately from him under a decree of separation or under any custom or usage without her consent shall be punished with imprisonment of either description for a term which may extend to two years and shall also be liable to fine.

Section 376-B
Whoever, being a public servant, takes advantage of his official position and induces or seduces, any woman, who is in his custody as such public servant or in the custody of a public servant subordinate to him, to have sexual intercourse with him, such sexual intercourse not amounting to the offence of rape shall be punished with imprisonment of either description for a term which may extend to 5 years and shall also be liable to fine.

Section 376-C
Whoever, being the Superintendent or Manager of a Jail, remand home or other place of custody established by or under any law for the time being in force or of a women's or children's institution takes advantage of his official position and induces or seduces any female inmate of such jail, remand home, place or institution to have sexual intercourse with him, such sexual intercourse not amounting to the offence of rape, shall be punished with imprisonment of either description for a term, which may extend to five years and shall also be liable to fine.

EXPLANATION-1
"Superintendent" in relation to a jail, remand home or other place of custody or a women's or children's institution include a person holding

any other office in such jail, remand home, place or institution by virtue of which he can exercise any authority or control over its inmates.

EXPLANATION-2
The expression "women's or children's institution" shall have the same meaning as in explanation - 2 to sub section (2) of section 376.

Section 376-D
Whoever, being on the management of a hospital or being on the staff of a hospital takes advantage of his position and has sexual intercourse with any woman in that hospital such sexual intercourse not amounting to the offence of rape, shall be punished with imprisonment of either description for a term which may extend to 5 years and shall also be liable to fine.

EXPLANATION
The expression "hospital" shall have the same meaning as in Explanation -3 to sub section (2) of section 376.

UNNATUTURAL SEXUAL OFFENCES

Section 377
Whoever voluntarily has carnal intercourse against the order of nature with any man, woman or animal, shall be punished with imprisonment for life, or with imprisonment of either description for a term which may extend to 10 years and shall also be liable to fine.

EXPLANATION
Penetration is sufficient to constitute the carnal intercourse necessary to the offences described in this section.

****

SOME COMMENTS ON IPC

Section 375 - 377[1]

1. It is no defence that the woman consented after the act. Consent as a defence to an allegation of rape requires voluntary participation,

---

1. The five comments that follow are quoted extracts from the comments by Ratanlal and Dhirajlal, Lawyers, who wrote the commentary for I.P.C., in a text published by Wadwa and Company Ltd.

not only after exercise of intelligence based on the knowledge of the act, but after having freely exercise the choice between resistance and assent. So a helpless resignation in the face of inevitable compulsion or passive giving is no consent

2. Where a man had carnal knowledge of a girl of imbecile mind, and the jury found that it was without her consent, she being incapable of giving consent from defect of understanding, it was held that this amounted to rape[1].

3. If a girl does not resist intercourse in consequence of misapprehension, this does not amount to a consent on her part. Where a medical man, to whom a girl of 14 years of age was sent for professional advice had criminal connection with her, she making no resistances from a bonafide belief that he was treating her medically, it was held, that he was guilty of rape[2].

4. Indecent assault upon a woman does not amount to an attempt to commit rape, unless the court is satisfied that there was determination in the accused to gratify his passion at all events and inspite of all resistances.

5. As in rape, so also in unnatural offence, even the slightest degree of penetration is enough and it is not necessary to prove the completion of the intercourse by the emission of the seed.

***

A CRITICAL SURVEY

The Indian Penal Code, for ordinary rape (12 years and above), has constructed the punishment range from 7 years to life imprisonment. For kid rapes, the imprisonment is 10 years to punishment for life. But, generally, the punishment given for these two cases is seven years and 10 years. Therefore the existing punishment in the opinion poll for the two above categories of rape had to be 7 and 10 years. Readers must realise that by asking whether the punishment for ordinary rape should be 7 years or life imprisonment, the question obviously stands whether 7 years punishment is enough, as given in majority of cases or should always life imprisonment be given. There is a miles apart difference between a scope

---

1. See Fletcher, (1859) 8 Cox 131.

2. See William's cae (1850) 4 Cox 220.

for life imprisonment, used for a very few cases or life imprisonment as the 'Only' punishment for rape.

*

Parental rape has rather been fitted, in some way or the other in the criminal code of the country. The analysis of this crime throughout the book has made it more than clear that the IPC should have a separate section, as for homosexuality and bestiality, for incest and incest crimes.

*

Sections 376(1) and 376(2) offer complete flexibility to the judge to announce his decision regarding the punishment.

376(1) has a punishment range of 7 years to punishment for life and the judge can announce the punishment period whatever desired. Same is the case with 376 (2) where the lower range is 10 years. Moreover, in the punishment clause of 376(1 and 2), there is a separate postulate saying:

> "Provided that the court may, for adequate and special reasons to be mentioned in the judgement, impose a sentence for a term of less than seven years".

Thus the compass of flexibility makes a full circle. This is a good clause, as rape is a multi-faceted phenomena and the crime cannot be included in a single punishment. However, I must mention a few points :

- Punishments should have a scope for, in addition, to any-term imprisonment;
    (i) execution.
    (ii) other measures such as crime-confrontation, psycho-counselling; if they stand a viable chance.
- In a flexible punishment structure, the judge should always be assisted by a jury, in the capacity of an advisor group, whose advice may wholly or partially, be dismissed or accepted. The jury must consist of :
    (i) psychologists.
    (ii) sociologists
    (iii) psychiatrists.
    (iv) sexologists

The International Perspective

(v) representative from National Human Rights Commission.

(vi) representatives from Women Commissions.

- Reduction of punishment from the 7 years or 10 years lower limit should have a viable reason for it. Punishment reduction must involve a lot of study and reasoning, as many-a-times punishments might be reduced because of wrong reasons.[1]
- Gender bias in courts can lead to wrong use of this power of flexibility. This must be kept in account.

These factors, if kept in mind, can enable the Indian Jurisprudence to extract a lot of benefit from the punishment structure.

Rape, in Indian Penal Code, has been very well defined. However, I.P.C. lacks, like many other countries, in either including marital rape or specifically defining what marital rape is and why/why not does India include it in its penal code.

In marital rape context, Section 376-A, comes up with many objections. These have been discussed in 'Part thirteen, Section IV: Development of Comparative Law Thought.'

Rape is forced sexual intercourse without consent. IPC has a very good definition regarding what "without consent" means. It also explains the meaning of sexual intercourse, as regards rape accusation. Sexual intercourse refers to penetration of penis into the vagina. It is not necessary that there is the emission of the seed. This is explained immediately below Point 6, Section 375.

Section 376(2) while defining custodial rape, does not include cases where a woman asks a lift from a Police Officer in uniform and he commits rape.

It must be taken to be equal to custodial rape, as:

(i) It is done by a Police Officer, who was trusted for his uniform and associated duty.

(ii) Registration of such a case might involve complexities that come up when complaints are made against a Police Officer to the Police.

---

1. See Part one, p. 17.

Section-III
RAPE LAWS ACROSS THE GLOBE

THE ISLAMIC NATIONS

In AD 600's, Prophet Mohammed gave birth to a new religion called Islam. The teachings of Prophet Mohammed from the knowledge he had received from God through the archangel Gabriel is compiled in the Holy Book, The Koran.

Islam today is the world's second largest religion after Christianity and is practised by millions of people around the world.

Many nations follow Islam as their code of political, social, religions, cultural and ideological conduct. These countries called The Islamic Nations are distinctly different from the rest of the world and strikingly similar among themselves. This characteristic of intra-similarity and inter-diversity makes them merge into a group.

The law of rape enters a new perspective and meaning when seen through nations where Islam is the code and where women, even when in league with the rest of the globe, are characteristically unique. Before beginning any argument that involves women in the Islamic nations, it is both inevitable and invaluable to understand the position of women in Islam. It is only when the woman is understood from the Islamic standpoint and is weighed by the eternal pages of the Koran that the knowledge how Islam wants her to be dealt with, is understood. It is thus made clear whether her treatment by a particular Islamic nation is a rude distortion of that holy religion's feminine dictates or an extension of divine theory into a pretty practicality. All this helps in much sharply understanding the right attitude to women in the crime of rape, by any nation and most especially Islamic nations. This customary prologue to any Islamic feminine study, which I am here giving in my own flavour, is a perfect approach to a comparative study on rape involving Muslim fair sex. To ignore it is perfectly synonymous to a gigantic Himalayan Blunder.

WOMEN AND ISLAM

From the Indus Valley to the Egyptian civilization, from the ancient times to the modern age, from the Arctic to the equatorial, from the Indus to India, from the anno domini to before Christ, Woman has been treated in varied ways and her long journey on the road of time has been walked on a bed a of roses and a ocean of thorns. If she has been adored, admired and respected as a friend, philosopher and guide; she has also been chided as a beast and treated as a sex slave.

Ancient Romans, Arabs, Frenchmen and Athenians lived in a cent per cent male dominated society. Their attitude towards women is one of the most discredited forms of female treatment, and represents the most barbaric stages of human civilization in which narrowmindedness and dwarfish intellectuality ruled, run by brains that seemed to be placed upside down in the body. Martyr Muhammed Jawahar Bahonar comments that these ancient societies treated woman as[1]:

- the creation of devil; and,
- non-possessor of human soul.

Even when the situation improved, woman was nothing but :

- a creature, whose deeds were not acceptable to God;
- a means of 'Satanic seduction', thus one who should be physically tortured;
- a evil compared to whom death, poison and fire were nothing;
- a creature worthy of being buried alive, if one wanted to wash away scars of disgrace; and
- a human being created to serve man.

This is a terrifying example of human barbarism in an ancient society. But, woman is not placed in Paradise in today's world either. A paper on women crime by Dr. Robert. A. Myers[2] proves that if ancient societies chopped women with their fanaticism; even today women are robbed of their basic rights, and their sex lives are tempered with. The issue in question is female genital mutilation in Southern Nigeria. Muslim girls are genitally mutilated; which is totally non-Islamic with neither the holy Quran nor any religious order permitting it.

---

1. Islam and Women's Rights. (Status of Women in Islam).

2. Female Genital Mutilation in Southern Nigeria; ex crepts from a paper by Robert A. Myers; Ph. D. Mahjubah, Islamic Magazine for women, Vol. 13, No. 8 (123), August 1994.

The six ethnic groups that practice it are Bini, Esan, Etsako, Ijaw, Ukwuani and Urhobo.

Bini (95%) and Ukwuani (67%) practise "traditional animist beliefs". Esan (75%), Ijaw (82%) and Urhobo (74%) are Christians. Etsako (94%) is Muslim.

Despite these religious differences and varied other differences, these communities meet at a consensus is mutilating females genitally.

There are varied reasons for mutilating women:

- Maintenance of custom or tradition (74%).
- Protection of baby at birth from the clitoris (24%)
- Cosmetic, asthetic reasons (14%).
- Increasing reproductive abilities (8%)
- Diminishing female desires (4.5%)
- Increasing or enhancing women's sexual pleasure (3%).

With all these wrong reasons, a wrong practice continues, shattering apart all norms and codes of conduct, and sexual parts of women are chopped at varied age groups differing from ethnic groups to ethnic group.

This is an example of male domination, barbaric custom and pseudo intellect, much more shocking than the ancient schools of thought on women.

These are instances were women have been humiliated, tortured and maltreated. But women have also led human civilization and life- Religiously as Mira Bai, Politically as Queen Elizabeth-I, Socially as Mother Teresa, and Creatively as George Eliot[1]. The feminist side of our civilization rather looks like a chess board, of black and white squares, where women have stood on both the blocks and have either moved and forged ahead gaining power and achievement or have been chopped and dismantled of their rights.

With this rather long introduction on the dual aspect of female treatment and female placing in history and contemporary times, we come

---

1. George Eliot is the male pseudonym of Mary Ann Evans.

to our main question - **How is woman placed in Islam?** This is the central question around which our complete argument on Islamic women and thus women related crimes in Islamic world, revolves. Because only the answer to this can answer how women are treated in countries where Islam and The Holy Koran are guiding light; most especially in Iran where the political, social and cultural facet of the nation is determined by the pages of the divine verses.

Before I forge ahead with my pen and draw a sketch of Women in Quranic context, I must make it clear that I will not comment or critically evaluate what Quran says on women. I will just state the facts. This is because firstly, talk on any issue related to any holy book, requires a deep and complete understanding of the divine text in question. At this stage of my career, I do not claim any authority on the same. Moreover, our main discussion being on rape, this might deviate us from our central issue. However, to understand any Islamic country and its law, knowledge if its feminist pole is inevitable. For this, I will endeavour in the paragraphs to follow, to outline Women in Islam that shall help in understanding the whole Islamic group of countries.

But, before discussing women status in Islam, it is essential to discuss some basic differences between a man and woman because many issues in Quran on women are based on these differences. These differences have come out after extensive research from a collection of papers, that came out on the eve of The Ten Day Dawn Celebrations in Iran in 1985, and dealt with the status of Islamic Women in Islam[1] :

- *Physiological*
- Women are more emotional. This difference can be related to their nervous system.
- *Anatomic*

---

1. (a) Women or half the Body of Society.
       by : Hojjatulislam M.T. Mesbah.
   (b) Islam and Women's Rights.
       by : Martyr M.J. Bahonar.
   (c) Women in a Quranic Society.
       by : L. Lamya-al-Faruqi.
   STATUS OF WOMEN IN ISLAM by Islamic Propagation Organisation, Tehran.

- Man's Brain is anatomically larger than women. Front half of the woman's brain is more than fifty cubic millimetres smaller than the man's.
  Women's brain is one hundred gram lighter. Man's brain also weighs 100 grams more.
- Man's lungs carry 300 grams more weight.
- Average weight of man is 4000 grams more.
- Heart of an average man is heavier by 500 grams[1].
- *Sexual*
- By and large, men cannot be forced to sexual intercourse. Forced sexual intercourse of woman is common and finds place in the history of all societies, all civilizations and all times.
- Man's sexual role is what may be defined as "instantaneous". Woman has to bear the weight of nine month pregnancy.
- Man becomes potentially reproductive in early puberty stage. He remains so till late in his life. Woman becomes barren after an average age of 50. A man may even stay potentially reproductive till ninety years.
- Man faces no 'natural obstacle' whether it is seasonal or non seasonal, in his reproductive behaviour. But many obstacles hinder a woman's reproductive role, like menstruation. Menstrual cycle occurs every month, lasting for a few days. All through this cycle, the female is not deemed fit for sexual coitus.

During pregnancy when the foetus is being nurtured by the womb and a few weeks following conception, a woman cannot rear new seeds.

- Girls become ready for marital relationships quite early.
- *Maternal*
- A woman is more inclined to her children, and often makes the more tender and caring parent of the two.

With these differences in mind, let us now study the status of women in Islam.

Both women and men are equally responsible for the holy merge in which the neutral sex is formed and life is created. Islam the places equal

---

1. Some critics believe that "these anatomical differences are reflected in the mental capabilities of the two sexes."

worth to them. There are hundreds of verse which "take the form of address, '!O mankind.' or 'O believers!' which cover both men and women".

It has been very clearly stated:

"O you men! Surely We have created you of a male and female[1]..."

and,

"O, mankind, fear your Lord Who created you from a single soul and from it created its mate, and from the pair of them scattered abroad many men and women[2]..."

Moreover, the holy pages say that:

"Whoever does right, whether male or female, and is a believer, we shall assuredly give them to live a goodly life; and we shall pay them a recompense according to the best they do[3]."

L. Lamya Faruqi, noted Islamic scholar says that "if Allah 'subhanahu wa ta 'ala' had not deemed the two sexes of equal status and value, such explicit statements of their equality in ethical obligations and rewards would not have been made in the Quran".

This indeed is the truth when we observe together the following verses from the divine text :

- "They are a vestment for you and you are a vestment for them[4]..."
- "To the men a share of what parents and kinsmen leave and to the women a share of what parents and kinsmen leave[5]..."
- "To the men a share from what they have earned, and to the women a share from what they have earned[6]..."

---

1. The Holy Koran, 49 : 13.
2. The Holy Koran, 4 : 1.
3. The Holy Koran, 16 : 97.
4. The Holy Koran, 2 : 187.
5. The Holy Koran, 4 : 7.
6. The Holy Koran, 4 : 32.

- "... the thief, male and female cut off the hands of both as a recompense for what they have earned and a punishment exemplary from God[1]..."
- "Lo! Men who surrender unto Allah, and women who surrender, and men who believe and women who believe, and men who obey and women who obey, and men who speak the truth and women who speak the truth, and men who preserve and women who preserve, and men who are humble and women who are humble, and men who give alms and women who give alms, and men who fast and women who fast, and men who guard their modesty and women who guard their modesty, and men who remember Allah and women who remember– Allah hatch prepared for them forgiveness and a vast reward."[2]

Thus Islam finds women of equal worth as men, and grants them equal duties in many fields of spiritual and material life. Regarding education in Quran, L. Faruqi says.

"It (Quran) repeatedly commands all readers to read, to recite, to think, to contemplate, as well as to learn from the signs of Allah in nature. In fact, the very first revelation to Prophet Mohammed was concerned with knowledge. In a Quranic society, there can never be restriction of knowledge to one sex. It is the duty of every Muslim and every Mulsimah to pursue knowledge throughout life, even if it should lead the seeker to China, we are told."[3]

Throughout Quran, says M.J. Bahonar, is a discussion of well known women in religious history and the description matches the objective of Koran. These women are twelve in number. One of the Surahs[4] of the Quran is named as "Surat-al-Nisa." This has highly glorified women.

However, even though the Quran tells us that men and women are deemed equally worthy in the eyes of Allah, and gives them equal rights and duties in many spheres, it also assigns both of them their separate responsibilities and thus, quoting a scholar we might say that "the society based on Quran is a dual sex society".

---

1. The Holy Koran, 5 : 38.

2. The Holy Koran, 33 : 35.

3. In "Islam and Women's Rights" by L. Faruqi.

4. Surah - (noun) : Chapter or section from the Holy Koran.

Men are assigned economic responsibilities and "Quran has restricted women's role in social affairs". Men are given greater role in maintenance of family, Men have the real right to divorce, women can only do that in special circumstances. Woman is given all household jobs and bearing of children.

It must be added, however, that woman can demand maintenance as an exchange for rearing children and providing for the family well being.

Polygamy is an exclusive right of men.

The women is ordered by Islam to cover herself from head to toe when she moves out.

Women are restricted from going to war and be seated on seats of justice.

These differences are attributed to the male-female differences as discussed in this essay. Restricting my role to giving 'news not views" here, I leave it to my readers to reason each division of labour to the two sexes and define it as right or wrong.

My own ideology, (free from Quran, Bible and Geeta), as individual's own ideology, is that women have proved themselves worthy of all affairs inside and outside the home and men and women, must merge equally in social, political and economic spheres and thus breed all facets of society, with a equal distribution an harmonious permutation of rights and duties.

There was one very sensible thing which I found in the papers for women status in Islam. It is a universal fact which goes for each and every religion. I submit for your inspection a whole passage from an illuminating analytical thought:

"One must not analyse the dictates of Islam on the basis of the action of some Muslims at a certain time or place. For instance, if some Muslims abuse the woman's rights, this injustice should not be attributed to Islam. Likewise, it would be wrong to affirm that Islam has ignored the legitimate rights of the woman on hearing or observing that somewhere or at a certain period, the Muslims have been denying the woman her legitimate rights. When one observes Islamic tenets being neglected in some Muslim lands, which prefer rather to copy western cultures, one should not conclude that the governing laws agree with Islam, even if millions of Muslims do follow these Westernised ways.

Again the distortions, carried so often to extremes and the wrong conceptions of the Westerners cannot be attributed to the religion of Jesus Christ. We know that some Christian sects hold that the woman is not a full human being and that she is a link between animals and making or that her soul (excepting that of Holy Virgin Mother Mary) is not eternal, eternal salvation being the purgative of man above. These far fetched conceptions cannot be attributed to Christ's teachings. So also, it would be totally wrong to associate the reigning corruption and prostitution in the Western World with Christianity".

This is a very viable point which must be kept in mind while criticizing any religion or faith. The real extract of the whole passage is that any religion whether Zoroastrianism, Islam, Hinduism or Judaism should be appreciated or criticized only through what is said in its pure source. It should always be ensured that nothing criticized about; is in actuality 'distortion' of the teachings of that religion but attributed as a fault of that religion. If a group of Buddhists engage in terrorism Buddhism is not at fault. Gutama Buddha preached Ahinsa.

Thus while discussing women's position whether in general or regards rape, in any nation of the world, the faults must be attributed to the nation's ideology and not religious ideology. Religion should only be condemned when purely at fault.

THE DIVINE ISLAMIC STANDPOINT ON DAUGHTER-FATHER SEXUALITY

> "Call unto the way of your Lord with wisdom and good exhilaration, and reason with them in the best way. Lo. Your Lord best knows those who astray from His path, and He knows best those who are rightly guided.[1]"
>
> God sits within you and everywhere around you. You can deceive yourself but He cannot be deceived in understanding you.

---

1. The Holy Koran, 16 : 125.

Thus our Father Almighty sits in a trance and watches the whole world. He observes our actions and decisions and delivers His perfect Justice, when we depart from mortal life and stand before him for our final judgement.

Those of us who rape our daughters, set our mortal eyes on them and rob them of their virginity - we might escape from our fellow men, we might escape from our law books and courts but where would we go when he shall demand an answer to our evil? The cosmos is infinite and yet wherever we shall go, we shall find him.

Thus nobody can escape him and one has to repay all the damage he does and all the destruction that he constructs.

Almighty Father however has always told us that life is like a board of chess, built of white and black squares. Using the shades of ethics and morals, He has sketched this board in front of us. We have been told about all the paths that can be taken with their routes and their final destination. After being told of the right and wrong, we have been left free by Him. We are supposed to think, judge and act. We can go wherever we desire. But, we cannot repent when we stand before Him in His Supreme Court of eternal justice.

Through the vehicle of Gabriel, God sent a message to Prophet Mohammed, that he must tell Man, what has been allowed and forbidden to be tucked with a nuptial knot. The holy prophet obeyed this eternal decree, and wrote the same on the pages of the Holy Koran.

He clearly explained Mahram - forbidden relationships in marriage.

This knowledge is a great standpoint; which clearly informs the forbidden in marriage. As we shall see, it has a far reaching importance for our argument. So, let us investigate this knowledge in the form of two tables[1] and then learn what has been passed to us.

Thus, we can clearly see that even marriage with one's daughter has been prohibited. Islam only allows one form of satisfying sexuality, which

---

1. The tables have been extracted from "A Manual of Islamic beliefs and practice" (by Ali Muhammed Naqui).

is with one's legitimate partner the spouse. This makes obvious that sex with daughter, even with consent, inside or outside marriage is prohibited. Where then shall we place rape of a daughter? I am more than sure that Prophet Mohammed would have pronounced a decree of execution for a father guilty of raping his daughter.

Though not necessarily so explicit as The Holy Koran, all other religions prohibit incestual marriages and incestual sex with consent. Lord Krishna and His Holy Geeta, Prophet Zoroaster and His Holy Avesta, Lord Jesus and his Holy Bible, all prohibit it. Sex has been explained by every religion as a holy merge where procreation and copulation symbolises life. It has been termed as a means of attaining the enlightenment. Sex is one of the highest steps of material life which gives way to spiritual life.

	Mahram for a male	Cause
1.	Mother	Kinship & suckling.
2.	Mother's mother	-do-
3.	Father's mother	-do-
4.	Daughter	-do-
5.	Daughter's daughter	-do-
6.	Son's daughter	-do-
7.	Sister	-do-
8.	Sister's daughter	-do-
9.	Brother's daughter	-do-
10.	Paternal & Maternal Aunt	No special reason assigned
11.	Wife's mother	-do-
12.	Daughter of wife when the marriage has been consummated, and her daughter	Relationship by marriage
13.	Son's wife and the wife of the son's son.	-do-
14.	Father's wife	-do-
15.	Wife's mother's mother	-do-
16.	Wife's father's mother	-do-

The International Perspective

	Mahram for a female	Cause
1.	Father	Knship suckling
2.	Father's father	-do-
3.	Mother's father	-do-
4.	Son	-do-
5.	Daughter's son	-do-
6.	Son's son	-do-
7.	Brother	-do-
8.	Brother's son	-do-
9.	Sister's son	-do-
10.	Paternal & Maternal Uncle	No special reason assigned
11.	Husband's father	-do-
12.	Husband's son and his son	Relationship by marriage.
13.	Daughter's husband and the husband of the daughter's daughter	-do-
14.	Mother's husband	-do-
15.	Husband's father's father	-do-
16.	Husband's mother's father	-do-

But sex as incest blackens sex and it doesn't create life ... it is a procreation and copulation giving birth to hell.

Incestual sex has been placed on the black box of the board of chess. You are free to step in. But remember, every move from there, leads to hell.

IRAN

THE INTRODUCTION FILE

Profile

- Official name : Jomhuri-ye Eslami-ye Iran (Islamic Republic of Iran)
- Capital : Tehran
- Continental Location : Southwestern Asia

- Neighbouring Countries : Afghanistan, Iraq, Quwait, Pakistan, USSR & Turkey.
- Religion Status : Theocratic (Islam).
  State Religion-Shi'ah Sect, approx. 90% practitioners.
- Economic Status : Developing nation, but economy severely affected, because of post-war (Iraq) effects.
- Total Population : 1986 Census - 48,181,463
  1996 estimate - 66,370,000
  Density : 35 persons per Km^2
  Distribution : 55% Urban, 45% Rural
- Official Language : Persian
- Political status : Constitution 'provides' extensive power to the leader. He is the supreme power and can even impeach President. All important appointment are under him and he reserves exclusive authority to declare war and grant pardon.
- Feminine status : Evaluated and treated by being placed in the Quranic perspective.
- Area : 1,648,000 Km^2
  Greatest distances–Northwest-Southeast: 2213 km and Northeast-Southwest 1370 km.
- Currency : Basic Unit - Rial
  Exchange Rate - .0007 US$
- National Flag : Divided into three equal stripes of green (top) which is the traditional Muslim colour, white (Centre) and red (Below). In the end of the green and the beginning of the red stripe, the inscription "God is Great" in Arabic is written, 11 times in each. In the centre is written Allah in Arabic.

- Coat of Arms : In the traditional Muslim colour green, the holy word "Allah", in Arabic.
- National Anthem : "Soroude Jomhuri - ye Eslami - Ye Iran", meaning "Anthem of the Islamic Republic of Iran."

The History and Times of Iran

BC
- 3000 — Settlements of the Elamites, and the first major civilization.
- 1400-1000 — Prophet Zoroaster lived & preached.
- 900 — Wandering tribes of Medes and Persians.
- 700 — Creation of the first state in the Persian plateau by Medes.
- 600's — Flourishing civilization of Medes.
- 550 — King Cyrus the great overthrows the Medes in ferocious battle.
- 545 — Cyrus captures the Kingdom of Lydia and gradually increases the empire, naming it Achaemenid Empire.
- 530 — Cyrus the great is killed.
- 525 — Cambyses, son of Cyrus, conquers Egypt.
- 522 — Darius-I, relative of Cambyses, becomes the ruler.
- 513 — Darius captures part of USSR and Southeast Europe.
- 490 — Darius sends force into Greece, but the army defeated by Athenians at Marathon.
- 486 — King Darius-I dies.
- 331 — Alexander defeats the Persian forces and ends the Achaemanid empire.
- 323 — Selecus, the general of Alexander, controls Persia after his death. Gives birth to the Seleucid dynasty.
- 155 — Parthians take control of Persia.

AD
- 224 — End of the Parthian empire by Ardashir. New empire starts in the name of Ardashir's Grandfather Sassanid.
- 600's — Rise of Islam. End of the Sassanid empire[1].
- 600's-900's — Mass conversion of Iranians into Islam.
  - Arabic becomes the official language.
  - Disintegration of Iran into small kingdoms.
- 1000's — Seljuk Turks take control of Iran.
- 1220 — Ghengis Khan destroys Turkish rule and lets loose a region of terror.
- 1501 — The Safavid dynasty is founded.
- 1722 — Safavid rule ends.
- 1730's — Nadir Shah takes control of Iran.
- 1747 — Nadir Shah is assassinated.
- 1750's — Karim Khan takes control of Iran
- 1827 — Russia defeats Iran.
- 1828 — Russia and Iran sign treaty of Turkomanchai.
- 1857 — Iran and Britain sign treaty of peace; Iran dismisses claim over Afghanistan.
- 1906 — Qajar Monarch Shah Muzaffar-al-Din gives the country the first constitution, under heavy pressure.
- 1914 — Iran remains neutral in the World War.
- 1921 — Qajar dynasty thrown.
- 1925 — Politician Reza gains power.
- 1941 — Invasion of Iran by Britain & Russia.
- 1951 — Oil industry nationalised.
- 1979 — The Great Revolution of Iran, Iran proclaimed 'The Islamic Republic'
  - Ayotollah Khomeini, revolution leader, becomes the supreme power.

1. Up till this point, the history of Iran is part of the history of Ancient Persia, which was great civilization in Iran and Afghanistan. Thus till AD 600's, it is not necessary that every important event happened within the present day international boundary of Iran.

- 1980 - Beginning of the Iran-Iraq war.
- 1988 - The ceasefire.
- 1989 - Death of Ayotollah Khomeini.

Looking Back
Looking Beyond

"The first impression is the last impression".

This line became a divine truth; when I was searching for knowledge on Iran. The country's dedication towards God leaves a very divine imprint about the nation.

The inscription "God is great" is written twenty two times in the national flag. In the centre is to work "God" in Arabic Script, which is also the national coat of arms.

When I received a letter from the Press Secretary of Iran, I noticed that the letterhead had on the top, in bold lettering, the words "In the name of Allah", which are the words to be seen in the first page of almost every literature published in the country.

Scanning through some issues of Mahjubah, the tops Iranian women's magazine, I was overwhelmed with admiration to read the following passage on the first page of every issue :

> "Throughout this magazine the names of God, Prophets and verses of the Holy Quran have been used. Please handle the magazine in proper manner".

Iran is a nation that is completely soaked in the nectar of Religious devotion. It is a beautiful truth; which leaves a lasting impression in any devout heart. Such sights are pleasant for the carnial eye, fragrant for the mental eye and divine for the spiritual eye.

THE FEMININE GLASS

I now turn to the position of women in Iran. Not having much knowledge about the nation, I cannot promise that my pen will be able to evaluate the status of woman there. Therefore, instead of evaluating woman's position, I just state some positive facets of woman status in Iran, which promise that the Iranian woman is certainly on the move, though exploitation of hers cannot be ruled out.

Iran guarantees to the women of the nation the following :

1. Establishment of favourable conditions for the fostering of the character of women and the assertion of her material and spiritual rights.

2. Support for mother, in particular, when they are with the child, child care and protection of children who are without guardian.

3. Establishment of a competent court for the protection of the existence and continuance of the family.

4. Establishment of special insurance for widows, elderly and people without guardians.

5. Awarding of the guardianship of children to worthy mothers for the benefit of children in cases where there is no legal guardian.[1]

After divorce, woman, if not a party to the guilty "is entitled to half the wealth earned during marriage".

The women can exercise right to divorce called Wakalah in the following twelve situations[2]:

- Abstention of the husband from spending on his wife or his failure to perform his marital duties - for a period of six months - and if he cannot be compelled to carry out his duties.

- Improper behaviour of the husband towards his wife to a point when she cannot endure living with him.

- The husband suffers from an incurable disease, serious enough to prevent a normal marital life.

---

1. Article 21, The Constitution of Iran.
   Note : Point 5 is directly from the Islamic Jurisprudence.

2. All the twelve situations have been quoted from an authoritative source.

- Refusal of the husband to comply with a court order to abstain from work which is determinal to the position of his family, not befitting his wife.

- When the husband is sentenced to at least 5 years imprisonment and/or fined such a sum which will prevent him from spending on his wife for five or more years. This will apply when court order is to be executed without delay, but not in the event of stay of execution.

- The husband's addiction to any prohibited drugs, that in the view of the court upsets the life of the family.

- Abandonment of his family for a period of six consecutive months without an excuse acceptable to a court of law.

- When a final order of imprisonment for fine is passed by court of law against him for committing a crime which, in the view of the court, is determinal to the position of his family or does not befit his wife.

- Sterility of the husband for a period exceeding five years.

- When a husband is missing for a period exceeding six months, despite efforts by the courts and the authorities concerned to trace him.

The woman's position is rising in Iran. The Ist Seminar of the country on Girls was held on 23rd-24th Jan. 1995, at the Artistic and Cultural Centre, Tehran. It was jointly organised by the Bureau of Women's affairs (Iran), UNICEF and UNFPA (United Nations Population Fund). Many important issues regarding women were discussed. Gender bias was criticized. It was reminded that even the Holy Prophet had a great love for his daughter Fatimah and had once said that she was an extension of his existence[1].

Prior to this, a workshop was held with an objective to establish a women's information network in Iran, from October 11 to October 13, 1994[2].

---

1. Based on a report in Mahjubah, Vol. 13, No. 2 (129) Feb., 1995.

2. Based on a report from Mahjubah, Vol. 13, No. 10 (125) October 1994.

The Iranian woman is now steadily moving in many spheres of work, with her talent. Here are some statistics of success[1]:

Percentage of Female Students in all the fields of Medical Sciences

Year	Students (Female)
1990-91	55.50%
1991-92	56.86%
1992-93	58.88%

Percentage of Women's Education level in three Universities

Level of Degree	The whole group	Control Groups
PhD.	34.2%	32.2%
MA & MS	59.6%	60.2%
BA or BS	5.3%	5.4%
Not decl.	0.9%	2.2%

Percentage of University instructors according to their Gender

Gender	Number	Percentage
Total	30,262	100
Men	24,723	81.7
Women	5,539	18.3

Percentage of Graduate Students according to Gender (1992-93)

Gender	Number	Percentage
Total	374,734	100
Men	269,067	71.80
Women	105,667	28.20

1. Extracted from the article "Women's Role in Productivity", Mahjubah, Vol. 13, No. 10 (125) October, 1994.

Percentage of Women Participants in Animal Raising

Sections	Percentage of women participants
Feeding	23
Harvesting for animals' food	41
Taking care of animals	42
Milking	86

Distribution of Home Production in Rural Families in Iran in 1988

Description	Number	Percentage
Carpet making	319,710	79.8
Cloth weaving	76,630	1.9
Sewing/weaving	14,231	3.6
Mats	13,049	3.3
Food stuff	35,527	8.9
Total	400,565	100.0

THE LAW FILE

The divine revelations given by God through the archangel Gabriel to Prophet Mohammed are the ultimate truth for the Muslim world.

The Prophet's revelations and their transformation into teachings are recorded in The Holy Koran. The Quran deals with all individual, social and political questions and states the laws for almost everything; from Marriage and sex, to fighting and economic planning. These laws are collected into a vast force that has ruled the working of Muslim dynasties for centuries: The Islamic Law.

Iran's laws are directly based on The Islamic Law and the law of Islam is the law of Iran. Same is the case with criminal offences that are social and individual in nature, and weighed in a moral perspective; like rape.

The position of rape in Islam is very peculiar. Unlike the internationally accepted criminology of rape as "sexual intercourse without consent", Islam defines as rape every illegitimate sexual relationship which includes pre-marital sex, adultery and forbidden married relationships. The only allowed sex relation is between a husband and wife; and every man and woman who are Muslim can marry except with certain forbidden relations[1]. All other sex relations are rape.

I am describing here the complete rape law in Islam.

MAHRAM

Execution for both, provided that both marry by consent, and neither one is forced into tying a nuptial knot.

ILLICIT SEX

1. *Crime and Punishment*

- If both are non-married, then 100 times flogging to both.
- If one is married and one is unmarried:
- Execution for the married one, as he committed two crimes in one of marital irresponsibility towards spouse and of illicit sex.
- 100 times flogging for the non married partner.
- If both are married, execution for both.

2. *Requirement for conviction and the convicting process*

- Four eyewitnesses to rape.
- One person can be an eyewitness to any one rape in his lifetime.
- Each of the four eyewitnesses are to be taken to a separate room by the judge and questions are to be asked as per requirement.
- Statement of eyewitnesses to be tallied and compared.
- Punishment only when the judge is fully satisfied.
- Punishment not to be differentiated on :
- male discrimination because of a male fundamentalist society.

---

1. See "The Divine Islamic Standpoint on Father-Daughter Sexuality", Mahram Tables. Part 13/Section III/Group A.

- female discrimination of grounds of comparative physical weakness of sex.
• Punishments are on the basis of crime and not on the basis of sex difference.

RAPE
(AS IN INTERNATIONAL TERMINOLOGY)

1. *Crime and Punishment*

• If a man rapes a woman then :
- woman would be left scot free with due respect and sympathy.
- man to be executed.
• If a woman rapes a man then:
- man to be left free with due respect.
- woman to be executed.

2. *Requirements for conviction*

Either of the following four requirements are necessary proof for the culprit's crime:

• Four witnesses[1].
• Confession by the culprit.
• Knowledge of the judge (subject to viable proof and is aided by the rest three factors).
• 50% of the people knowing both of them take oath in the name of God, that they are assured of the culprit's crime.

The judge is however free in exceptional cases, to dismiss the case even if the above 1st, 2nd and 4th reasons are fulfilled and he is not satisfied. His reasons however, must be viable and in line with law.

3. *Special Iranian addition to the law*

Medical examination of the victim is allowed and supports the judgement of the judge[2].

---

1. Procedure synonymous with the one for illicit sex.
2. The complete outline of the law told by Mr. M.A. Ghazi.; moulded, placed and explained in the writer's own words.

A CRITICAL SURVEY

The Islamic law for rape (rape as in International Terminology) has been made flexible on grounds that the crime is more serious and the punishment more necessarily needed.

However, it needs some changes in the light of deep study on the crime:

- Execution may not necessarily fit every rape crime. The case might be an exceptional instance of psychological complexity.

- Marriage is the only allowed relationship in Islam, which is a very viable placement of sex in spiritual perspective. However, marital relationship in itself, sometimes stands questioned and marital rape must be considered for inclusion.

I am intentionally leaving the rest of the argument on illicit sex, as it is not in line with the book's argument and discussion.

PAKISTAN

THE INTRODUCTION FILE

Profile		
• Official Name	:	The Islamic Republic of Pakistan
• Capital	:	Islamabad
• Continental Location	:	Southern Asia
• Neighbouring Countries	:	India, Iran, Afghanistan and China
• Religion Status	:	Theocratic (Islam)
• Economic Status	:	Developing Nation.
• Total Population	:	1981 Census - 84,253,644 1996 estimate - 141,599,000 Density - 154 persons per Km^2 Distribution - 68% rural, 32% urban.
• Official Language	:	Urdu
• Political Status	:	Parliamentary Democracy, affected by long years of military rule.

The International Perspective

- Feminine Status : Women burnt by the acid of male fundamentalism and pseudo religious advocacy.
- Area : 796, 095 Km²
  Greatest Distances:
  North - South - 1, 505 Km
  East - West - 1, 287 Km
- Currency : Basic Unit - Pakistan Rupee
  Exchange Rate - 04 US $
- National Flag : 1/3 of the flag is white (from the left) and the rest is green. This represents the Muslim majority of the nation. The green part has a white crescent in middle and a white star above it, both being traditional Islamic symbols.
- Coat of arms : All green in colour. A narcissus wreath which is the national flower of the country encircles a shield having four divisions containing traditional symbols.
- National Anthem : "Quami Tarana" meaning National Anthem in Urdu.

The History and Times of Pakistan

BC
- 2500 - Beginnings of the Indus Valley Civilization.
- 1700 - Collapse of the Indus Valley Civilisation.
- 1500 - Aryans enter through passes in the mountains.
- 500's - Conquest of Punjab and its inclusion in the Achaemenid Empire. Chandragupta Mauraya Annexes it later.
- 230 - Cracking of the Maurayan Empire that had controlled the Achaemenid parts in 500's.
  - Greeks from Bactria invade the Indus Valley.
- 100 - Scythians come to Baluchistan and Sindh.

AD
(From its origin as a separate nation to present)

- 1947 — India is partitioned and Pakistan is born.
- 1948 — India and Pakistan go to arms against independent Kashmir.
- 1949 — Ceasefire on Kashmir issue, catalysed by the United Nations.
- 1956 — Becomes a republic.
  - Major General Iskander Mirza becomes the first President.
- 1969 — Work begins for the construction of one of the world's largest dams, the Tarbela Dam on the river Indus.
- 1970 — Severe cyclone and tidal waves kill 266,000 people in East Pakistan.
  - East Pakistanis accuse the centre of ignoring their plight.
- 1971 — President Yahya Khan postpones the National Assembly's first meet.
  - Civil war breaks out in East Pakistan and it declares itself a separate nation called Bangladesh.
  - India joins war on the Bangladesh side.
  - Pakistan suffers heavy losses.
  - Yahya Khan resigns, succeeded by Zulfiqar Ali Bhutto.
- 1972 — Withdraws from the commonwealth of Nations in Objection of British ties with Bangladesh.
  - India agrees to withdraw troops from Pakistan territory but remains firm on Kashmir.
- 1973 — New Constitution makes President, the head of the State and PM, the Chief Executive.
  - Bhutto becomes the PM.
- 1975 — Tarbela Dam is completed.
- 1977 — Bhutto wins election.
  - Gen. Zia Ul Haque declares martial law and removes Bhutto.

The International Perspective

- 1978   -   President resigns and Zia becomes the nation's President.
- 1979   -   Zulfiquar Ali Bhutto hanged.
- 1985   -   President Zia ends martial law.
- 1988   -   Gen Zia is killed in a severe plane crash.
  - Ghulam Ishaq Khan becomes President.
  - Parliamentary elections and Benazir Bhutto becomes PM. The dark years of military rule end.

Looking Back
Looking Beyond.

As you read the Pakistani law against rape in 'The Law File' of this section, you would only be amused if you are a passionately obsessive male fundamentalist and religious advocate of a distorted, decayed and depraved character. In all other cases, you shall be shocked to the core. Because no other nation in the world perhaps has such an ugly criminal code produced by the distortion of its religious principles, against so sensitive, delicate and traumatic issue as rape.

Pakistan represents one of those nations that adhere to their religion to a point of obsession and eccentricity. One word for the betterment of their faith or a syllabic displacement in their religious literature is awarded by a execution decree. But at the same time, the nation's fundamentalists, of conservative and thus suffocative wisdom, will act opposite to their religious tenets if it means nurturing and supporting their decayed ego and monopoly.

The law on rape is a striking example. Pakistan was the first Islamic country whose law I had read. I had a rough idea that the Islamic code gives a death sentence and further that Islam like all other religions respects woman. In all Islamic nations, therefore, the sensitive issue of rape was supposed to be dealt with some wisdom and sobriety. But where shall you place the Pakistani requirement to book a rape culprit, that is so ugly and unfeministic that it vomits barbarism. Prophet Mohammed explicitly says[1] that the only legitimate sex relationship is marriage. Is it needed, then, to

---

1. Read "The Divine Islamic Standpoint on Father Daughter sexuality", part 13/Section III/A.

explain where the Prophet would have placed rape? Why then does a country that runs on the dictates of the great Mohammed occupy Satan's chair in rape criminal law? The tragedy here is that the ugly law is produced not by going against Quran but moulding Quaranic law to suit the wishes of fundamentally suffocative society.

The greater paradox perhaps is the Pakistan sponsored Afghanistan terrorist Mast Gul's attack on the holy shrine of Charar-e-Sharief, which was burnt to ashes. The nation which is Islamic burns down one of the most holy shrines of Islam - a symbol of purity and a passage to reach Allah ......? So paradoxical and yet so simple. These are the natural actions of conservationists who do not adhere to religion but rather misunderstand, misinterpret and misuse it.

We, in India, are all ashamed that the domes of Babri Masjid were brought down. And barring a few fundamentalists, the whole nation was clouded in shame. Pakistan, in order to avenge the bringing down of the mosque domes, exactly a year after, remote controlled a train mishap in India. Paradoxically, only one Indian was killed. He was Muslim.

Pakistan was created from India in 1947 and the two countries are sharply in contrast to each other. The bridge of ideology that separates them spans a greater length than is between the elements of the sky and the elements of the earth.

Pakistan was created as a theocratic state, allowing only Islam, with 97% if its people being Muslim. India was created as a secular state, allowing and promoting the co-existence of all religions. Where Pakistan has been stung by years of military rule, India has been one of the world's most successful nations, as regards continuance of democracy and democracy till date has been perpetual in India. India is one of the largest centres of education and culture in the world and its schooling is deemed as one of the very best in the globe. Pakistan, tragically, has a very poor education network and where India believes education to be a renaissance, Pakistan has a wide gap between people and learning. According to statistics, only a fourth of all the populace of 15 years or order can read or write. The children going to school are less than half of the total kid populace. India, on the other hand has 5,000 colleges and 85% of its children attend primary and pre-primary education in thousands and thousands of schools that span across the nation.

India through Pandit Jawaharlal Nehru, one of the country's pearls, introduced to the world, the five point peace plan–The Panchsheel. Pakistan contributed to the world three bloody wars attacking India, all of whom we won. Because India is a nation that loves and talks peace, and acts peace, but to defend herself has the world's bravest and most dedicated stalwarts.

Pakistan has sponsored terrorist campaigns in Kashmir and was also behind the bloody Punjab terrorism. It feels, perhaps, that through such meanly activities and a proxy war, that indicates the deep decline of its international fundamentals, it can take Kashmir into its own territory. It then must be told that a crown of a country can never be lifted from its head. In this case, firstly because it only fits our quantitatively large and qualitatively deep nation. Secondly because crowns are meant for kings and not robbers. Pakistan's policy is against God and religion. Bloodshed is the greatest crime in the face of God and invites His harshest punishment. Moreover, a nation that sets fire on his neighbour's abode can never herself save her own from being burnt down to ashes. Karachi is full of riots and murders and this day, the 25th of June when I am writing this piece, 39 innocent people have been killed there. I still hope that may Allah bless this nation, that once was such a beautiful part of an eternal culture.

India has believed in peace and that is why, perhaps, the world has believed in us. But if the cries of our Kashmiri countrymen shall rise above our limits of endurance, our love shall compel us to leave our white robes and engage in a holy defence. We shall not spare the nation then, that we have been forgiving time and again.

But for the meanwhile our diplomatic strength is enough. Our two outstanding Parliamentarians Mr. A. B. Vajpayee and Mr. Khurshid gave Pakistan a taste of our diplomatic superiority and strength when we made Pakistan an international joke at U. N. Human Rights Commission at Geneva, in 1994. Let Pakistan remember that Ashoka the great, was a prototype of India. One form of his was the spiritual escalator and another the eternal warrior.

Where will a country like Pakistan, were morality cries and humanity weeps, go ......? If Pakistan doesn't wake up, it shall have to enter its final sleep. For God has said that where all ethics die, death immediately and spontaneously occurs. The reasons for it are mere catalysts in the reaction of granules of immorality as reactants and particles of death as products.

THE LAW FILE

In his article "Peculiar Paradox" Christopher Thomas, of the Times, London[1], informs thus of the Pakistani criminal law against rape :

"Four male Muslim witnesses must testify that there was penetration before a man can be charged with rape. A woman complaining of rape, unable to prove her case, risks being jailed for fornication".

A CRITICAL SURVEY

We have learnt that Islam doesn't make it necessary that four male witness testify a penetration. It is just a part of a four point requirement, in which any of the one is sufficient to convict a person. The 4 witness requirement is necessary only for illegitimate relationships of adultery and premarital sex, which Islam includes in the crime of rape; where firstly both men and women are convicted and which is secondly of a different parameter. It is clear that the Islamic code has been compressed to suit the male class and thus contribute to a heinous female exploitation.

Forget what punishment shall be offered to the rape culprit, for, with such a law, probability can rest on the bed of assurance, that barring bizarre exceptions, with such laws no culprit shall be booked.

Such criminal laws are not penal codes. They are rather codes of escape. Such laws are made when it is wanted that nobody should be booked for a particular crime but it should have a place in the law book for the sake of it.

Wherewith can a woman find four witnesses to rape ....? To top it all, the four witnesses also are to be males. Male witnesses in a country where perhaps only three male types can be found. One, those who are depraved fundamentalists, to whom no crime to woman exists because woman is only meant to bow and endure their dictates and passions. Such people instead of acting as a woman's witness to rape shall kill her for objecting to rape. Second, those who are good but so passively good that the tongue of their goodness lies frozen beneath the ice of terror. Third, those to whom rape is an enjoyment basis. In addition, as Christopher

---

1. The article by Christopher Thomas was produced in The Hindustan Times, Sunday Magazine, March, 5, 1995, p. 1.

Thomas says, in Pakistan "the testimony of women carries little legal weight". Where then will a witness come from? And then, rape may - a–times has no witness.

This is the ugliest law that I have read. I have included it because it is the sharpest contrast in our comparative study on rape law. Rather than approaching this law for suggestions. I rather suggest Mrs. Benazir Bhutto that being a woman she should understand the meaning of rape to a victim and rather than being a remote controlled politician of feminist issues, existing on the dictates of conservationist males and mullahs, should make courage rise in her, and as true follower of Prophet Mohammed, bring solace to rape victims in her nation.

B. CONTINENTAL CULTURES

If quality would have been the only criterion of a continent, Greece would have always existed not as a nation but perhaps the largest continent of the world. The depth and variety of Greece is so captivating and authoritative that it commands and controls an extraordinary powerful culture of a continental class.

This was the reason that Greece had to be included as a separate group, as it is a culture of the depth of a continent[1].

GREECE

THE INTRODUCTION FILE

Profile		
• Official name	:	Elliniki dimokratia (Hellenic Republic).
• Capital	:	Athens
• Continental location	:	Southern Europe.
• Neighbouring countries	:	Albania, Yugoslavia, Bulgaria and Turkey.

---

1. The word "Continental culture" has its own meaning here, as indicated, and has no relation with any other meaning with which it might have been associated and recognised.

- Religion Status : Official religion "Greek Orthodoxy", 95% of the populace a member of the Greek Orthodox Church. Grant of freedom of worship to all, irrespective of faith.
- Economic Status : Expanding economy with rapid development, though weak as regards European perspective.
- Total Population : 1981 Census : 9,740,151 people
  1966 estimate : 10,138,000 people
  Density - 76 persons per Km^2
  Distribution - Urban 63% and Rural 27%
- Official language : Greek
- Political Status : Republic
- Feminine Status : Equal rights granted by the Constitution.
- Area : 131, 990 Km^2
  Greatest Distances :
  North-South : 587 Km
  East-West : 555 Km
- Currency : Basic Unit - Drachma
  Exchange rate - .005 US $.
- National Flag : White cross covering left most corner. Rest blue and white stripes. White cross symbolises the Greek Orthodox religion. Blue stripes stand for the sea and the sky. The white ones represent purity of Greek independence struggle.
- National Emblem : The emblem has a white cross in square like shape with blue base. It is surrounded by a circle or necklace of green leaves called "laurel wreath".
- National Anthem : "Imnos pros tin Eleftherian" ("The Hymn to Liberty").

The History and Times of Greece

BC
(Ancient Greece)

- 3000 : Beginning of the first civilization also called Minon culture
- 1450 : Domination of Minoan culture ends, and Mycenaeans take over.
- 1200 : Mycenae wins a war in Asia minor against Troy. Base for inspiration for major works like Illiad by Homer.
- 700's : Birth of city States.
- 600's - 300's : The tactic of phalanx, one of the greatest forms of battle and warfare in use.
- 500's : Democracy originates in city states.
  : Origination of Greek Philosophy.
  : Persian empire expands, Greek states conquered in Asia minor.
- 508 : Cliesthenes puts up a proposal for a constitution. Athens is converted to a systemized democracy.
- 400's : Athens becomes a successful democratic state.
  : Building of the great temples at Aexopolis in Athens.
  : Democritus put the theory that everything consists of atoms.
- 499 - 494 : King Darius-I of Persia crushes Greek revolts against Persian control in Greece.
- 477 : Greek Alliance in Athens against Glean League.
- 477-431 : Golden age of Ancient Greece.
- 300's : Plato finds the Academy.
- 399 : Athenian jury sentences Socrates to death
- 338 : Macedonia defeats Greeks in the Chaeronean battle.
- 334 : Alexander the Great starts his expansion Plans in Persia.
- 323 : Death of Alexander and the beginnings of the Hellenistic Age.

- 200's : Aristarchus of Samos theorises that earth revolves around the sun and not the contrary.
- 140's : Rome extends it's Greek influence.

AD
(Modern Greece)[1]

- 1453 : The Byzantine capital, Constantinople is captured by the Byzantine Turks.
- 1700's : The national revival of Greece
- 1821 : Beginning of the Greek war of independence.
- 1827 : France, UK, and USSR agree to make Greece a "self governing" area of the Ottoman empire by their combined strength and tact.
- 1832 : The Bavarian prince Otto becomes the first king of Greece.
- 1844 : Greece is established as a constitutional monarchy.
- 1864 : New constitution comes to effect, giving major power to the Parliament.
- 1909 : The Great revolt of the Military League.
- 1917 : Greece joins World War-I on the Allies side.
- 1940-41 : World War-II completely devastates Greece.
- 1952 : Greece joins NATO.
  : Women given right to vote.
- 1967 : Army officer's seizure of government. Constitution suspended.
- 1968 : New constitution for Greece.
- 1974 : Parliamentary election after 10 years. Formation of civilian government.
- 1981 : Greece joins the European community.
  : Panhellenic Socialist movement (PASOK) party wins; leading to the first socialist government.

---

1. AD doesn't begin the modern era in Greece. However, I have highlighted only those developments in AD that are a part of modern Greece.

Looking back
Looking beyond.

In ways more than one, Greece has been the centre of gravity of civilization. It has been the nucleus of ascent development, achievement, magnificence, splendour, search and breakthrough. The turning points of Greece have turned the tide of the globe and the Greek origins have been the doors to the golden horizon.

The Greek man has been a fanatic searcher and a eccentric creator, and this fanaticism and eccentricity has given birth to the divine forms of human endeavour and achievement. The names that adorn the golden corridors of Greek history are perhaps numerable but still innumerable. Alexander the Great, Alcibiades, Archimedes, Cimon, Euclid, Hipparchus, Hippocrates, Olympias, Zeno of Citium, Pythagoras, Plato, Solon .....the list is too vast to end!

The Muses, holy daughters of the Zeus[1] and Mnemosyne[2], and Goddesses of science and arts blessed Greece with their divine blessings and eternal power - goddess Calliope of Epic Poetry, Erato of love poetry, Euterpe of lyric poetry, Clio of history, Malpomene of tragedy, Thalia of comedy, Terpsichore of dance, Urania of astronomy and Goddess Polyhymnia of sacred songs blessed to birth some of the world's greatest genius, from this great nation.

When the world was intellectually sleeping in the Bronze Age, in Greece was fought the Trojan War[3], which was penned into an immortal saga called "Illiad" and later led to its sequel "The Odyssey"[4]. Thus Greece gave the world two epics which formed examples of the zenith of lyrical creation. Homer became the father of epic poetry and the intellectual guide of the writer's tribe. He was adored, admired and respected by the greatest of the writers and John Milton who composed the two holy epics - Paradise Lost and Paradise Regained; thus assuming the role of the world's spiritual teacher, praised Homer for his wit and creativity.

---

1. Zeus (Greek mythology)– The King of the Gods.

2. Mnemosyne (Greek mythology)- The Goddess of memory.

3. Possibly in 1250 BC.

4. Illiad and Odyssey were both possibly composed in the 700's BC.

Sophocles penned over ninety plays and the ones existing have proved that he was the master of tragic Drama. With Aeschylus and Euripides, Sophocles made drama a masterpiece of literature. Aristophanes and Plautus guide d the world in comedy, and thus not just was drama born in Greece but the birth was properly nurtured to make it reach its full maturity and magnificence.

Greek language is a member of the Indo-European family of languages and one of its oldest members. Many of its symbols like alpha, beta, gamma, delta, iota, lamba, pi, sigma and omega have become internationally accepted symbols of science and mathematics, besides having an immortal place in their language's expression and communication.

Greek philosophy has shaped the entire philosophical tradition of the West and sketched the Western intellectual throught. The Greek philosophy is the blueprint for the western philosophy. Socrates, his disciple Plato and Plato's disciple Aristotle gave birth to a great philosophic thought that amazingly uncovers some of the world's greatest questions in spirituality, ethicality, intellectuality and politics.

Greece gave the world the system of democracy and Athens inculcated this system hundreds of years before Christ. Alexander the great, at 13, set on his mission to conquer the world and the world had to salute him with a great bow. World politics acquired their centre stage in Greek soil.

Pythagoras with his Pythagoras theorem and other logical theories developed mathematics to zenithal heights. Archimedes ran naked on finding one of the bare scientific truths, making Greek science as noble and as pure as a new born babe. Greece outshines in the cosmos of science for giving birth to the most earnest, genuine and dedicated scientist whose happiness of discovery was greater enough to superimpose over his sense of clothes;

The extraordinary achievements of the Greek sculpture are evident from the fact that three of the Seven Wonders of the Ancient World are from Greece.

"The temple of Artemis" to Esphesus, was build in 550 BC. The great architect Cheriphron and his son, Metagenes designed it for worship of the Greek Goddess Artemis. The almost entirely marble temple had 106 columns, each stretching to a height of 12 metres.

"The Statue of Zues" was made of pure creativity and its majesty perfectly suited the great God. The robe and ornaments were of gold and the body resembled the spirituality of the divine form in being gleaming white, built out of ivory.

"The Colossus of Rhodes" was in honour of the Sun God Helios built by Greek sculptor Chares, standing a majestic 37 metres high.

It is thus no wonder that Renaissance was actually a revival of Greek and Roman Culture.

But what is Greece today?

Greece certainly has preserved its great heritage but some cracks can be seen in this vast civilization. A very tragic fact is that a country which produced out of its womb, democracy, had a majority of undemocratic governments. 1967 and 1973 have been jet black years when Army has captured the government giving a severe jolt to politics, by bringing the foul wave of monopoly, aggression and dictatorship. But it is good to note that Greece today has a purely democratic government.

Greece has also proved its strength to the world by recovering from the second world war damage, when it's economy had been totally devastated. Thus the days after the second global war, when the shattering of the nation had been but too short of the post traumas of a nuclear bomb explosion, are now over and gone for ever. The picture today is of expansion, which reflects will, a spirit of strength and the desire capability of keeping the head high. After all, Greece always has travelled alone.

THE LAW FILE

Mr. Evangelos Theophilou, Attache in The Embassy of Greece, informed me of the Greek criminal law regarding rape. I am reproducing the extract of his letter that deals with the same :

"The Greek Penal code (Law No. 1492 dated 17 August 1950, as modified subsequently) provides in Article 336, titled rape, that the person who compels a female to extramarital coition, through corporal force or threat of serious and immediate danger, is punished with imprisonment.

According to Article 340, if the action committed as per Article 336 resulted in the death of the victim, at least ten years imprisonment or life imprisonment is inflicted.

Again, according to Article 344, in case of Article 336, the criminal prosecution takes place only upon indictment; however indictment is not required if the action created a scandal or aroused the public curiosity."

A CRITICAL SURVEY

Execution as a punishment is not included in the Greek criminal law on rape. However, Article 340 must have capital punishment for rape, in both the two following cases :

- If Greece has capital punishment for murder, then rape resulting in death has two crimes been committed-first, rape; which in the light of traumas to the victim and violation of her sexual privacy assumes the form of a very serious crime, in itself equal to murder, Second, death of the victim by being rapes is the murder of the victim. Thus, it is a case of double murder and makes capital punishment necessary.

- If Greece has no capital punishment at all, even then rape and murder is a very serious offence. As murder is often considered the most severe offence and rape is the deepest bruise on a woman's personal rights; it necessities the penalty of execution.

In fact, the case that Article 340 refers to must have execution as a punishment, in very country of the world, excluding the very high exceptions. In this double crime, even psycho patients stand a slight chance, if any, to be spared of the gallows.

The line "...... the person who compels a female to extramarital coition .....? Is very debatable. Does it mean that a person can compel a female to marital coition? How can marriage give one the right to force his spouse to a sexual intercourse? If a couple vows to live together, it is on the basis of respect for each other's rights and a mutual co-existence, without use of any force, whether emotional, physical or sexual. Like almost very country, Greek also offers the same narrowminded and paradoxical view on marital sexual relations and doesn't recognise marital rape.

The International Perspective

C. SOMERSAULT REGIMES

As time takes a turn there are many issues that take a somersault. This is an established fact, proved by time and recorded by history.

However, there are many cultures - vast and deep, of the size of a country that take a complete somersault; and it seems as if time completely washed away what was in existence and from some remote part of space brought in a new, distinct culture.

The same is true of Soviet Union. What was until 1991, a communist regime has now transtitioned into a loosely governed confederation of states on democratic lines. And it is not the only time that Russia, on the floor of time, has staged a spectacular somersault. In the first quarter of the twentieth century it had tossed to oblivion the stale monarchy of the czar, as if Russia was just placed on a game of chess where displacements and new placements were made by a band of socialists at their will.

Russian Federation certainly deserves the credit of being separately included in a group.

RUSSIAN FEDERATION

THE INTRODUCTION FILE

Profile		
• Official name	:	The Republic of the Russian Federation.[1]
• Capital	:	Moscow
• Continental Location	:	Exists both in Asia and Europe. Covers two fifths of the Asian continent and half of Europe.
• Neighbouring countries	:	Iran, Afghanistan, Pakistan, Mongolia, Finland, Poland, Romania,

---

1. It is remarkable that even today, the country is recognised the world over as Union of Soviet Socialist Republic.

- Religion status : China, Turkey, Hungary and Czechoslovakia.
  All curbs on religion now lifted, granting freedom of worship. Major Religion - Russian Orthodox, practised by about half the populace.
  Other religions : Islam, Roman and Ukranian Catholics and members of Armenian Church.

- Economic Status : Once a superpower, now try to come from the economic slump after the transition process.

- Total population : 1989 census - 285, 688, 985
  1996 estimate - 299, 450,000
  Density - 13 person per Km^2
  Distribution - 68% urban, 32% rural.

- Official language : Russian, other languages also have a partial official status. They are Ukranian, Uzbek, Tartar, Kazakh, Azerbaijani, Armenian, Georgian, Moldavian and Tajik.

- Political Status : Revolutionary transitions from 1991. Now a loosely governed confederation of independent states, headed at the centre by the President. Armed forces are common and all the states are joined by mutual co-operation though each state is managed by an independent government.

- Feminine status : Woman on the move.

- Area : 22,228,000 Km^2
  Greatest distances
  North - South - 5,150 Km
  East - West - 9,656 Km.

- Currency : Basic Unit - Ruble
  Exchange rate - 1.68 US$

- National Flag[1] :

The International Perspective

- Coat of arms[2]   :
- National Anthem   : A "classical melody" by illustrious Russian composer Mikhail Glinka. An all Russia contest announced in 1990, for the best text for the anthem. The contest stands uncompleted as yet.

The History and Times of Russia

BC
- 1200   - Habitations of the Balkan people called the Cimmerians in the north of Black Sea, now south Ukraine.
- 700   - Defeat of the Cimmerians by Scythians, Iranian tribe from Asia.
- 200   - Sarmatians, a Iranian tribe, defeats Scythians.

AD
- 200   - Goths conquer the region.
- 370   - Huns defeat Goths
- 500's   - Avars, an Asian tribe, related to Huns, begins to rule.
- 800's   - State of Kiev Rus established by Eastern Slavs.

---

1 and 2. The official powers of Russia have not yet arrived at a consensus on the issue of the flag and the emblem (coat of arms). I reproduce here the following statement from a short article on Russian symbolics, faxed to me by the Russian information Department:

"The new symbols were widely introduced after the Decree of the President signed in December, 1993. But the draft Federal Constitutional Law "on the State symbols of the Russian Federation" which the President submitted to the Parliament's Power Chamber, the State Duma, has not been officially endorsed because the Deputies can't agree on the question. Some of them hold the red flag and the sickle from the country's former Soviet life sacred, other object to the transfer of the old monarchic symbols."

It is thus, not proper, at the moment, to write on the symbolics of Russia.

- 882 — Kiev captured by Oleg, starts ruling as prince
- 900's — Kievan ruler comes to be known as Grand Prince.
- 988 — Grand Prince Vladmir-I converts to Christianity, Eastern Slavs themselves being Pagans worshipping idols representing forces of nature.
- 1237 — Grandson of Ghengis Khan, a Mongol, invades Russia.[1]
- 1240 — Kiev destroyed, Russia becomes part of Mangol empire, included in a "section" called "Golden Horde".
- 1300's — Prince Yuri of Moscow marries daughter of Golden Horde's Khan.
  - Moscow increases in economic strength and political power.
  - Golden Horde's power decreases.
- 1480 — King Ivan-III the great, of Moscow, breaks away from Mongolian influence.
- 1547 — Moscow's grand prince or ruler comes to be called the Czar. King Ivan-IV, also called Ivan, the terrible, crowned the first Czar.[2] Makes power of Czar all over Russia.
- 1547-1897 — Death of Czar Ivan-IV followed by "Time of Troubles" because of problems on heir to the throne.
  - Crimean war breaks between Russia and Ottoman Empire. Russia defeated. Suffers losses.
  - Russian expansion in Asia.
  - Formation of political organisations opposed to monarchy - liberal constitutionalists, social revelationists and Marxists.

---

1. Here Russia refers to the city and not the country.

2. Those interested in Russian history must read about King Ivan - IV. He was extremely ill tempered, brutal and may be insane. He even killed his eldest son in anger.

Czars and Empresses of Russia : 1547 - 1897

- Ivan - IV : 1547 - 1584
- Theodore-I : 1584 - 1598
- Boris Godunov : 1598 - 1605
- Theodore-II : 1605
- False Dmitri : 1605 - 1606
- Basil Shuisky : 1606 - 1610
- Michael Romanov : 1613[1] - 1645
- Alexis : 1645 - 1676
- Theodore - III : 1676 - 1682
- Ivan - V : 1682 - 1696
- Peter - I : 1696 - 1725
- Catherine - I : 1725 - 1727
- Peter - II : 1727 - 1730
- Anne : 1730 - 1740
- Ivan - VI : 1740 - 1741
- Elizabeth : 1741 - 1762
- Peter - III : 1762
- Catherine - II : 1762 - 1796
- Paul : 1796 - 1801
- Alexander - I : 1801 - 1825
- Nicholas - I : 1825 - 1855
- Alexander - II : 1855 - 1881
- Alexander - III : 1881 - 1894
- Nicholas- II : 1894 - (1917)

- 1898 - Formation of Russian Social Democratic Party
- 1899 - The great economic depression.
- 1903 - Russian Social Democratic Party splits into two parts, Bolsheviks and Mensheviks. Bolsheviks lead by Lenin.
- 1905 - Revolution of 1905, government kills hundred of rebels on Sunday, January 22, thus called Bloody Sunday.
  - General strike in the country.

---

1. In 1610, Moscow came under Polish control. The Polish were driven out in 1612. In this period, thus, there was no czar.

	- Revolutionaries form the 'Soviet or council.
	- Nicholas grants Duma legislative powers.
• 1914	- Germany attacks Russia on the Ist August in World War - I.
• 1917	- The great revolution of 1917.
	- Czar Nicholas-II overthrown.
	- Lenin becomes dictator.
• 1921	- Lenin established the NEP or New Economic Policy to enable Russia to overcome the economic depression and starvation.
• 1922	- USSR is established.
• 1924	- Death of Lenin.
• 1927	- Stalin becomes the Supreme power.
• 1928	- First Five Year Plan
• 1930's	- Stalin orders an action programme called "The Great Purge". 20 million estimated to be killed.
• 1945	- Japan surrenders to Allies which includes Russia. World War-II ends. Russia suffers highest casualty, statistically 7.5 million people killed, 5 million wounded, 3 million captured or died in Nazi Camps, millions of civilians dead.
• 1953	- Stalin dies.
• 1956	- Khrushchev criticizes Stalin, renames all towns and structures named on him, disbands the reign of terror, allows freer atmosphere.
• 1960	- Crisis over American confession on USR spying
• 1963	- USSR, USA and UK sign joint treaty prohibiting all nuclear tests excluding underground ones.
• 1985	- Mikhail Gorbachev becomes the supreme premier
• 1991	- Strategic arms reduction ties (START) signed between Mikhail Gorbachev and George Bush, US premier.
	- Communist rule ends.

Looking Back
Looking Beyond

Soviet Union is a land of great change. Its profile graph changes so rapidly and takes so unprecedented and unbelievable turns that this nation seems too transient to be contained in a definition. In one single century this country has changed from monarchy to communism to a loosely held government on democratic lines. It was once under great economic slump, recovered from it majestically to be a stable and prosperous economy, was again struck by economic famine and is now trying to come from the deeps, Once ignored as an entity, it rose to become the world's greatest super power and lent many a nation a support of its iron bane. Suddenly, she is seen learning to support herself. They very many distinct states were combined by Czar Ivan-IV, were again disjointed by the separating fibre of political moves, were binded by Lenin and are now again loose and more disjointed than joined. Soviet Union is the most perfect example of the theory of flux. It is a land meant for the mentally stable and emotionally strong. Peace as stability has not been given a place here.

But Russia is also a beautiful personification of Darwin's theory of "survival of the fittest". It certainly has survived against all waves, all turbulence and all the severe tests of time. It has stood for centuries as a geographic and biological spectacle, where both man and land has wonderstruck the world.

The tragic thing however is that Russia's somersault changes have only come when the existing politics and the issues that adhere to it have become stale, depraved and far beyond endurance. The historic revolution of 1917 was prompted by years of brutal autocracy, ocean wide gaps between the elite and the poor and a "Bloody Sunday". Similarly, it was dictatorship, terror and butchering of innocent men in the guise of holy Marxist thought and socialist benevolence that toppled the socialist turned communist regime.

It is thus praise worthy that Soviet Union has survived against all odds and each time managed to be a super power. However, it is tragic that this nation becomes so easily rotten to invite series of revolutions in a single century. One wishes that this great nation of geographical diversity and mammoth area, great cultural inheritance and several thousand calendars deep heritage, reaches that zone of stability where there is love, peace and equality, whose fragrance grows each hour.

The world desires Soviet Union to take no more somersaults. For when an athlete jumps, the audience are wonderstruck. But each granule of the body has to suffer the pain of travelling an upside down journey before coming to rest.

THE LAW FILE

Though Soviet Union has politically changed, this has not led to the change of issues that have no relation to a communist regime's topple. Rape is one of them.

The law on rape remains by and large the same.

Law on rape has been extracted from the article "Provisions of Soviet Criminal Law safeguarding personal rights of women" by Professor A. Michailov, in the book "Crimes and Punishments in New Perspective". It is necessary that this file, before introducing the law, devotes some stanzas in establishing the nation's attitude to women, as an independent entirety and in relation to males. The article written by a Russian authority on law fulfils both the needs and combines the nation's constitutional attitude to the fair sex and her treatment by the jurisprudence.

The USSR Constitution has laid down the foundations to safeguard individual's rights by criminal law, without discrimination of origin, social or property status, race, nationality of sex.

The USSR Constitution provides for the equality of men and women in all spheres of life. All this contributes to creating an atmospheres of life. All this contributes to creating an atmosphere of respect and equality for both the sex. *As a woman is absolutely independent and equal in her citizens rights, she is free to decide herself the questions of sexual relations.*

No one is allowed to impose his will on the woman and force her to sexual intercourse. This right of the woman to her private sexual life cannot be challenged by factors such as financial dependence or subordinate position in office.

As rape might mean alienating women as inferior human beings, existing only for sexual lust, rape is also a direct challenge to social equality.

Rape or any means of sexual assault are considered as *"Socially very dangerous acts"*, and thus are considered to be a specific part of criminality.

The characterization of criminals committing rape is immoral behaviour, alcohol consumption, violations of the norms of social interactions and unhealthy family relations.

The Presidium of the Supreme Soviet of the USSR emphasized in this decree that in order to reinforce the rule of law, crimes of rape will be punished with the deprivation of liberty for the term from 10 to 15 years, while rapes of juvenile as well as rapes committed by a group or rapes resulting in serious consequences will be punished by the deprivation of liberty for the term from 15 to 20 years.

In 1959-1961, this was slightly changed by a provision for a shorter term of maximum period of deprivation of liberty upto 15 years and not 20 years.

On February 15, 1962, a new Federal Decree on Reinforcement of responsibility of crimes for rape was enacted. *This decree provided for capital punishment as an "exceptional and extraordinary measure for rapes" committed either by a group of persons or by an especially dangerous recidivist or for rapes with extremely grave consequences. The decree provided for capital punishment also in cases when victims of rapes were juveniles. Later on, the legislator considered it appropriate to mitigate responsibility for rapes of juveniles, but for infant victims, punishments remained very severe, including capital sanctions.*

Judicial practice knows cases treated as crimes of rape, when the criminal in order to petrify the will of the victim and her resistance, fraudulently made her take some soporific medicine or drugs, thus depriving her of the possibility to resist.

Law provides for "enforced responsibility" in case the rape was done by threat to kill or by causing grave bodily injuries to the victim.

With due regard to social status, which is equal to that of men, USSR legislation does not qualify as rape compelling a woman to sexual intercourse with a person with whom she occupies a dependent material or professional position. Such a compulsion is treated as an independent corpus delicit, which is liable to punishment of deprivation of liberty for the term upto 3 years.

The violent criminal must be accountable for the following :

He should be accountable for his *conscious intention to commit a sexual act against the will* of his victim.

He should be accountable for the *use of force or threats of violence in order to oppress his victim's resistance,* or for taking advantage of his victim's helpless state because of which she can't put up resistances to the rapist.

The subject of the crime of rape may be *criminally imputable person of the male sex,* not younger than 14 years.

Lastly, practical application of criminal laws regulating questions of responsibility for rapes proceeds from the principle that forcible encroachment on sexual immunity of persons of the male sect should be treated whether as forcible homosexual act, or as hooliganizm, or as causing of bodily injuries. Such actions, though being criminal, do not constitute corpus delicit of the crime of rape.

A CRITICAL SURVEY

There are two very notable points in the Russian criminal jurisprudence against rape :

It is a very accurate understanding that rape of women might mean "alienating them as inferior human beings" and thus "is a direct challenge to social equality".

Indeed, when a woman is raped, the criminal in one way or the other treats her just as an object of sexual lust. The women feels being ostracized in society as one of those social beings living without her virginity. Thus equality is broken in two ways. First–as woman is treated as a sexual object and not a human being with her own rights and self governed private existence. Second - rape snatches from her the guarantee to stand equal to men as per official, emotional, legal and sexual rights.

The International Perspective 229

It is praiseworthy that Russia understands rape as a "socially dangerous act", which is certainly is.

- Russia includes the punishment of execution. The punishment of execution seems to be included while deeply understanding its use and is done when among others, the following factors are there :

(i) Extremely grave consequences ; which includes intense traumas and death of the victim.

(ii) Infant victims.

We have talked of execution clause throughout the book, deeming it a necessary punishment for certain types of rape and certain types of culprits. Russian Law not only acts as a good proof of the book's advocacy but also gives a good study point in case the rape law needs to be amended in any nation (and thus India) and punishment of execution is studied for inclusion.

D. SUPERPOWERS AND DEVELOPED NATIONS OF THE WEST

There are countries where science seems to have been crowned with majesty and recognised as a royalty. Supersonic jets penetrate the sky at unbelievable speeds, and cars of the latest technology ride on superscientific roads, going from one modern skyscraper to another. Computers have invaded each granule of official and personal life and multimedia rules the sky with hundreds of channels.

This extraordinary technology has made these regimes superpowers and helps them to outshine others. They lead the world in armed strength, scientific powers and financial stock.

Superpowers have a distinct characteristic of their on and these fair cousins from the west thus merge into a separate and distinct group, in this international study. After all, power is the product of society and culture and gives it a new aura that travels across both the sides of the evaluating line.

THE UNITED STATES OF AMERICA

THE INTRODUCTION FILE

Profile

• Official name	:	United States of America
• Capital	:	Washington, D. C.
• Continental Location	:	Occupies entire middle position of North America; Northwest America and the Pacific.
• Neighbouring Countries	:	Canada and Mexico.
• Religion Status	:	Freedom of religion
• Economic Status	:	The Supreme Superpower of the World.
• Total Population	:	1990 census : 249,632,692 1995 estimate : 259,259,000 Density : 27 persons per Km^2 Distribution: 74% Urban, 26% Rural
• Official Language	:	No official language English the most spoken language, followed by Spanish.
• Political Status	:	Federal Republic, Capitalist Economy
• Feminine Status	:	Paradoxical, with one of the highest feminine development and attitude of permissiveness towards fair sex; and at the same time a very high woman oriented crime rate.
• Area	:	9, 372, 571 Km^2
	:	Greatest distance :[1] North-South - 2,572 Km East - West - 4,517 Km
• Currency	:	Basic Unit - US$ Exchange Rate - 1

---

1. Area of USA main + Alaska + Hawai. Same for greatest distances calculation. (According to international calculation).

The International Perspective

- National Flag : The left most corner has a blue square, covering about a fifth of the flag, with white stars. Rest is red and white stripes, beginning with red from the top.
- The Great Seal : On both sides. Side one - Eagle holding olive branch and arrows, which symbolises that the nation prefers peace, while at the same time having the ability to wage war.

  Side two - An eye of Providence, representing God and a pyramid, dated 1776.
- National Anthem : "The Star Spangled Banner".

The History and Times of the United States

BC
- 20,000 Yrs. Back : People from Siberia cross into America.
- 10,000 Yrs. Back : Melting of ice in the ice age brings changes, in the geography, biology and human life.
- 7,000 : Beginning of agriculture
- 6,000 : Habitation at the southern tip of South America.
- 5,000-2000 : People in Mexico improve in agriculture.
- 2,000 : Beginning of permanent villages
- 1,200 - 100 : Development of a calendar and counting system.
- 100 : Building of large cities like Monte Alban and Teotihuacan.

AD
- Till 500 : Building of large burial mounds and ceremonial centres.
- 700 : Flourishment of an advanced civilization in the Mississippi Valley Area.
- 1000 : Vikings from Greenland discover American continent.

- 1300 : True establishment of the great Aztec empire by the foundation of its capital Tenochtitlan.
- 1492[1] : Christopher Columbus discovers America
- 1607 : First permanent English settlement founded, and named Jamestown.
- 1620 : Puritans separated from Church of England, called separatists, lay foundation of second British colony called Plymouth Colony.
- 1775 : American revolution begins between Britishers and Colonists.
- 1776 : United State of America formed.
- 1781 : A federal government set up under laws called "Articles of Confederation"
- 1783 : Revolution ends by Treaty of Paris.
- 1787 : Writing of the constitution of the United State of America.
- 1791 : The Bill of Rights, concerning individual rights, becomes law.
- 1797 : Birth of the historic XYZ affair[2]
- 1799 : USA and France reach a peaceful agreement.
- 1800 : Washington, D.C., becomes the capital of the country.
- 1812 : War with Britain over shipping interference.
- 1814 : Treaty of Ghent on December 24 ends the war, with both sides suffering equal losses.
- 1815 - 1820 : The Era of Good Feeling[3].
- 1820 : Slavery dispute ends with Missouri compromise.
  : Massive expansion till date in the west.

---

1. Up till this point, it is not possible to bifurcate history of the United States from the history America, the continental landmass.

2. John Adams, the President of USA sent diplomats to France to resolve tension between the two nations. The diplomats were insulted by three agents, whose names were not revealed and were only called X, Y, Z.

3. In these years, there was a growth in nationalism and the triplet of "peace, unity and optimism" reigned,. Thus, the term coined by the historians.

The International Perspective

- 1835 : Oberlin College becomes the first college to admit women.
- 1848 : Married women allowed to have property.
  : Woman Rights Convention in Seneca Falls, New York formally appeals for "woman suffrage" or right to vote.
  : Gold rush on its discovery is California.
- 1850 : The 1850 compromise brings a temporary end to a slavery question of national character.
- 1860 : Pony express riders start carrying mail to far lands of the West.
- 1861-1865 : Civil War between North and South America.
- 1865 : The 13th Amendment bans slavery.
- 1867 : Alaska annexed from Russia.

- 1873 : Economic Depression.
- 1884 : Economic Depression.
- 1893 : Economic Depression.
- 1907 : Economic Depression.

- 1876 : Graham Bell invents the telephone
- 1886 : AFL - The American Federation of Labour is formed[1].
- 1901 : Roosevelt gives an outline of his foreign policy through the historic line - "Speak softly and Carry a big stick", helps US become a superpower.
- 1917 : Joins World War-I against Germany Wins the War.
- 1929 : The greatest economic slump paralyses the economy
- 1933 : Roosevelt begins the "New Deal" programme to tackle the economic slump.
- 1941 : U. S. joins World War-II
- 1945 : First atomic bomb of the word dropped on Hiroshima and later at Nagasaki.
- 1947 : Trueman Doctrine, announced by President Trueman, pledging the States 'and to nations threatened by communism.

---

1. Now called AFL- CIO, American Federation of Labour - Congress of Industrial Organisations.

- 1969 : Neil Armstrong becomes the first man of Moon.
- 1990 : Helps Kuwait in its war against Iraq.

Important Presidents of the States

- George Washington   : 1789 - 1797
- Abraham Lincoln   : 1861 - 1865
- Theodore Roosevelt   : 1901 - 1909
- Woodrow Wilson   : 1913 - 1921
- Franklin D. Roosevelt   : 1933 - 1945
- John F. Kennedy   : 1961 - 1963
- Richard M. Nixon   : 1969 - 1974
- Jimmy Carter   : 1977 - 1981
- Ronald Reagen   : 1981 - 1989
- George Bush   : 1989 - 1993
- Bill Clinton   : 1993 -

Looking Back
Looking Beyond

'What lies beyond ....?'

This is one of the central questions which has determined human existence. Man is never satisfied with the limit, the limitless and the infinite is the food for his grey crop. This passion made him travel to new lands and thus every country has had to suffer invasions and penetrations from outside. New cultures have been superimposed over existing cultures and they copulated and merged into a new, distinct cultural pattern. Religions with an authoritative existence have had to endure the coming of new faiths, adding more flavour and colour to the patterns of belief and worship.

Though every country has added to its social, cultural, ethical, religious and political mixture several new colours and shades to form at regular intervals a new permutation, adding to its prowess of contributing to the antithesis of its ethos, the United States is perhaps nearest to being called an everybody's land.

By and large, the States today is inhabited by the descendants of those who came here a couple of centuries back - some in search of spiritual gold and some in search of material gold. The Mayas and The Aztecs that ruled the vast Americas for hundreds and hundreds of years, those cultures that civilized the mammoth land mass in the prehistoric times, those cultures that survived "in the year of our Lord", they now habitat the country's vast museums and libraries. The descendants of those cultures are few and are perhaps the least known. Because the moment a human at this corner of the globe thinks of America, the gentleman with golden hair and white skin comes to the mind who is a descendant of the people who lived somewhere in London or Lisbon, and some centuries back colonized here.

Christopher Columbus indeed had created a wave when he had discovered this gigantic land mass. People from all around the western part of the globe, took their ships and boats, and with their oar of hope sailed to this land and built their dream castles. America is indeed a United States. Philosophically, a million states of emotional, cultural ethical, geographical, political, intellectual and individual patterns are united into this vast reservoir of people, flora and fauna. It has been nurtured by the dose of several cultures, and the 'Ab aeternno[1]' of Latin tongue, the 'Celui qui veut peut[2]' of French tongue, the 'Che sara sara[3], of Italian tongue and the 'Danke Schon[4]' of Geman tongue have been fed to the taste buds of American ethos. It is indeed a composite spectacle.

But, what has been the contribution of this cultural mixture to the Mother Earth? How has this unity born by diversity, fared in the test of time?

The States was born in 1776, an year after the great revolution. In two hundred years and two decades, she had managed to become a

---

The meaning of these phrases from foreign languages do not hold importance here but are given for the sake of information.

1. Ab aeterno - From eternity.
2. Celui qui veut peut - One who has the will, has the skill.
3. Che sara sara - What will be, will be.
4. Danke Schon - Many thanks.

superpower and the most important nation of the world. She has followed perfectly the policy of Theodore Roosevelt "Speak softly and carry a big stick". Softly she advises and very politely she interferes in the international affairs and internal issues of some nations but the stick of power that she carries is so big that almost immediately her wish becomes a dictate.

America has given a notable contribution to the world culture and this composite heritage has in ways more than one been the building blocks of the global cultural pattern. A very easy way to prove it is a look at the Nobel Awards File for various faculties.

The Nobel prize for economics was established in 1969. From 1969 to 1990, an American has in sixteen out of twenty one times captured this glorious award. From 1970 to 1973, four times in a row, from 1978 to 1983 six times in a row and from 1985 to 1987 three times in a row.

The Nobel Prize[1] for all other faculties were established in 1901. Physics has an American thirty five times out of ninety. In Chemistry twenty six times, the American has brought his country pride and honour. Thirty seven times American has won the glorious Nobel in Physiology and medicine - 1952 to 1954 three times in a row, 1966 to 1972 seven times in a row, 1975 to 1977 three times in a row, 1978 to 1981 four times in a row and 1988 to 1990 three times in a row. Thirty times America has contributed to the world peace of Nobel Standards, with this award being won four times in a row from 1970 to 1973. Four times the States has produced a nobel winer in literature. In all, USA has won one hundred and forty eight Nobel prizes which is a magnificent achievement, and hints at the varied zones of horizon that this composite culture has attained[2].

However, America's role today as the supreme superpower is questioned by many. Ideally, a superpower ought to act like a Godfather, support other nations and guide them to success and peace. Many feel that America goes away from her ideal and uses its superpower for its selfish means, supporting and suppressing economies at her pure will. Her attitude towards Vietnam War has been extremely controversial.

---

1. Excluding literature, which is till 1991, all other Nobel statistics are till 1990.

2. Though the nobel statics are from highly authoritative source giving complete list of Nobel prizes, and have been rechecked, the writer does not accept responsibility for the authenticity of the same.

But at the same time, it is also true that USA has nurtured with her resources many poor economies, especially in Africa. It is hoped that in the years to come the United States shall take her contribution as a superpower to perfection, catalysing world harmony, flourishment and peace.

THE LAW FILE

Before defining the law on rape, it is natural and essential, that the definitions of rape, other sex offences and sexual assault is understood in the American legal perspective.

RAPE IN USA

Rape is defined as "sexual intercourse with another person by forcible compulsion or threat of such or with a person 'incapable' of consent".

Rape is now defined in American criminology as forcible rape, to distinguish it from "statutory rape".

Statutory rape consists of sexual intercourse with a person "who is under a statutorily specified age (16 yrs., example gratia) whether the person consents or not". It is said that persons, in this age are immature and thus "incapable of understanding the full implications of giving consent". It is very important to note that in American law "mistake as to the age of the person, is ordinarily not a defence to statutory rape".

American law has now started giving attention to victims.

SEX OFFENCES EXCLUDED FROM THE RAPE CATEGORY

In U. S. A. many other sex offences are listed which do not come under rape.

- *Indecent exposure*
  This is generally defined as *exhibition of one's genitals* which is under circumstances "where such conduct is likely to cause affront or alarm and for the *purpose of arousing or gratifying the sexual desires* of the exhibitionist or other". It is usually *referred to as a "misdemeanour"*.

- *Indecent assault*

    This is referred to as *sexual contact with a person not one's lie partner,* when:

    (i) He knows that the contact "is offensive to the other person".
    (ii) The other person is not aware that such a contact is being done.
    (iii) The person cannot resist being in a drugged state.

- *Corruption of a minor*

    Any act which corrupts the morals or "contributes to the sexual delinquency" of the minor.

- *Prostitution*

    Prostitution is, as is generally known, engaging in sexual activity as a business. Prostitution is done both by male and females. It is considered "as an offence against public decency" and not against any person. In USA it is understood to be a "victimless crime".

    However, it is a crime to engage directly in prostitution or promoting, compelling, procuring, encouraging or soliciting it[1].

THE AMERICAN JURISPRUDENCE ON SEXUAL ASSAULT

- Volume 6

    Assault and Battery to Attachment and Garnishment.[2]

23. Mere words and mere preparation distinguished.

It appears to be settled that mere words are not sufficient to constitute the overt act required for a criminal assault, however insulting, abusive, or violent, the words may be. It has also been held that a man who merely asked a woman an improper question, unaccompanied by a show of violence, threats, or any display of force, did not commit a criminal assault against her. The threatening words should be accompanied or followed by an actual battery, the crime is committed if the words are accompanied or followed by either an offer to do violence or an attempt to do it.

---

1. Based on "The American Legal System", 2nd Edition, by Blair J. Kolasa and Bernadine Meyer.

2. A multivolume series on complete American Jurisprudence as it exists; by Jurisprudence Publications.

The International Perspective

It seems also to be settled that mere preparation to commit a violent injury on the person of another, unaccompanied by a physical effort to do so, does not constitute an assault, to constitute an assault there must be an attempt or offer, though interrupted, to an act, which, if not prevented, would produce the battery.

24. Sexual Assault

The indecent conduct of a man towards a woman or a man towards another man may under certain circumstances, amount to a criminal assault, or to a criminal assault and battery. In such a case, the threat or danger of physical suffering or injury in the ordinary sense is not necessary, the injury suffered by the innocent victim may be the fear, shame, humiliation, and mental anguish caused by the assault. However, particularly in jurisdictions where lewd, obscene, or indecent conduct as such is a statutory crime, for a certain conduct of an indecent sexual nature to amount to a criminal assault, the indecent sexual conduct alone is not sufficient; it must involve the elements required for a criminal assault. It has been held that since there can be no crime which is not defined and denounced by statute, there can be valid prosecution under a statute declaring an indecent assault to be punishable, which does not define what constitutes an indecent assault.

The phrase "indecent liberties", used in statutory definitions of sexual assaults, has been held to be as difficult to defines accurately as it is to define "fraud", or "dupe the process of law". It has also been held that the phrase is self defining[1].

It is generally not an essential element of a sexual assault that it should produce shame or other disagreeable emotion in the alleged victim, except where the statutory definition of the sexual assault includes this as an element of the crime.

25. Of man against woman.

A man who takes indecent liberties with a woman may be liable for criminal assault. But not every indecent act of a man towards a woman constitutes a criminal assault. Thus, applying the general

---

1. For this see State V Kunz, 90 Minn 526, 97 NW 131.

rule that words alone are not sufficient to constitute a criminal assault, and that an additional overt act is required, it has been held that a mere indecent proposal made by a man to a woman is not sufficient to constitute a criminal assault. The courts vary considerably in regard to the added factors needed to support a charge of assault. In some jurisdictions the courts have gone very far in applying the principle that a sufficient overt act must be involved. According to some authorities, it is a sufficient overt act to support a charge of criminal assault, that a man, by his indecent behaviour towards the woman, puts her in fear, although he does this merely by words.

Where a indecent proposal is accompanied by actual or attempted physical contacts, it is generally held that an assault has been committed.

26. Against unchaste Woman

Some statutory definitions of sexual assault or aggravated sexual assault expressly include the chaste character of the victim as an element of the offence or expressly exclude a prostitute as a possible victim of the particular crime. It has been stated, however, that it is not universally true that an indecent assault cannot be made by a man against a woman unless she is absolutely chaste, but, that each case must be judged under its particular circumstances. In jurisdiction, the view is taken that they sexual assault of a man against a woman not consenting thereto is criminal even though the woman has a bad reputation for chastity or is actually unchaste.

Proof of the unchaste character of a woman allegedly assaulted by a man affords some presumption that she consented to indecent acts, and might reasonably aid the jury in weighing the evidence concerning the existence or lack of consent.

27. Of man against man

A man who takes improper liberties with the person of another man without the latter's consent may thereby commit the crime of assault. It is not necessary that the acts taken, be of such a nature as to put the person thus assaulted in fear; it is sufficient if they arouse his indignation. Where the victim is a boy who because of his youth, cannot, as a matter of public policy, be considered as validly consenting to such an act, the defendant may be guilty of the crime of sexual assault although he committed it with the consent of the victim.

In a jurisdiction where an indecent assault is defined by statute as "the taking by a man of indecent liberties with the person of a female without her consent and against the will, but with no intent to commit the crime of rape", it has been held that the crime of indecent assault could not be committed by taking indecent liberties with a male juvenile. But a statute providing that a person over the age of 18 years who assaults a child under the age of 16 years, and wilfully takes indecent and improper liberties with the person of such child, without committing or intending to commit the crime of rape upon such child, or wilfully makes improper exposures of his person in the presence of such child, commits a felonious assault, has been held to be applicable to an assault upon a male child as well an assault upon a female child.

Where, on a charge of sexual assault upon a man, the defendant categorically denied that he had touched the alleged victim, it was not error on the part of the trial court not to instruct the jury that a merely accidental touching of the other person by the defendants would be a good defence.

CRIMINAL LAW ON RAPE

THE UNITED STATES CODE

Chapter 99
Rape
Sec.

2031. Special maritime and territorial jurisdiction

Whoever, within the special maritime and territorial jurisdiction of the United States, commits rape shall suffer death, or imprisonment for any term of years or for life.

(June 25, 1948, c. 645, 62 Stat. 795)

Important Comments on Section 2031[1]

---

1. Comments are based on a United States Code multivolume series, published by West Publishing Group.

- *Rapes within Section - generally.*

    This section "has been interpreted" to define rape as defined at common law, that is "carnal knowledge of female by force or threat of force."

- *Homosexual rapes.*

    "There is no federal statute punishing specific acts penetrated by homosexual rapist".

- *Intent.*

    Only intent which is necessary in rape cases "is intent to have carnal knowledge of prosecutrix by force and without her consent".

- *Use of Force*

    It is not necessary that the person who was attached and threatened with rape, must fight to the last ditch.

    Threats of bodily harm with some degree of physical force is sufficient.

- *Lesser included offence, excluded from rape*

    A "charge of assault with intent to rape" is different and thus not included in the charge to rape.

- *Intoxication as a defence*

    "Where there was testimony that defendant charged with rape on an Indian reservation tore away clothing of victim who suffered maxillary bone, bruise on lower lip, and loosened teeth, testimony that due to his intoxication defendants was impotent and incapable of rape did not preclude conviction for assault with intent to rape".

Section
2032. Carnal knowledge of female under 16

   Whoever, within the special maritime and territorial jurisdiction of the United States, carnally knows any female, not his wife, who has not attained the age of 16 years, shall, for a first offence, be imprisoned not more than 15 years, and for a subsequent offence, be imprisoned not more than thirty years.

Comments [1]
- *Constitutional v/s Unconstitutional*

This section does not "unconstitutionally discriminate" with males.

A CRITICAL SURVEY

The American criminology has introduced a new term called "forcible rape" The term might evoke surprise as the very definition of rape is "sexual intercourse without consent".

Actually, the word "consent" is very tricky. The whole discussion on rape is based on consent.

In cases involving an adult victim, consent means agreeing to have an intercourse.

However, women till a specified age (generally 16), are deemed incapable of giving consent. Sexual intercourse with them thus assumes the form of rape, in any circumstance. However, as in any way the accused didn't use force, it cannot be called rape but "statutory rape". Rape in the purest form can occur only in the former case, now called "forcible rape".

This inclusion, in the criminology of each nation, must be brought out.

In America, there is a new wave under which attention has started being given to the victims. USA thus has moved beyond other nations in understanding that while right punishment to the culprit is a very essential counter reaction by the law, it must also involve the parallel treatment of victim counselling as rape causes a massive breakdown in the psycho-emotional structure of the sexually attacked individual.

Sexual assault is understood in the United States as an action which causes harm or something that would have caused grave consequences had it not been stopped. It is quite logical a definition for sexual assault.

The concept of injury as regards sexual assault has been very well understood. It need not only be a physical harm, it might also be mental or

---

1. See Footnote 1, p. 241.

psychological, emotional or psychiatric harm that can be placed in a sex perspective.

The case of sexual assault or even rape, enters a very heated debate when the victim is of an unchaste character.

The accused's defence counsel in such a case uses he argument that the fact that the alleged victim is an unchaste woman gives a hint that sexual assault might not have been committed on her, as she being of loose character, gives high indications of agreeing to any indecent proposal.

This, however, is by no means a taken for granted situation that an unchaste woman cannot be sexually assaulted. It is infact quite illogical to assume that an unchaste woman shall give assent to every decent and indecent proposal for sex.

GREAT BRITAIN

THE INTRODUCTION FILE

Profile

• Official Name	:	United Kingdom of Great Britain and Northern Ireland.
• Capital	:	London
• Continental Location	:	Northwestern Europe
• Neighbouring Countries	:	France, Ireland, Norway, Denmark, Netherland and Belgium.
• Religion Status	:	Freedom of worship. Two national or established churches - Church of England (Episcopal) and Church of Scotland (Presbyterian).
• Economic Status	:	Developed Economy
• Total Population	:	1981 Census : 55,638,455. 1995 Estimate : 58,123,000. Density : 235 person per Km^2 Distribution: 92% Urban, 8% Rural
• Official Language	:	English
• Political Status	:	Constitutional Monarchy

The International Perspective 245

- Feminine Status : At league with men
- Area : 244,100 Km²
  Greatest distance -
  North - South : 970 km
  East - West : 480 km
- Currency : Pound (also known as pound sterling)
  Exchange rate - 1.71 US$
- National Flag : Blue background on which are two crosses, the one below in the shape of X and the one above in the shape of Jesus Christ's cross. Both crosses are in red bordered by white. The flag in known as British Union Flag or Union Jack.
- Royal Arms : Bears the arms of England, Ireland and Scotland.
- National Anthem : "God Save the Queen"

The History and Times of United Kingdom

BC
Palaeolithic Age
- 250,000 : Earliest Settlements
- 70,000 : Last of great glaciations; only "mild" settlements of human ancestors.
- 12,000 : Ending of the Ice Age; several great Palaeolithic Art forms like Dancing Man of Creswell Crags associated with this period.

Mesolithic Age
- 8,000 : Immigrants from Denmark; settlement at North Yorkshire and Star Carr.
- 5000 : English Channel and North Sea formed; Britain looses land link with Europe;

Neolithic Age and Bronze Age
- 4,000 : Tribes from Western Europe migrated to U. K.
- 3,000 : Neolithic people use graves of stone to bury the dead.

- 3000-2500 : Beginnings of the use of meta,
- 2700 : The Great monument of stone, Stonehenge, begins at Woltshire.
- 2,000 : Use of Bronze begins.
- 1400 : Stonehenge is completed.
- 700 : Celtic migrants invade Britain, bringing in the technology of iron.
- 200's : More Celtic migrants invade Britain and bring weapons and ornaments

Roman Britain (55 BC-410 AD)

- 55 : Julius Ceaser invades Britain

AD

- 43 : Claudius, the Roman emperor, invades Britain
- 209 : The first Christian martyr of England, St. Alban, killed.
- 368 : Pictish tribes damage Hadrian's Wall.
- : Romans abandon Cambria Forts.
- 407 : Roman soldiers leave Britain.
- 410 : Britain requests Rome for protection against Saxons, request turned down.

The Dark Ages (410 AD - 1066 AD)

- 597 : St. Augustine brings Christian faith to Kent.
- 664 : Pope declared as head of Celtic Church.
- 789 : Vikings, seafaring Scanidavians, raid Sussex coast.
- 827 : Claim by Egbert of Sussex to be the king of England.
- 851 : Vikings settle in England.
- 870 : Vikings conquer complete England; excluding Wessex.
- 1042-1066 : Rule of King Edward, the Confessor.

The Norman conquest (1066 AD - 1337 AD)

- 1066 : William I crowned king of Westminster Abbey (London) on the Christmas day.
- 1086 : "Domes day Book" records the wealth of Britain.
- 1215 : King John signs the "Magna Carta".

Magna Carta now stands at a monument along river Thames. At the time it was signed, the document did the function of checking royal power and bringing king under law. Later it became the mould for constitutional government development. King John was forced by the English Barons to sign it.

- 1314   : Robert Bruce frees Scotland from England.

The Conflict Years (1337-1485)

- 1337   : The Hundred Years War between England and France begins.
- 1348   : The evil plague, "The Black Death" coasts death in England
- 1453   : Ending of the Hundred Years War.
- 1455   : War of Roses between Lancastrians and Yorkists begins for the thrown.
- 1476   : The first printing press set up.
- 1485   : War or Roses ends.

The Horizon years (1485 - 1603)

- 1549   : Publication of the 1st English prayer book.
- 1558   : Elizabeth-I becomes queen.
- 1560   : The Church of Scotland becomes Presbyterian.
- 1603   : Union of Scotland and England under James-I.

The Years of Constitutional change (1603 - 1714)

- 1605   : The Gunpowder Plot.

The Gunpowder Plot (1605) was a plot by Roman Catholic fundamentalists to kill King James-I, a Protestant. It was foiled.

- 1611   : Publication of authorised version of Bible.
- 1628   : Petition of rights passed by Parliament.
- 1633   : William Laud, becomes Archbishop of Centerbury, spiritual capital of Britain.
-                : Clergies forced to use the Prayer Book.
-                : Puritans flee to North America.
- 1629-1640   : Charles-I rules but without Parliament.
- 1640   : Recalling of Parliament by Charles on invasion of Scots.

- 1649 : Charles-I is beheaded.
- 1649-1660 : England is called "The Commonwealth", Parliament rules as supreme power.
- 1660 : Monarchy is restored.
- 1707 : Act of Union ; England - Scotland united, Britain becomes United Kingdom of Great Britain.

The Transition Years (1714 -1837)
- 1733 : The flying shuttle invented.
- 1764 : Spinning jenny invented.
- 1801 : Act of Union; country's official name changed to United Kingdom of Great Britain and Ireland.
- 1832 : The first reform act passed.
- 1833 : Slavery is banned.

Years of transition lead to many far reaching changes and development. In Arts, Swift wrote the great Gulliver's Travels and William Hogarth became the master of painting. Robinson Crusoe was written. Sir Newton discovered law of gravity.

The Progress Years (1837-1906)
- 1840 : Establishment of penny post.
- 1858 : Government of Britain takes India under direct control.
- 1859 : "Origin of Species" by Charles Darwin published.
- 1879 : Opening of Britain's first telephone company.

The Modern Times
- 1908 : Old age pensions act passed
- 1914-1918 : Britain fights against Germany and allies, wins in the war.
- 1939-1945 : Second World War, Britain fights against Germany wins.
- 1973 : Britain joins European Community.
- 1979 : Margret Thatcher assumes office as first woman Prime Minister.
- 1990 : John Major becomes the Prime Minister.

Looking Back
Looking Beyond

"The Sun of England never sets".

In the days when imperialism was the global obsession and when the English rule spread far and wide–from the dark lands of Africa to the austerely beautiful deserts of Asia, and when the Union Jack stood on the top of the Himalayas; it was then that the Englishmen with their heads high, used to speak this statement now and then; as a hallmark of their imperials supremacy.

What was meant was quite simple. The English had such a vast empire that if the sun was drowning in the blue waves of the sky at one place, it was being born in red and gold, at the other.

But, let us widen the horizons of this sun a little more, so that we are able to give a complete definition of the United Kingdom; and see whether the sun of Britain indeed has never seen the dusk or is this authoritative claim a mirage, spun by the waves of vanity and illusion.

If we look at the Hall of Literature in the museum of the grand, old man of time, we shall see that Britain indeed claims a majestic respect.

Literature of Britain is a conglomerate of depth, variety and substance. It reached the zenith of poetry when the immortal British poet John Donne became one of the major forces to give birth to the Metaphysical School of poetic thought, a school of philosophical poetry where meanings and lyrical sensitivity breeds new horizons. Where existing truths are crossed to achieve a new world; and with it a new sense of creative life.

Charles Lamb with his mysterious pseudonym of Elia has mesmerized the complete literary cosmos and William Shakespeare seems to have made his presence as an inevitable necessity. The Literary Sun of Britain has neither sunk into death and infamy nor has been stung by the peril of dormance and inactivity.

In many other spheres of culture and heritage, Britain has prospered with a similar dawn of perpetual existence.

But, why is it that the white robes of peace and humanity, benevolence and universal brotherhood seen too big to fit Britain? May be because while the Imperial Britain had geographically expanded to infinity, it had ethnically shrunk to an infinitesimal consciousness. Men deemed inferior on the basis of colour were made slaves, and fed on filth and dirt and tortured by being mutilated, both mentally and physically. Did Britain notice that when it had shrieked aloud from the top of the Himalayas that the British Sun never sets, Jesus had cried?

The British sun of benevolence did set and sink to alarming deeps and lay immersed for centuries in that filth, pampered by the spirit of superiority complex.

It is only a matter of carnal synonimity and mental disparity in eyesight, when a glass with water makes one say that it is half filled and the other that it is half empty. Similarly if the sun of Britain never did set; then in that way it never did arise also.

Britain has come out of the obsession of imperial passion and is now member of the new wave of global thought. If Britain has to make the British empire be ruled by sun that never sets; it must insure that in this global market it usher in the magic of love and peace and not set up Satanic forces like the East India Company.

THE LAW FILE

In the absence of the British Penal Code, the British law on rape was extracted after a deep study of some authoritative books on the law of Great Britain.[1]

The law relating to most sexual offences has now been consolidated in the Sexual Offences Act, 1956. This law has been amended several times thus clarifying, changing and adding several points. The most serious of such offences, is rape.

---

1. "Outlines of English Law" by Marsh.
   "Introduction to English Law" by Phillip S. James.
   "Law: A Modern Introduction" by Paul Dehman.
   Many of the statements have been quoted in the rape section.
   The section on incestual rape has been entirely quoted.

RAPE

Rape carries a maximum penalty of imprisonment for life. Rape arises when a man has sexual intercourse with a woman without her consent.

The "consent" must be a real consent. The following cases cannot be covered under the postulate of consent:

(i) Consent induced by fraud - as, where man induces a married woman to have intercourse with him by impersonating her husband.

(ii) Sexual intercourse with a woman who is unconscious, for then she is incapable of giving or of withholding her consent.

(iii) Woman unable to give or withhold consent because of being under the influence of drink or/and drugs.

A man cannot be guilty of raping his wife, unless they are living apart under a separation order or perhaps even under a separation agreement.

In England a man cannot otherwise be deemed guilty of raping his wife. Sir Mathew Hale, one of the most eminent English personalities in the field of law, says that "by their mutual matrimonial consent and contract, the wife hath given herself in this kind unto her husband, which she cannot retract", *There is however a scope of a husband guilty of "assault" if he uses force to win intercourse with her wife against her will.*

It is also an offence to have sexual intercourse with a girl under the age of sixteen. If, however, the girl is between the age of 13 and 16, and consents to the intercourse, a man under the age of 24, may successfully plead, 'on one occasion only', that he had reasonable grounds for believing the girl to be over the age of sixteen.

Under the 1956 act (s 2) procuring a woman to have sexual intercourse by threats or intimidation is a separate offence from rape. This punishable by upto two years imprisonment.

In the same way, procuring by false pretences or representations is punishable with two years. Both offences may be committed in any part of the world. Threats or intimidations, may not only be to the person concerned, they may be directed to a third party in whom the victim has a interest.

There is a vast difference between fraud and false representation, however it is not easy to differentiate between the two. In the former, consent was never given but in the latter it was given on a misleading information.

To administer drugs to a woman in order to overpower her and have an intercourse is also an offence.

To have intercourse with a girl under 13 is unlawful, which is punishable with life imprisonment.

It is an offence to have unlawful intercourse with a mentally defective woman suffering from "sever mental impairment". It is also an offence to procure such a woman for such purposes.

A person who permits the use of premises for unlawful sexual intercourse with a girls under 13, under 16, or with a mentally defective woman, is a crime under law.

INCESTUAL RAPE

- Under the 1956 Act it is a crime for man to have intercourse with a woman he knows to be his daughter, mother, sister, or granddaughter, whether she consents or not. If consent was not forthcoming, he will be guilty of rape.

- It is also an offence for a woman over 16 yrs. to allow a man whom she knows to be her grandfather, father, brother or son to have sexual intercourse with her by consent. A brother may include a 'half-brother' and a sister a 'half-sister', but an adopted child is not capable of an incestuous relationship; however, illegitimacy is not a bar to a prosecution.

- The maximum punishment is seven years' imprisonment, but life if the female is under 13.

- Under the Criminal Law Act 1977, it is an offence punishable by upto two years for a man or boy to incite a girl to have sexual intercourse with him if that girl is under 16 yrs. and if he knows her to be his granddaughter, daughter or sister.

- A prosecution for incest may only be brought by the Director of Public Prosecutions or with his consent.

A CRITICAL SURVEY

The law on incestual rape raises several interesting points, which are of considerable importance to the book:

It is a very wise approach that the prosecution for incest can only be brought by the Director of Public prosecutions or with the consent of him.

Incestual rape is a very complex menace. And perhaps, therefore needs a direct handling from a very high government authority.

There is however, another solution to it. A separate department run by a staff especially trained for handling the incestual rape and incest problems should be opened. It should have a very fine network, spread like arteries and capillaries throughout the body. Because, while the above condition in the British law, enables incest to be handled by a high profile, competent authority, it somehow makes a large gap between the law and the public. Also a post like director of public prosecutions and its equivalent is a very responsible and eminent force in the law, but as incest needs a vast force of psychologists, sociologists and sexologists also, there remains a vacuum that need to be filled.

It is very questionable as to why the maximum punishment for incestual rape is only seven years (life imprisonment in only exceptional cases involving minors) whereas rape has life imprisonment attached to it.

Study of incest gives rise to the fact, that it is a much more severe crime than rape whether in spiritual, social or individual perspective, and some cases offer scope only for the punishment of execution as the perfect means of delivering justice.

This might be perhaps because Britain in its incest law has joined together the crime of incest by consent and incest by force, which are miles apart in their causes and implications.

Britain should have a separate law for the two. The same should be the approach of all nations regarding the crime of incest.

The question also arises as to why is incest with consent, even in the case of adults, a crime? It is because, as we have learnt, neither nature not ethics permit the same. From genetic disorder to social chaos, incest is metered by any parameter, only as a force of chaos and destruction.

E. SOCIO-COMMUNIST REGIMES

Till 1991, Russia was the most powerful communist regime of the world. The fact that Russia was the greatest country in terms of geography and power, made it the centre stage of the communist conglomerate.

However, communism was dismantled from Russia and the country today is a democracy.

Communism still survives in many countries of the world, and this political ideology with its stiff and stern principles, breeds atmosphere which is in a league of its own. Communism as the ruling political thought of a nation has a very deep impact on the heritage, culture and social ethos. It makes the country strikingly distinct and markedly different, so that the communist regimes merge into a group. It many a times seems that the communist countries and the rest of the world have a different existence and the earth is a dipolar civilization.

CHINA

THE INTRODUCTION FILE

Profile		
• Official name	:	Zhonghua Renmin Gongheguo (Peoples Republic of China)
• Capital	:	Beijing
• Continental Location	:	Eastern Asia
• Neighbouring Countries	:	Vietnam, Laos, Burma, Bhutan, Nepal, India, Pakistan, Afghanistan, USSR and Mongolia.

- Religion Status : Religion not encouraged by the communist regime. Important religions Confucianism, Taoism, Buddhism. Islam and Christianity are minority religions.
- Economic Status : Ultra developing economy.
- Total Population : 1990 Census - 1,133,682,501
  1995 estimate - 1,173,659,000
  Density - 115 people per Km^2
  Distribution :
  79% Rural : 21% Urban
- Official Language : Northern Chinese, called Mandarin or Putonghua.
- Political Status : Communist nation. Domination of three organisations : Chinese Communist Party, the Military and the State Council. The communist party controls the country.
- Feminine Status : Placing on both extremes.
- Area : 9,572,678 Km^2
  Greatest distances–
  North - South -4023 km
  East - West - 4828 km
- Currency : Basic unit - Yuan
  Exchange Rate .19 US$
- National Flag : Background in red, with a big yellow star in the leftmost upper corner, surrounded by four yellow stars in the shape of semi circle. The big star stands for the leadership of the communist party and small ones stand for the workers.
- National Emblem : Shows gate of heavenly peace surrounded or "framed" by grains of wheat and rice. In the centre of this circular frame is a cogwheel, representing industry.
- National Anthem : "March of the volunteers".

The History and Times of China

BC

- 10,000 : Development of New Stone Age cultures.
- 3,000 : Yangshao a new stone age culture, at the zenith of its development. Alongwith Longshan led to the development of the great Chinese civilization.
- 1,700's : The Shang dynasty is born from the Longshan cultures.
- 1,122 : Zhou people overthrow the Shangs.
- 500 : The great Chinese philosopher Confucians develops a system of ethics and values, giving rise to the faith of Confucism.
- 221 : Qins develop first central government of China.
- 221-206 (?) : Qin Emperor Shi Huangdi plans and orders the construction of the Great Wall of China.
- 202 : Qin dynasty collapses, Han gains control of the nation.

AD

- 8 : Han official Wang Mang seizes throne.
- 25 : Hans regain control.
- 220 : Han dynasty falls, China disjointed by distinct political cultures.
- 581 : Sui dynasty reunifies China.
- 618 : Tang dynasty gains power from the hands of the Sui.
- 907 : Fall of the Tang empire, leading to disjointment of China.
- 960 : Song dynasty reunifies China.
  Far reaching Song Dynasty Developments
  - System of civil examination established, power snatched from aristocracy and placed in the hands of talent.
  - Neo Confucism comes into being, combining Confucism with Buddism and Taoism.
- 1279-1368 : China under the rule of the Mongols.
- 1368 : Mongols overthrown, Ming dynasty gains power.

The International Perspective 257

- 1644 : Qing dynasty established by the Manchurians.
- 1842 : Treaty of Nanjing after British victory in the China-Britain opium war. Island of Hong Kong given to Britain and five ports opened to British trade and stay.
- 1851-1864 : The Taipang Rebellion against the Qings, millions killed.
- 1899 : United States catalyses the international acceptance of "Open Door Policy" giving all nations rights to trade with China.
- 1900 : The Boxer Rebellion against Westerners and Christianity.
- 1912 : Manchurian rule ends, as all provinces declare their independence and the six years old Manchu emperor Pu Yi leave the throne
-   : Establishment of the Republic.
- 1922 : Failure of the Republic.
- 1928 : Nationalists Unite China
- 1949 : Communists defeat nationalists, set up Republic of China
- 1962 : Indo-China War
- 1989 : Rebellion by people against communist dictatorship, overthrown by the military.

Looking Back
Looking Beyond

I have never been to China. Yet, whenever I think of the nation, my heart and my senses respond with such a deep sense of belonging, that it seems as if I have lived in the nation for centuries.

This is because whenever I think of China, I think of Chen Ling Ling, my classmate for years and my friend.

As I go down the memory lane and try to recall those days when a two and a half year old kid, submissive and shy, is moving with a schathel to kindergarten, it seems that I am trying to see a pretty house clouded in deep depths of fog and mist.

But, I still distinctly remember meeting Chen, a typical Chinese girl, with glowing white colour, red cheeks and 'stretched' features.

We used to fear Chen because of her robust strength and for years she was popular throughout the school as the best monitor of all classes. Yet, she was also a friend of ours and we used to share and multiply our fun and frolic with her.

We used to be crazy about her being a Chinese. In many a free periods, we used to compel her to write some English words in Chinese, and used to be fascinated seeing the Chinese alphabets. The greatest fun was when she used to tell us about what some words in our language meant in Chinese and all of us used to tell the same to our mothers on reaching home.

I have shared with Chen, hundreds of anecdotes of her Chinese life and she was good friend and also a good sister, till I left her after changing my school in tenth and doesn't know when I shall meet her.

It is Chen, that has made me reach the soul of Chinese culture and heritage and even while living in India, I have tasted the sweet Chinese breeze, watched the landscape from it's Great Wall.

When I think of Chen, I think of the pretty fact that she and my class got so immersed in each other, that even while belonging to two markedly different places, we subconsciously exchanged our culture, while in the conscious it never even once came that we were any different.

So, why can't we all live like one ? Why do we have to exist only as a part of a group, whether being an Indian and Chinese or a Hindu and Confucian ...? Instead of a global economy, why not a global culture, where these silly international borders are broken off and people live and enjoy with each other to realise that they are all one. We have made ourselves so different and we have been so deeply framed by Hinduism and Christianity and Chinese and English; that we don't have time to recall that we are humans — a single species stretching across the entire globe.

THE LAW FILE

Before coming to the Chinese criminal law on rape it is essential to explain the terms "fixed term imprisonment", "life imprisonment" and "execution", as they stand in the Chinese legal context because only the proper understanding of the same can lead to the proper understanding of the law of China.

THE CRIMINAL LAW OF CHINA

Sec. 4. Fixed Term imprisonment and life imprisonment.

Art. 40

The term of fixed term imprisonment is not less than six months and not more than 15 years.

Art 41

A criminal element sentenced to fixed term imprisonment or life Imprisonment is to have his sentenced executed in prison or in another place for reform through labour, Reform through labour is to be carried out on anyone with the ability of labour.

Art. 42

The term of fixed term imprisonment is counted as commencing on the date the judgement begins to be executed; where custody has been employed before the judgement begins to be executed, the term is to be shortened by one day for each day spent in custody.

Sec. 5 Death Penalty

Art. 43

The death penalty is only applied to criminals who commit most heinous crimes. In the case of a criminal element who should be sentenced to death, if immediate execution is not essential, a two year suspension of execution may be announced at the same time the sentence of death is imposed, and reform through labour carried out and the results observed.

Excluding judgements made by the Supreme People's Court according to law, all sentences of death shall be submitted to S.B.C. for approval.

Sentences of death with suspension of execution may be decided or approved by a high people's court.

Art. 44

The death penalty is not to be applied to persons who has not reached the age of 18 at the time of crime committed or to women who are pregnant at the time of adjudication. Persons who have reached the age of 16 but not 18 may by sentenced to death with a 2 years suspension if the crime committed is particularly grave.

Art. 45

The Death penalty is to be executed by means of shooting.

Art. 46

If a person sentenced to death with suspension of execution truly repents during period of suspension, he is to be given a reduction of sentence to life imprisonment upon the expiration of two years period if he truly repents and demonstrates meritorious service, he is to be given a reduction of sentence not less than 15 years and not more than 20 years of fixed term imprisonment upon the expiration of two years period, if there is verified evidence that he has resisted reform in an odious manner, the death penalty is to be executed upon, the order or approval of the supreme People's court.

Art. 47

The term for suspension of execution of sentence of death is counted as commencing on the date the judgement becomes final. The term of sentence that is reduced from the death penalty with suspension of execution to fixed term imprisonment is counted as commencing on the date of the order reducing the sentence.

RAPE : THE CHINESE JURISPRUDENCE

THE CRIMINAL LAW AND THE CRIMINAL PROCEDURE LAW OF CHINA

PART-II : Special Provisions.

Chapter-IV : Crimes of infringing upon the rights of the person and the democratic rights of citizens.

Art. 139

Whoever by violence, coercion or other means rapes a woman is to be sentenced to not less than three years and not more than 10 years of fixed term imprisonment.

Whoever has sexual relations with a girl under the age of fourteen is to be deemed to have committed rape and is to be given a heavier punishment.

Whoever commits a crime in the preceding two paragraphs, when the circumstances are especially serious or a persons injury or death is caused, is to be sentenced to not less than ten years of fixed term imprisonment, life imprisonment or death.

When two or more persons jointly commit rape in succession, they are to be given heavier punishment.

A CRITICAL SURVEY

One of the very important points that was discussed by me while critically evaluating the Greek Law on rape was that why does Greek Law not include execution in case rape leads to death.

It is heartening to note, that the Chinese law realises that rape and death or rape and murder is equal to a double murder, or at least of a much severe category than murder, and therefore needs execution. Death punishment has been included in cases where rape leads to death or is accompanied by murder of the victim.

The clause for reform and reduction in the execution punishment in Chinese jurisprudence, is a differentiating factor of Chinese law. China give a scope to the culprits to reform in the two years suspension period[1]. This brings in ethical, spiritual and moral factors in the Chinese law.

F. ROYAL REGIMES

History is a vast kaleidoscope of events, characters and happenings. If we glance at the medieval and ancient times, we will hear the galloping of horses, slaying golden chariots in which are seated Kings decorated in pearls and diamonds, followed by a thousands soldiers. The eyes of imagination can still see royal palaces, sparkling with magnificence, splendour and glory; framed in the natural beauty of the royal garden and filled with the aroma of roses and sunflowers.

All this now is almost a distant past that now exists in the land of oblivion. The present is the time of Presidents and Prime Ministers, Chancellors and Dictators, that pass through the modern city streets in cars, surrounded by a fleet of securitymen.

---

1. I am sure that my readers have observed that this opportunity is not given to all culprit, but depends on the crime graph and the culprit's profile.

However, there are a few countries where there are still Kings and Queens, and royal dynasties, though that royalty may have now worn the cloth of modernism.

BHUTAN

THE INTRODUCTION FILE

Profile

- Official Name : Bhutan
- Capital : Thimpu
- Continental Location : South-Central Asia.
- Neighbouring Countries : India and China
- Religion Status : Official religion–Buddhism; Hinduism also a major religion.
- Economic Status : Developing Economy
- Total Population : 1969 Census : 1,034,774
  1996 Estimate : 1,737.000
  Density : 33 persons per Km^2
  Distribution : 95% rural, 5% urban.
- Official language : A Tibetan dialect, Dzongkha.
- Political Status : Rule of a King, who is the most powerful person and who is appointed by inheritance
- Feminine Status : Placed in the measure of jurisprudence that rightly understands her. Mixed stride of achievement and exploitation. On the move
- Area : 46,500 Km^2
  Greatest distances.
  North-South–177 Km
  East-West–322 Km.
- Currency : Basic Unit : Ngultrum
  Exchange rate : Data not available
- National Flag : Diagonally cut into two halves of yellow (above) and orange (below).

	White dragon in the centre, with jewel in each claw.
• National Emblem :	Called "The Royal Crest". In the top, the symbol of "sacred jewel", In the centre, crossed Vajras or diamond sceptres. The male and female turquoise thundergragons embraced in unity, symbolizing the name of the Kingdom.
• National Anthem :	In the Thunder Dragon Kingdom/ Adorned with sandal wood/The Protector who guards the teachings of the dual system ....

The History and Times of Bhutan

AD

- 800's : Invaders from Tibet conquer the Bhutia Tephoo, the original inhabitants.
- 1500's : The descendants of the Tibetans control Bhutan from many places.
- 1600's : Tibetan Lama takes power of spiritual and social life into his hands, giving Bhutan a distinct entity.
- 1700-1800's : Bhutan raids Sikkim and other parts of India.
- 1907 : Ugyen Wangchuck becomes the first King of Bhutan.
- 1910 : British Govt. of India takes over the external affairs of Bhutan.
- 1949 : India agrees to assume responsibility for Bhutan's defence and external affairs.
- 1959 : China conquers parts of Bhutan.
- 1972 : Death of King Jigme Wangchuk, succession of his son to the throne.

Bhutan's Ballet of existence

A King, with supreme powers, controls Bhutan. He is appointed by inheritance. Bhutan has no legal political parties. The Prime Minister, the

Council and the national assembly are in their supreme capacity only advisory forces.

Bhutan has two major religions, Buddhism and Hinduism, practised by Tibetan descendants and Nepalese descendants respectively. The people are almost wholly rural with a slender, five percent urban existence.

Bhutan has a flourishing natural habitual of mountains, plains and river valleys, together producing severe extremes in climate.

A modernization process was begun in Bhutan, leading to the construction of varied specimens of modern age, ranging from a power station to a factory to a network of roads.

India is the best friend and most powerful ally of Bhutan and one of Bhutan's a major policies is to be closely associated with the Indian government and people.

Looking back
Looking beyond

Can a country exist in isolation? Surely it can. Its millions of people will interbreed thus leading to the survival of the human species. The heritage and culture produced by its millions will run like a pendulum between stability and change, stability produced by the issues of universal acceptance and change produced by the permutations and combinations of ethical, moral and spiritual clash over the times. The people in themselves would preserve and nurture their art and architecture, science and technology and the arteries and capillaries of the mammoth geographic body will thus survive, pumped by inputs of social, cultural and spiritual life.

But neither will such a country benefit from the inputs of external culture nor the outer world from the outpours of its heritage.

A country being a large mass of life and society, is capable of a self sufficient existence but without any contribution from the positive facets of the outer globe, might well find herself out of the league, in a negative fashion, by being left behind. That sadly, out of it's own choice.

Bhutan has a glorious history of art, culture and society. But sadly it remained for a long time in isolation, keeping away from the give and take policy of the entire world. Jubilantly enough, it has come out of its self imposed exile and both Bhutan and the world can now benefit from the barter system of culture.

India regards Bhutan as one of its best friends and younger brother. We are proud to tall Bhutan, that in every time of her danger, Indians will leave no stone unturned to protect and preserve her ethos, her entity and her existence.

THE LAW FILE

Before reading about Bhutan's law on rape, it is necessary to know certain terms exclusive to Bhutanese jurisprudence

- GAO-GAO means Divorce settlement.

  In the law of Bhutan on rape, you will read the line "Pay the amount of "GAO" according to the various sections of the marriage act".

  This means that the amount in money or equivalent has to be paid, equivalent to the money paid in divorce settlement, the exact amount to be decided by the court, according to various sections of the marriage act.

- Thrimthue - is compensation in lieu of punishment. So, in the Bhutanese law, thrimthue is compensation, however, it is not in lieu of punishment, but along with the punishment. The actual amount of compensation is decided by the court.

AMENDMENTS FOR THE OFFENCE OF RAPE UNDER THE MARRIAGE ACT

Whereas, it is expedient to amend the certain sections of the Marriage Act 1980 dealing with the offence of rape, it is hereby enacted by the National Assembly of the Kingdom of Bhutan as follows:

BA 2. RAPE ACT

Ba 2.1 Definition

BA 2.1.1 A person shall be guilty of the offence of rape when he/she has sexual intercourse with a person under any of the following circumstances :
- Without his/her consent;
- Use of any force; or
- With his/her consent when the consent is obtained by putting him/her in fear of death or of harm.

Penetration is sufficient to constitute sexual intercourse of the offence.

2.1.2 The age of a person shall be calculated on the basis of actual date of birth.

BA 2.2 Rape

BA 2.2.1 Whoever commits the offence of rape shall :

Pay compensation equivalent to fifty percent of "thrimthue" for one year to the victim of rape; and be imprisoned from one to five years.

BA 2.3 Gang Rape

BA 2.3.1 If a person has given consent to have sexual intercourse with another person and if the latter person and one or more persons have sexual intercourse against the will of the former person, all the persons committing the sexual intercourse shall be deemed to be guilty of rape, and each of them shall:

Pay compensation equivalent to fifty percent of "thrimthue" for one year; and be imprisoned from three to seven years.

BA 2.4 Raping a married person

BA 2.4.1 Whoever rapes a married person shall :

Pay the amount of "GAO" according to various sections of the Marriage Act; Pay compensation equivalent to fifty percent of "thrimthue" for one year to the victim of rape; and be imprisoned from one to five years.

BA 2.4.2   It shall constitute a sexual offence not amounting to rape if a spouse commits sexual intercourse with his/her spouse without consent, if they are living separately while a divorce suit filed against him/her is pending in a Judicial Court. Such an offender shall pay:

> Compensation equivalent to fifty per cent of "thrimthue" for one year; and "thrimthue" for one year as fine.

BA 2.5 Gang Rape of a Married person

BA 2.5.1.   If a married person has given consent to have intercourse with a person and that person is responsible for rape one that person by one or more than one person, then the person who is so responsible and all other persons who commit rape shall each :

> Pay the amount of 'Gao' according to the various Sections of the Marriage Act;
>
> Pay compensation equivalent to fifty percent of "thrimthue" for one year; and be imprisoned from three to seven years.

BA 2.6 Raping Minor

BA 2.6.1   If a girl/boy who is above 12 years and below 16 years is raped, the offender shall :

> Pay compensation equivalent to fifty percent of "thrimthue" for one year; and be Imprisoned from five to ten years.

BA 2.6.2   If a girl/boy below the age of 12 years is raped, the offender shall :

> Pay compensation equivalent to fifty percent of the "thrimthue" for one year; and be Imprisoned from ten to thirteen years.

BA 2.7 Gang rape of a minor

BA 2.7.1 If a girl/boy who is above 12 years and below 16 years is raped by more than one person, then each of the offenders shall :

Pay compensation equivalent to fifty percent of "thrimthue" for one year; and be Imprisoned from then to fifteen years.

BA 2.7.2 If a girl/boy below the age of 12 years is raped by more than one person, then each of the offenders shall:

Pay compensation equivalent to fifty percent of "thrimthue" or one year; and be Imprisoned from fifteen to seventeen years.

BA 2.8. Injury

BA 2.8.1. In addition to other punishments prescribed under this Act, if the victim of the rape is injured as a consequence of rape, then the offender/offenders shall together pay :

All expenses for the period during which the victim receives medical treatment or is hospitalized.

BA 2.9 Rape and Murder

BA 2.9.1 If a person is raped and murdered, the offender shall :

Pay the amount of "GAO" according to various sections of the Marriage Act if that person was married; Pay compensation equivalent to fifty percent of the "thrimthue" for one year to the surviving spouse or next of kin;

Pay an amount equivalent to fifty percent of the "thrimthue" for five years to the surviving spouse or next of kin for the last rites of the deceased; and be imprisoned for life.

BA 2.10. Gang Rape and murder

BA 2.10.1 If a person is raped and murdered by more than one person, then each of the offenders shall:

Pay the amount of "GAO" according to various sections of the Marriage Act if that person was married;

Pay compensation of an amount equivalent to fifty percent of "thrimthue" for one year to the surviving spouse or next to kin;

Pay an amount equivalent to fifty percent of the "thrimthue" for five years to the surviving spouse or next of kin for the last rites of the deceased; Be imprisoned from seventeen years to life; and The leader of that group shall be imprisoned for life.

BA 2.11 Reporting

BA 2.11.1   In case an offence of rape is committed, a report of the commission of the offence shall have to be submitted either to the nearest Court of Law or Police/hospital/ Chimi/Gup/Mang Ap as soon as possible after the commission of the crime.

In case of the latter, the Police/Hospital/Chimi/Cup/ Mang Ap shall submit the report to the court of law without delay.

BA 2.12 Requirement of Proof.

BA 2.12.1   In a rape trial, no one shall be convicted of rape unless proven guilty.

BA 2.13 False Accusation

BA 2.13.1   No one shall be subjected to false attack on a person's character and reputation. Therefore, whoever is responsible for false accusation of the rape shall :

Pay compensation of an amount equivalent to fifty percent of "thrimthue" for one year; and be Imprisoned from three months to three years.

A CRITICAL SURVEY

Bhutan's law is extremely well developed and many points outshine and outsmart the other legal structures. It gives indications of being developed from deep research and accuracy; wisdom and foresight, and its positive facets shall be of use to the comparative rape study, in being capable of a positive contribution to rape criminology around the globe.

This survey, deals with a remark on Bhutan's uniqueness and suggestions from the distinct pattern.

- Bhutan's law is a dual law that deals with rape of women and rape of men. Thus, the customary line "if a woman is raped ..." is replaced in the Bhutanese rape criminology as 'if he/she has sexual intercourse against his/her will ...' etc.

- Bhutan has unique punishment structure in which alongwith imprisonment a victim is also required to pay a fixed amount. This is a good clause, as though the same amount can undoubtedly not bring back the Victim's respect but can be of use to her for her treatment and related needs.

This clause might be taken up for observation, while amending the legal structure on rape.

- It is a very praiseworthy and accurate approach that if injury is done to a victim, than the "offenders" shall be required to pay all medical expenses and dies expenses during hospitalization; all this being in addition to imprisonment.

This is a good clause, where raped victim, suffering from pangs of pulsating privacy, is saved from the burden of expenses and finance.

It is a good observation point in our comparative study.

- Bhutan understands the gravity of rape and murder, and even though it doesn't allow execution to enter in this particular case, necessities the next-in-line punishment, life imprisonment. It further raises many important points that I must highlight, to capture the attention of law throughout the world :

(a) Culprit pays for the last rites of the deceased. This is a right approach as he was accountable for his death.

(b) He supports the "surviving spouse or next of kin", leading to financial assistance in case of family breakdown, resulting from the victim's death.

(a) and (b) are two invaluable clauses, as pointed by the reasons that follow:

I. The rule of "eye for an eye and tooth for tooth" goes as a perfect ethical approach in some special cases. In this case of victim murder and also in the former, of victim injury, as the culprit wholly contributes to the injury and death, he/she should be accountable for the expenses arising out of the same. This is an accurate reciprocation and counter reaction of the law.

II. Expense approach is a good one, as culprits might fear in raping a man/woman which will lead them to financial trouble.

- Section BA 2.13 dealing with false accusation is the right approach. If rape results in a vast trauma for the victim, false accusation leads to great insult and infamy for the innocent. To be a false accused in a rape case is equal to being a victim of rape, as regards damage of respect, shattering of personal status and chaos in the mental build up.

G. AFRICAN REGIMES

Africa is a mammoth land mass of geographical diversity, biological wonder, cultural zenith, artistic splendour and human's super human wonder. It is rich in variety, depth and rarity.

Africa is the first of the very firsts. Historians conjecture that around 2,000,000 BC, the earliest human being lived and existed in the African land mass.

Geography has spread its sheets of spectacle on the African land. The Sahara desert, stretches longer than the United States, spreading its austere beauty throughout and its sand and cactus hold a rare fascination. The Nile flows to the longest length, cutting across valleys and forests.

Equatorial rain forests house a wealth of flora and fauna and contain species that have an exclusive existence in these hot and wet floral masses.

African geography has lead to birth civilizations that represent the Zenith and have achieved wonders that are unbelievable and can be placed only in a Homeric epic or a Grimm's tale.

Egypt became the eternal combination of the rare, the distinct and the outstanding. Ancient Egyptian civilization's spiritualism and religion has a unique place in human faith and mythology and its Gods and Goddesses; the great Amon-Re, Re Osiris, Isis, Horus and Ptah are immortal; not just because they are believed to be, but because they are placed so in history and spread in golden colour in the historical corridors. The Pyramids represent the biggest architectural festival on a human death and are the most majestic imprint of a human genius and the best graves for a homosapien. Africa has housed many more civilizations and the Kush civilization is just one more example of the numerous worth remarking symbols of human life and society.

The animal life in Africa leaves one wonderstruck. There is a mesmerizing variety ... Barbary Ape, Porcupine, Dorcas Gazelle, Fennec Aoudad, Jerboa, Dama Gazelle, Dromedary, Vulture, Eland, Lion, Spotted Hyena, Hippopotamus, Dina Monkey, Elephant, Baboon, Ibis, Crocodile, Zebra, Leopard, Okapi, Guereza Monkey, Gorilla, Cheetah, Giraffe, Flamingo, Serval, Impola, Ostrich, Rock Python, Cape Buffalo, Cape Seal, Jackass Penguin Mamba ...!!!

No less is the plant life. Atlas Cedar, Cork Oak, Olive, Date Palm, Papyrus, Elephant Grass, African Mahoony, Bubinga, Kola, Aligna, Red Ironwood, Africa Tulip, Silver Tree, Stapelia, Myrrh, Coffee, Papyrus, Mangroves, Kafir are the pearls of vegetation that decorate the continent.

Such a wide variety and such a wide depth gives rise to a myth. Whether Africa really exists ... ! Even then this spectacle, this wonder creation of the Almightly Father, has borne the burnt of the meanest treatment by the fellow humans.

The Europeans, for centuries, exploited Africa; robbed it's natural wealth and chopped its people. Africans, with the same infinitely powerful wisdom, due to dark colour produced by the scorching heats, were discriminated by the fair Europeans and in their own land, which they had habitated and loved as their mother, were treated as animals, used as slaves, and rewarded by being chained, chopped and fed on flith.

The "Dark Continent" called so because of its dark jungles and lack of information to the outer world, became the centre stage of the darkest human decline and the personifications of all the evils inherent in the human gene. Imperialism tied its nuptial knot here and bred innumerable serpents of racial discrimination; so that even now, when racialism has at last bade good bye, the scars have for ever, found a place and home in Africa.

The distinct African culture, its deep diversity and its inhumane treatment makes it a group in its own. An African with his jet black colour, out of league features, short hair, stout and solid growth, all accompanied by the halo of imperial past that shines behind him like fires of hell; makes him stand apart.

ETHIOPIA

THE INTRODUCTION FILE

Profile	
• Official Name	: "Hebretesebawit Ityopia" or People's Democratic Republic of Ethiopia.
• Capital	: Addis Ababa.
• Continental Location	: Northeastern Africa.
• Neighbouring Countries	: Somalia, Kenya, Sudan and Djibouti.
• Religion Status	: Majority of people follow Ethiopian Orthodox Church (Christianity) and Islam, with equal following. Traditional African religions and Judaism also practised.
• Economic Status	: Developing Economy.
• Total Population	: 1984 Census : 42,169,203 1997 Estimate : 56,348,000 Density : 40 persons per Km^2 Distribution : 87% rural, 13% urban.

- Official language : Amharic[1]
- Political Status : EPRDF, known as Ethiopian People's Revolutionary Democratic Front overthrew the military regime in 1991, leading to the birth of democracy and political freedom.
- Feminine Status : In a direction of its own. Characteristically unique and markedly different feminine laws and legal parameters.
- Area : 1,221,900 Km^2
  Greatest distances :
  North-South - 1,642 Km
  East West - 1,666 Km
- Currency : Basic Unit - Birr.
  Exchange rate - .48 US$
- National Flag : Three stripes of green (top), Yellow (centre) and red (bottom), of equal area and spread horizontally.
- National Emblem : The Emblem has been dismissed[2].
- National Anthem : "Whedefit Gesgeshi Woude Henate Ethiopia", meaning, "March Forward, Dear Mother Ethiopia, Bloom and Flourish".

The History and Times of Ethiopia

BC
- 2 Million years ago : Oldest human beings roamed in Ethiopia, as indicated by fossils.

  1. Amharic, one of the oldest surviving languages, is a member of the Afro-Asian family of languages. Afro-Asian family is spoken by 220 million tongues, or 4% of the global populace.

     Amharic is a "Semitic language". It is part of the Southern Semitic groups. Other Semitic languages are Akkadian, Hebrew, Aramaic, Elabite and Arabic.

  2. As told by Mr. Arvind, Secretary, Embassy of Ethiopia.

The International Perspective 275

- 400's : Inhabitations of Crishites - farmers and nomadic shepherds and Semites-traders.

AD
- 200's : Establishment of a developed State called Akusum, in the Ethiopian City of the same name.
- 300's : King Azana of Akusum Kingdom takes the civilization to great heights. Christianity inculcated as the chief and official religion.
- 600's : Influence of Arabs and Islam; Kusumian power declines.
- 1137 : Rise of the Zagwe' dynasty.
- 1270 : Zagwe' empire overthrown by Yekuno Amlak.
- 1500's : Disintegration of the Ethiopian Empire.
- 1889 : Reunification of the Ethiopian empire by Emperor Menelik-II
- 1896 : The Great battle of Adwa, with Italy. Italians defeated
- 1913 : Grandson of Menelik, Lij Iyasu becomes emperor.
- 1916 : Lij Iyasu overthrown with the help of UK, France and Italy.
- : Menelik's daughter, Zauditu becomes empress.
- 1930 : Death of Zauditu.
- : Tafari becomes emperor and takes the title of Haile Selassie-I.
- 1931 : Haile Selassie-I forms the first Constitution of the nation.
- 1935 : Italy invades Ethiopia.
- 1936 : Italians conquer Adis Ababa
- 1941 : Italians overthrown and outdriven.
- 1970's : Ethiopian-Somalian war over territorial dispute on Ogden region.
- 1972-1973 : Severe famine.
- 1974 : Military regime takes over; Haile Selassie rule ends.
- 1991 : EPRDF overthrows the military rule.

Looking back
Looking beyond

1991 became a vital turning point in Ethiopian history. The Ethiopian People's Revolutionary Democratic Front, known as EPRDF, overthrew the military regime. Seventeen ghastly years of military dictatorship, inhumane dictates, civilian butchering, rights' censoring, marshall laws and barbaric political thought came to an end. Arvind, the Ethiopian Secretary in the embassy, said that Ethiopia had undergone historic changes.

Let me ask a question: What is a historic political change? I am not asking this question in the Ethiopian context or the Indian context, I am asking this question in the global political context.

Historic political changes are not just toppling of political structures, political regimes and political monuments. A historic political change is not just a change from Czarish rule to socialist regime, or from British Imperial India to a democratic independent Bharat. Each historic political change involves a change of ethics and principles–class difference are broken or made, religious discrimination is done or undone to lead to a secular atmosphere, rights are imparted or taken away. A historic political change is a change that changes the methodology to extend the heritage and culture.

It is this aspect of a historic political change that is important. A change from military regime to democracy will become meaningless if democracy corrupts to merge with evils done by the military dictators. Democracy will become a sin if it would mean freedom of rights and negligence of duties, leading to a rights clash and social chaos.

A historic political change must involve penning down of real values, and sketching of golden horizons, not just on the constitution's papers and canvases of speech, but on the soul, body and mind of every countrymen so that the country indeed reaches a golden age.

Historical changes otherwise are meaningless. We say we live in modern times, and have developed the best political thought. Then why is the Golden Age of Guptas not seen in India today ? Why does Greece not relive its golden age of ancient times ?

Ethiopia, its good to see that you have shaken off your military rule. Your activated spirit and strength ignites our freezed prowess. But, your national anthem–"March Forward, Dear Mother Ethiopia, Bloom and Flourish", must become real in its pure form, otherwise your democracy would become more stale than the dark years of military dictatorship and Hitlerian dictates.

THE LAW FILE

Ethiopia has no law on rape.

A CRITICAL SURVEY

The Ethiopian law is the sharpest contrast to our comparative study. It is almost unbelievable to think that rape, that has been an universal postulate of civilization and which is done once in each second of the clock, in some countries, can be excluded from the law of a nation.

We had begun to think that rape as a crime can never be excluded from law books, it being a regular news contributor and virginity shaker. But Ethiopian jurisprudence compels us to give a second thought and observe and analyse, whether it is possible to shrink rape in the modern society to an infinitesimal existence.

Taking a general case, the following conditions act as inhabitors to the same:

- Social prowess in the form of ostracization of culprit, and accurate response to the victim. In addition to it, social strength as regards inhibition of open attack on virginity in the form of eve teasing and molestation.
- Marital acceptance of the victim, leading to breaking of the fear of Spinsterhood for a raped female, leading to a open society, freely talking and complaining of rape.
- Female equality to a high extent, leading to the dismissal of the inferior sex tag on the female being.

Ethiopian law proves that expulsion of rape law from a nation's jurisprudence is not a day dream of a person who is passionately optimistic or who has tied a nuptial knot with mirage and illusion. It is very much real to dream that rape laws might not be needed in a 'rapeless' atmosphere. All that is needed is the right mixture of sociological and psychological response and its harmonious merge with the ethos of the human civilization.

THE INTERNATIONAL SYNTHESIS

The comparative study on rape criminology brings to the fore many sharp contrasts; and these antimonious pairs, if studied together, will rejuvenate the rusted understanding of the crime.

As reflected by the introduction files and pin-pointed in the critical surveys, the rape jurisprudence in the international perspective twists and turns in all directions, and the main contrasts are caused by extraordinary characteristics of some countries' laws, caused to effect by the socio-political-cultural ideology of the nation in question.

While Ethiopia has no law on rape, Pakistan's law is lawlessness in disguise and the most barbaric form of feminine butchering. Many laws are completely flexible in their rape structure but Islamic law on forced sex is a unpunishment structure. Islam goes against all forms of jurisprudence on rape; and the customary explanation of rape being "forced sexual intercourse without consent" is extended in the Islamic penal code, making every illicit relationship a rape case. Most countries do not recognise that mean are raped but Bhutan gives it a full recognition. Bhutanese law also differentiates itself from most of the other criminal codes, by including "thirmthue" and medical expenses in its punishment structure. Homosexuality is permitted beyond a statutory limit in some countries, whereas India and the like, define it as illicit, offering the stringent punishment. Victim's treatment is at present beyond the reach of the wisdom and foresight of most laws, with only a few countries like the United States, directly referring to a need on victim counselling. Incest is not recognised separately by most, but some countries penalise, through a special clause, incest by consent and force.

Rape is subdivided in countries like America to define as statutory rape, sexual intercourse with consent, involving a minor.

The comparative synthesis merges into a synonymity with almost all countries deeming as sufficient, penis penetration into vagina, for a rape accusation and citing the debate on degree of penetration or sperm emission and its proof, as unnecessary.

This is a short sketch of contrasts and similarities, pointed out by 9 selected nations. Important issues are extensively discussed in the coming section.

Ardent seekers on this issue, must have realised the invaluability of this study by now, and in addition to extracting benefit from my inferences, shall also deduct and develop many new issues from the analytical power, imparted by their grey cell charge.

Section - IV
DEVELOPMENT OF THE COMPARATIVE LAW THOUGHT

OUTLINE

After studying laws of different countries, we come across many issues that are common to all nations. A deep research of laws on a particular issue, gives us an indication of perspectives that need a discussion, as the discussion can be to the benefit of all nations around the globe.

Our international study include India and several other nations that have a sharp contrast to each other. As a result, some issues have piled up, which need a pride treatment from my pen, and I have faith and hope that I shall be doing fair justice by the same.

However, only one issues is exclusively about parental rape, others are about markedly different rape perspectives. But a sharp reader shall realise that all the issues indirectly and in ways more than one, like this complete part; are invaluable to our central argument. Their need and value is as high as that of well written appendices to a book.

MARITAL RAPE

In "The Sexological View", I fully developed my argument on marital rape and explained to the reader what it means. I have also explained the viable importance of this discussion to our central thought.

Marital rape is a well conceived thought. It does not lack substance, rather it is one of the most occurring phenomenon in forced sexual intercourse, which has been wrapped beneath layers and layers of taken-for-granted right sexual relationship.

Argument on marital rape leads us to a conclusion that it should be included in the law, with the punishment at least equal to that of an ordinary rape.

However, if a country recognises the question of marital rape, it is only when a husband rapes his wife, when they are living under a decree of separation.

Please reconsider the concerned sections from the Indian Penal Code and British Jurisprudence :

> "Whoever had sexual intercourse with his own wife, who is living separately from him under a decree of separation or any custom or usage without her consent shall be punished with imprisonment of either description for a term which may extend to two years and shall also be liable to fine".

(India) (Section 376 A of IPC)

> "A man cannot be guilty of raping his wife, unless they are living apart order a separation under or perhaps even under a separation agreement".

(United Kingdom)

Now, first of all let us discuss the most important question. We agree that this is insufficient. But is even this a clause of marital rape?

Decree of separation means, that a couple has to live as 'strangers' (Mark this word) for a time, stipulated by the law. Thus here a stranger rapes a stranger. Therefore, the punishment. It clearly indicates that if they had been living together, the law was not concerned even if the husband had forced sexual intercourse.

But the question - Why?

Sir Mathew Hale, as I have already quoted, says that it is because of the "mutual matrimonial consent" of which the wife is an equal part.

Agreed. However, cannot one be deceived in giving matrimonial consent? If one can be deceived by one's partner in business, why not in marriage? Sex is a much more sensitive issue than even money, industry, power or land. If such reasons are viable then the law might tell a petitioner that he cannot report against his business partner of using his consent by force as he was in equal part to the mutual agreement.

The Indian Penal Code's punishment of 2 years is highly unsatisfactory. It is a crime equal to rape. And, at least, in this case the couple is living under a separation decree, the wife clearly retaking her mutual consent. Then, why a lenient punishment for a forced intercourse?

The reason is clear. The law gives a lighter punishment because the woman in this case is still the wife. This shows that women have to pay a high penalty of marrying a wrong man.

We must involve a separate clause for marital rape. But, while developing the same, it will have to be kept in kind that the identification process shall have to be very sharply developed, not enabling cunning wives to trap their innocent husbands by duping the law.

SUGGESTIONS TO INDIA

- Section 376 (A) is highly unsatisfactory and poorly developed. Needs re-consideration.
- Supreme Court must reconsider the whole issue and using its eminence, set up an independent penal to look into the whole perspective. The various postulates that might be considered are :

(i) Can marital rape be included, keeping in mind both the dangers inherent and the traumas of the wives.

(ii) If not a separate clause, can the judge be given a special provision for the same, if marital rape is clear in a case brought to him?

EXECUTION

Execution is one of the most heated debates in the whole world. The discussion has been pin-pointed from all directions and it has been branded as "the most needed" and "the most barbaric" practises of all times.

So, where should the pendulum of our standpoint rest? I need not discuss this here again; as pages of the book have made it more than clear that execution can never be the only punishment for rape but its scope surely is there. Infact, its inclusion is imminent if the jurisprudence of any nation wants to construct a full circle of justice with the compass of its criminal code.

SUGGESTIONS TO INDIA

- A high level committee of judges and lawyers; psychologists and sociologists must study the reasons for the inclusion of execution in the rape law of many religions and nations. Culprits executed for rape and their victims must be analysed. This can help a lot in sealing execution in right light.

- Severe rape cases must be thought of with execution in mind. The question "What can happen by it" is certainly a mind opener.

INCESTUAL CRIMES

Incest has been dealt very differently around the world. Many countries do not have any separate clause for incest and cases of such crime are rather fitted in their Penal Codes, and punishments given. It certainly cannot be hoped that full justice by such hit and trial method can be imparted. This is an example of a blunt judicial process, undesired by both sides of the judgements table.

Incest crimes, like parental rapes, are very savage realities. Deep studies, like this book, have indicated that it requires a completely different handling and not only should a separate law be made but also the code should be developed after extensive research, done by a diverse panel of people that can scan the crime from all angles possible, thus bringing it to a right synthesis, developing the perfect graph from the perfect data. Infact, the whole menace of rape requires the same treatment.

Some countries do have separate sections for incest related crimes, but they give rise to quite funny situations. To be frank, in many instances of such incest jurisprudence, one can find no reason behind their making and it indicates a very rash understanding of the whole crime.

Take for instance, Great Britain. It is highly appreciable that it has a separate Clause for the crime. But for what reason is the punishment for most of the incest crime much lower than even an ordinary rape ....?!! There certainly seems to be no logic behind it all.

I am not challenging the British law. Though at the same time as nothing is perfect, nothing has the right to wish to stand unchallenged. I am rather hinting that throughout the world the understanding of law towards incest crime lacks positive substance. Each nation must awaken up to this ugly menace and develop a proper code which is a product of a lot of wisdom, giving it the right to be accepted by one and all.

SUGGESTING TO INDIA

- Develop a separate incest crime package.
- Set up an independent research panel, working jointly or separately under a very high authority.
- Mobilise public opinion.
- Decentralize the rape punishment clause much more than at the moment. Diversify it as much as possible as different rapes have completely different parameters attached to them.

MAN-RAPES

It happened once that in a foreign country a man entered the Police Station complaining that he had been raped. The complete legal structure was taken aback. What could they do with the victim? There was no clause in their law books for men being raped....!

Some years back this true incident might well would have become a capital joke. But today, it is an instance of a great legal complexity.

Even though rape is largely a woman crime and may be so shall remain, but cases have started to be reported to the police by men, that they are raped. And the law can do nothing but put up a blank face as a reaction and a blank smile as a sympathy.

What happens is anybody's guess. The case is somehow fitted in the law books, and using the hit and trial method, justice imparted. Or the culprit persuaded by being pleaded, to withdraw the case.

Both instances pinpoint at a inefficient handling of a crime by judiciary. In the first case it is an incompetent system trying to solve a riddle, by joining the pieces so that they somehow all fit together, no matter what shape they produce. In the second case, is a handicapped system, pleading the victim to withdraw his case because of their incapability.

Tragic indeed. Is this a judicial system that is expected to give justice? In this case, it can't even justify its own capability.

Now, man-rape is a well recognised crime. Therefore a postulate can surely be developed for the same. Besides, there is no harm. Like all crimes, it can be put in use whenever needed and put to sleep whenever desired.

Besides, law should not be made on grounds that a particular crime occurs in a vast measure. Law must deal with every crime, even it happens once in a millenium.

Let me add, that a raped male's trauma is as much as that of a female. May be more, for it breaks his ego that his sexual privacy and freedom has been guaranteed.[1]

SUGGESTIONS TO INDIA

- Include a separate clause. For the moment stretch the rape law regarding women rapes to include the same for man rapes.
- In the event of such a case being brought out, judge might take suggestions form a jury comprising of people from psychiatry and law.

HOMOSEXUALITY : THE PRO AND THE CONTRA LAW

For a long while, homosexuality was considered a sin and was termed illegal. Strict laws were made against it.

But in the recent times, a mega discussion has opened up regarding homosexuals.

---

1. A man in Noida, some two-three years back committed suicide, after being raped by three women.

The discussion in divided into two groups, exactly opposite to each other. Their principles, ethics and arguments constantly clash with each other and the world seems to be divided into two hemispheres allowing inclusion of either of the two schools of thought regarding homosexuals.

THE PRO GROUP

- Homosexuality is a person's private affair. Law should not interfere.
- Abnormal sex definition is controversial. Sex is just a pattern of procreation, whether with the opposite sex or the same sex.
- Homosexuality is a minority but can be called a practice. It has a right to be included in the normal traffic.
- Homosexuality is a universal phenomenon, in the sense that it has always been there, since the very beginning. Thus calling it abnormal stands challenged.
- Accepted homosexuality is a two side accepted behaviour. It harms no one.

THE CONTRA VIEW

- Homosexuality is not a private affair. It undercuts society by breaking the codes of control, ethics and morals.
- Sex is procreation but with the opposite sex. The very base for making a male and a female is to make them merge to form a unisex–the code of life. All other forms are abnormal.
- Even if homosexuality is a practice, it is a great threat to society and civilization and must be curbed.
- It is a universal antithesis to rape; a product of sexual fantasy.
- It is wrong to say that it harms no one. Homosexuality is a risk factor in AIDS. Moreover, it is definitely an unethical dirt made of the bacteria of yearnings.

India equates homosexuality with a crime. However countries like U.K. permit adults to practise homosexuality in private with certain restrictions.

Homosexuality has an indirect connection with parental rape. If we grant homosexuality the tag of normal practise, then incest by consent can also be normal. This treatens the complete argument on parental rape.

I strongly take the contra view on homosexuality and I feel that homosexuals should not be allowed in the normal social traffic as it is bound to create a severe jam and dismantle the entire social structure.

In India, there is a recent flow of argument on homosexuality, which till now enjoyed a more or less universal view of being unethical. Some months back, there was great uproar on the question of distributing condoms to the Tihar inmates, more than eighty percent of whom are homosexuals, to prevent the AIDS risk. Gay Activists have put up this issue with the country's law, with a wish to include it in the normal perspective. The Government recently allowed the first ever gay conference to take place.

SUGGESTIONS TO INDIA

- India's law is quite good as regards homosexuality. Changing it is bound to cause a lot of socio-cultural danger and is totally opposite to the Indian ethos and heritage.

- The building blocks of our heritage have never allowed homosexuality. The sudden spurt of the so called open minded wave on gay activities; appears to be a western influence and it is not necessary to change our culture for the sake of globalisation.

SECTION V
THE INTERNATIONAL CASE BOOK OF RAPE

EXECUTION AND RAPE

Country : The United States of America.

Court of Appeal : The Supreme Court.

Year : 1977

Case Name   : Coker V/S Georgia.

Source   : Reproduced with slight amendments from "Significant Decisions of the Supreme Court: 1976-1977 term" by Bruce E. Fein Attorney with the U.S. Department of Justice. By American Enterprise Institute for Public Policy Research, Washington D.C.

THE CASE

Coker was serving three life sentences in a Georgia prison. These were two twenty years terms, and one eight year term for the crime of murder, rape, kidnapping and assault. After running from prison and being re-apprehended, he was found guilt of rape of an adult woman, a capital crime under Georgia law. A jury found that two circumstances justified the capital punishment on Coker for his rape conviction on the adult woman. First, "the rape occurred during the commission of another rape felony". Second, "Coker had a prior conviction for a capital felony". On appeal, the Georgia Supreme Court affirmed the death sentence over the claim that "it constituted cruel and unusual punishment proscribed by the Eighth Amendment".

THE EIGHTH AMENDMENT
(Plurality opinion by Justice White.

Vote 7-2, Powell, Brennan and Mars-hall: concurring; Burger and Rehnguit : Dissenting).

The Eighth Amendment has prohibited those criminal sentences that are "grossly disproportionate" to the severity factor in the crime committed by the culprit. Thus "public attitudes concerning a particular sentence–history and precedent, legislative attitudes, and the response of juries reflected in their sentencing decisions are to be consulted".

USA today, no longer accepts for raping an adult woman, the punishment of death. At present, only Georgia authorizes it in contrast to 18 States in 1925. In addition, sentencing juries in Georgia have declined to impose in ninety percent cases, capital punishments for rape.

Some critics hold and some judgements point out that the prevalent atmosphere is that, capital punishment is "grossly disproportionate". The writer of this case source says:

> "Although the crime of rape is "highly reprehensible", unlike murder it does not cause death. Rape, with or without aggravating circumstances, cannot be punished by death as long as the rapist spares the life of the victim."

THE COMMENTS CONGLOMERATE

I am not concerned with the conflicts going on in the US Jurisprudence. I have included this case in the international case book because it asks a very significant question, on the answer of whom, rests our entire execution debate:

> Can death sentence be given to the culprit if the life of the victim is spared?

The view of a substantial part of the US lawyers' lobby is that because rape does not cause death, as in murder, it cannot be punished by a death sentence. It is based on the age old rule-"Eye for an eye and tooth for a tooth", which has always been eyed by the bull of controversy.

This argument on the execution debate, not only represents a very shallow understanding on the part of the law analysts, it is also a very rude indifference to the rape victim and a complete reversal of the truth.

Let me answer this question by beginning from where the contra view group to execution debate has begun. The life of the victim, according to them is spared. So, let us try to define life. What is life?

Is life only an intake and outpour of breath? Is life only a mere consciousness? Is life only a three word recurring phenomenon of eat, sleep and drink?

It is very wrong to believe that this is life. This is existence. A mere wave of consciousness trailing on the rails of time.

Life is a synonym of aim and meaning; values and ethics. One lives life with certain fundamental rights, out of which sexual privacy is the most

The International Perspective 289

delicate and the most cared for among all. One lives for certain meanings. One lives life when he is psychologically, mentally, emotionally and physically his oneself. When all these powers are in perfect health and co-ordinate to a form a harmonious living system.

What happens when one is raped? We have seen it all in "The Victim's Defence". But, let me shortly, cluster the whole sequence of facts.

Physically, the victim may have abdominal pains, sexual diseases and AIDS; imparted by the culprit.

Mentally and emotionally she may have paranoia, depression, madness, fits, sense of foreshortened future.

Psychologically she may have hatred of sex, sexual perversion and conversion to that unholy order of prostitutes.

What is created when such emotional, psychological, mental and physical waves unite? Is this what one calls life....? To me it is rather a confusion in consciouness.... If a victim:

- In pro rape situation was a moral human being but rape makes her embrace prostitutism;

- In pro rape situation reacted normally to sex, now hates it;

- In pro rape situation was normal as regards her sexual attitude but now is a sexual pervert;

isn't this a complete reversal of her life? Or 'death' of her life leading to a new life or what is a rigmarole of depressions, hatred and perversions.

NAKED QUESTIONS

- If a victim is imparted AIDS, which is incurable, is this equal to murder?

- If a victim commits suicide prompted by the outside cause (culprit) is this murder?

- If a victim looses her mental balance, leading to complete destruction of mental life, is this murder?

CULPRIT AND HIS PRIOR ROMANCE RELATIONSHIP WITH THE ALLEGED VICTIM

Country : The United States of America.

Court of Appeal : The Supreme Court.

Year : 1991

Case Name : Michigan V/S Lucas.

Source : Reproduced with amendments, from "The Supreme Court Yearbook: 1990-91" by Joan Biskpuc; Congressional Quarterly Inc; Washington D.C.

THE CASE

This case comes under "Rape Shield Law" (U.S.A. Jurisprudence).

The culprit can use to his advantage the fact that he had a "prior" relationship of romance with a woman, who now alleges to be a victim of his sexual lust.

But the confrontation clause of the Sixth Amendment (US Law and Justice) does not give any guarantee that any "alleged rapist 'may' introduce evidence of a prior romantic relationship with the alleged victim". The accused in this case was barred from introducing such evidence. The reason was that he had failed to meet the rule that he notify the prosecutors "within ten days arraignment that he would seek to introduce such testimony".

The defendant (or alleged culprit) argued that the ten day rule violated his constitutional right to confront his accuser. The majority of the Jury (decided by a 7-2 vote on the 20th May, 1991. O'Connor wrote opinion; Stevens and Marshall dissented) said that the "state's notice and hearing requirement served legitimate interests of protecting rape victims against surprise, harassment, and unnecessary invasions of privacy".

THE COMMENTS CONGLOMERATE

This case indeed is a very significant court conflict and offers valuable contribution to the United States Jurisprudence. However, it at the same time, opens up a universal question on rape, common to all countries of all continents, no matter what political, social and ideological breath makes them survive.

The central question arising out of this case is:

Does a prior romantic relationship of a culprit with a victim open up a viable defence ground?

This defence clause has both the negative and positive aspects hidden in it and offers a scope of protecting innocence and tearing innocence.

THE PRO VIEW

Rape cases must also be thought on grounds that a culprit might have been wrongly accused by the victim, and being a feminist does not prevent me from highlighting this truth.

In this case this defence can be of a very powerful use to him. He can present before the court that since he was a lover of the woman, how can he rape her? If he is somehow able to present proofs of the victim's faith in his trustworthiness, he might be able to save himself from being put behind the bars for committing a crime never committed.

THE CONTRA VIEW

The same defence shield can be used by the culprit to wrongly prove that he is innocent.

It is never a guarantee that a woman's lover can not run into a rapist. We all try to be perfect but "to err to human". Every woman wants a lover who protects her virginity and offers her true love, true satisfaction and ever lasting warmth. In other words, it's a woman's dream to find a man who is both physically young and mentally handsome. But she might realise after a time that her lover is the harbinger of her ultimate doom. And the realisation might come in the form of a rape.

UNIVERSAL SUGGESTIONS

- This is a very good law and provides a defence ground with sustainable hope to an innocent man produced as a culprit. It is worth of inclusion in a nation's jurisprudence.

- The dangers of this law are also imminent, inevitable and apparent. The law thus must be introduced with certain clauses that cut the wings of its misuse.

- The advance information to the jury for introduction of this defence, is a good requirement. It might aware the victim beforehand, and in case it is a culprit's misuse, the victim's bench can think of measures to counter attack the culprit's move.

MALE CONSENT ISSUE IN SEXUAL RELATIONSHIPS

Country	:	The United Kingdom
Court of Appeal	:	Data not available.
Year	:	1981
Case Name	:	Faulkner V/S Talbot.
Source	:	Quoted case reference. By Paul Dehmam for his book–"Law : A Modern Introduction".

THE CASE

The defendant invited a 14 year old boy to sleep with her. When they were in bed the boy resisted attempts by the defendant to put her hand on his penis, whereupon she pulled the boy on top of her, and put his penis inside her vagina. The defendant argued that since there was no specific provision that made the act of sexual intercourse between a woman and a boy under 16 unlawful, the touching of the boy as a preliminary to sexual intercourse was not an indecent assault. This argument was rejected and it was held that the boy being under 16 could not consent to an indecent assault.

THE COMMENTS CONGLOMERATE

The case raises several objections:

- In the first place, when the case was being judged on the question whether touching of the penis is an indecent assault, then the case would also have been judged on the question whether pulling of the boy on her top by the defendant, was forced sexual intercourse and

The International Perspective

thus rape. If the boy is resisting attempts on his penis being touched, the question arises about his reactions (and thus unwillingness maybe) on the copulation that followed.

If a case can be opened on touching of the penis, then the events that follow, certainly invite a debate.

- If according to the court, "boy under sixteen could not consent to an indecent assault", how can he consent to a sexual intercourse, which in this case appears to have been unwilling?

Special provisions in every nation must be made that fix a limit for a boy's consent to a girl's approach for sex.

If the boy resisted the lady's attempts to lay her hand on his penis it is very much possible that he had no idea as to what sexual intercourse really meant. It is very much possible that he felt that a lip kiss is the greatest limit to sex. The case arises a strong and sustainable proof of a half banked sexual maturity, which gets fully baked up in such controversially warm situations. The real danger is that this cake of sexual knowledge baked in such a oven of sexual heat might leave wrong impressions in his brain leading to undesirable changes in his sexual behaviour. Puberty period gives rise to a sexual heat and pacifying it in that half baked age makes it re-emerge with a far greater pull and force and to satisfy it a youth can take varied paths, of which one is rape. Parental rape might be a postle effect, seen after many years, after a series of incidents and consequent changes, coming from a wrongly led sexual life.

- The argument of the woman defending her point that the boy cannot accuse her of indecent assault since there is no permitting age for a boy is a wrong defence. The question is not merely of a permission by law. The real argument is that of a consent. The permission of law is only limited to sexual intercourse with consent. If that consent vapours away, and the defendant tries to resist attempts, it is rape or molestation or any form sexual indecency. Thus, that two people are in bed with consent doesn't mean that rape cannot occur. If that consent breaks and still one party continues with it, the perspective assumes the form of rape or molestation.

This definitely is very tricky. A person might have intercourse with someone with consent and then shriek–"rape". But then, here, it was certain that the boy did not want his penis to be touched (and so may be a resistance for copulation....?). Even the defendant seems to agree before the court that this happened. Here the question that whether an intercourse with a certain age person is lawful or not, is actually a otherwise viable question brought in a situation deeming it a misfit. The Touching of the penis is an indecency. Not because law doesn't permit it. But because the boy, the equal partner in the sex relationship, doesn't permit it.

DRESSED UP INDIA

Where sixteen year old boys instead of going to school go to a woman's bed; where boys move court not on the question of insufficient education system but sexual indecency; where sex at sixteen is satisfied and life destroyed; what will happen to the culture and the ethos....? Are such lame teenagers any nation's future citizens?

We do not want such a naked India. My dressed up motherland better suits me, which asks it's sixteens to wear the clothes of control and patience and not throw them for consummation in the fire of lust.

Part Fourteen

WHEN I'LL BECOME A FATHER

WHEN I'LL BECOME A FATHER

As I come to the concluding lines of this book, a fear haunts me–Will my daughter treat me with the love my paternal love shall demand?

Today at 19, I am a bachelor. But one day, after some years, I shall be married. I might even have a daughter. I shall love my daughter with all the love and care a father can give. But, in today's world, with the black shade of parental rapes preventing the glorious light of a sweet, innocent life to touch your being, I think of my daughter with a lot of anxiety and terror.

May be, when my daughter shall grow up to understand sex and rape and that shall be nearly about 20 years from now, parental rapes might have become an everyday phenomenon. Would she, with such a father's world, have full faith in me? Would she believe me if I shall say that I'm sick and want to lie on her lap. I have my suspicions.

May be in that world of tomorrow, in that earth of the 21st Century we dream of in a million forms, a father-daughter's relationship would be limited to a handshake; kiss and hugs being looked as sexual and not paternal instincts.

I suddenly do not want to live. Somehow I don't want to hope for future–if future is so black. At the best, I don't want to have a daughter if the daughters of tomorrow shall behave like that.

I am not being negativistic or a pessimist–I at least, can't bear life with such a gift from parental rapes.

If to daughters, parental rapes or its possibility comes as a shock because the relationship they looked for protection breaks leaving marks of dirty sexual yearning; such suspicions about innocent fathers are also not charming incidents of life. A father to whom the daughter is more than life—who sits at her bedside when she is ill, makes all his wishes secondary before hers and traps all the warmth of life for her—such a sweet, innocent, lovable, adorable father....! How will he feel if he is suspected of being capable of a parental rape? I would, at least, not live to see another day.

That is why from the day I read the case of Jeet Singh Chauhan, I have wanted to write this research. For each day and each night I have hoped that Jeet Singh's case be the last one. Because, I know if this doesn't happen the future is very black and I can see that future right in front of my eyes.

A father-daughter's relationship for centuries has remained a sweet blessing of mother life. Please, let this scent of purity and paternal fragrance remain. Let not the acid of sexual passions decay it to death.

A father may not give birth to a daughter. But she is born out of a part of him. How can he kill what is a part of him by pressing her virginity to death.

If we fathers of today or tomorrow, who love our daughters as we do our breath, want them to love us, let us see that parental rapes die so that a daughter's blind faith on her father lives.... lives to see the final day of mankind.

But as I don't have full hopes that parental rapes would end, I end my book with a small poem for my daughter who shall come after some years. If she will suspect me; as a loving, caring and shocked father, I shall give her this poem to let her blind faith for me stay.....

> O' my daughter,
> The soul of my being,
> The life of my life,
> The shine of my sunshine,
> The laughter of my happiness,
>
> The glow of my living,
> I am your father,
> And have loved you as a father,
> Please love me as a daughter,
> Suspect me not.

O' my daughter,
You were born of me,
You are in me,
If not you, what's worth for me?
By suspicion of yours,
Kill me not,
Love me as a daughter,
Suspect me not.

My love for you,
Is innocence of a lamb.
Your ugly suspicions,
On me shouldn't be stamped.
From your heart,
Fade me not.
Love me as a daughter,
Suspect me not.

As I end this book, I can't wish you Good Morning, Good Evening or Good Night. The mornings, evenings and nights are no longer good in India.

APPENDIX

APPENDIX

THE BLACK HOLE OF DEATH

It has always been one of the foremost weapons of pseudo moralists, to misguide people in the form of theories and philosophies that appear as the agents of salvation and exist as agents of annihilation.

Morality is a very important issue–to such a large extent that it has assumed a very delicate form. On the hands of morality rests the entire culture. Morality in itself is a perpetual guide to the great Omnipotent but people who misinterpret morality and thus misrepresent it, misguide the entire society to destruction and make it merge into oblivion.

Society is a submarine. It's dipped partly beneath the water of evil and partly above it, in the zone of eternal air. Morality brings it further up, pseudo morality forces it further down. If pseudo moralities are not recognised and their largeness abbreviated to nothingness, the social submarine shall merge beneath the waters.......

Reading the histories of philosophy and religion, one encounters theories fantastic and magnificent, populist and well acclaimed, noble and humanitarian; but one close look and beneath the benevolent layers you can see Satan laughing.

There are some theories that misrepresent goodness, logic and Providence, using sharpness of Philosophy and weakness of human psychology to penetrate in the social ethos. They do not prohibit but promote evil.

Naturalism is a theory that evolved in the 1800's and through novels and drama, has taken an almost integral place in the human world.

This theory totally dismisses the Supernatural. It believes that a man is completely influenced by environment or heredity or both. These factors totally contribute to the making of him and he has no control over his urges.

Naturalism has been portrayed by many dramatists and writers, especially Zola in "The Experimental Novel" and many other works. Maxim Gorki, one of Russia's most influential writers has used this theory in his works and even one of the greatest genius in literature Leo Tolstoy; besides many other works in different parts of the globe.

No amount of qualitative and quantitative greatness can cover the dangers inherent in this topsy turvy philosophy of a misdirected creative power and human imagination.

If it is believed that the power punch of environment and heredity completely superimposes a human being to perpetually detach him from all forms of control over his urges and actions, than he can be accountable for no actions committed by him. Thus we arrive at a perfect excuse for all parental rape culprits, homosexuals and murderers. Infact, the characters of naturalistic form of literature are a perfect puppet of their passions, having no coordination with the rational, and in a chaotic state sway like a pendulum form one urge to the other.

If such misrepresented philosophies, born of pure imagination and pure falsehood, dominate the society, the human shall become a perfect synonym for a beast.

Can it be doubted, that this theory is wrong? It is perhaps a complete falsehood and misrepresentation, and all logical minds shall dismiss it spontaneously and perpetually. The human brain, testified to be the reservoir of infinite power, that is capable of witnessing the entire cosmos in a state of trance, will not even allow an urge to be born if controlled properly, positively and strongly. It is not the outer environment or heredity; but a evil deviated brain that weaves evil and plays havoc with his life using the dice of urge and yearning. The outer environment merely contributes as a catalyst if the rectants of yearning in the gray sense are pulsating to reach the waters of evil satisfaction. As far as genes are concerned, or what is better understood as heredity, it must be understood that though one is born with certain preferences, likes and dislike, which may be immoral, he becomes perfectly conscious of their being on the wrong side. This becomes possible because the brain being sharp, at once conceives the knowledge of right and wrong, and imparts it to the person. Moreover the conscience is always the supreme judge. Preferences, moreover, are never uncontrollable and can be regulated or inhibited. A very logical proof of this is that good people are seen to become bad after a time and also, the vice-versa. Thus, though heredity and outer environment contribute to the making of an individual's ideas and actions, they can not make a man their puppet.

Such theories are great dangers to the social structure of the civilization and are vast antiwaves that act as black holes to trap the entire human species and compress it to oblivion.

Urges are human born and evil actions are remote controlled by the human mind.[1] Naturalism is also a theory imagine and formed as a charter of destruction by a human brain, to be liked and supported by all evils frantically searching for a moralist fundamental to prevent them from reaching the dock. It must be displaced from the civilization to be replaced by the logical and moral synthesis of principles. Otherwise the final hour of your species shall very soon give a knock.

Severe problems occur when many theories are consciously or unconsciously misunderstood.

Predestination has been a controversial theory and one of the major problematic forces, because it has been understood (and perhaps so portrayed by most) with the concept of the predetermined factor.

Predestination says that "only a selected race will be saved and the rest damned", as willed by God. It is mostly believed that it has been predetermined, even before an individual's birth that he would be damned. This brings a danger, cosmically grave in its full power.

If all this is believed to be true than people might tend to believe that they can do anything, since they have been already choosen for the eternal Paradise or the perpetual blackness and fiery disturbance of hell.

There are many other theories that hold that man is not accountable to any of his actions, whether good or evil, as whatever he does is determined by God.

Thus these theories place God equal to Satan in the sense that if God is responsible for all of man's actions, that he is so for all evil.

---

1. Read "Man's Sexual Fantasy" in "The Sexological View".

Plato realised the inherent danger in making God completely accountable to man's actions and dismissing man's free will. He decries the same with the help of a very powerful dialogue in The Republic:

Socrates : ".... God must surely be represented as He really is, whether poet is writing an epic, lyric or tragedy".

Adeimantus : "He must".

Socrates : "And in reality of course God is good, and He must so be described".

Adeimantus : "Certainly".

Socrates : "But nothing good is harmful, is it?"

Adeimantus : "I think not".

Socrates : "Then can anything that is not harmful do harm?"

Adeimantus : "No".

Socrates : "And can what does no harm do evil?"

Adeimantus : "No again".

Socrates : "And can, what does no evil be the cause of any evil?"

Adeimantus : "How could it?"

Socrates : "Well then is the good beneficial?"

Adeimantus : "Yes".

Socrates : "So it must be the cause of well being".

Adeimantus : "Yes".

Socrates : "So the good is not the cause of everything but only of states of well being and not of evil".

Adeimantus : "Most certainly".

Socrates : "Then God, being good, cannot be responsible for everything, as is commonly said, but only for a small part of human life, for the great part of which He was no responsibility[1]........".

---

1. The Republic, Part Three (Book Two); Education : The First stage, 379(a)-379(d).

After all, will you place God as accountable for an incestual rape....?

Then there are the schools of thought of Hobbes and Mandeville saying that men are essentially and completely depraved. Thus, instead of diminishing the human's evil, they glorify it to universality and perpetuality.

Where man is said to be in control of his urges and God is responsible for his evil, where man's decision is nil and predestination is the everything and where depravity is an essentiality, incest exists as a glorious form and books like "When Fathers Rape" become meaningless. If books like mine, are to be beheld like a woman's Bible and spiritual and cultural rejuvinator, such philosophies shall have to be given a swing at the gallows. But that seems too much to ask from our civilization.

Utopia is a land totally perfect. The Utopic dream is a great imagination and if society merges with Utopia to be it, how great it would be. How meaningful all the years of mankind on Earth would then seem.

But when sex beyond control gives salvation and such philosophies reign, it is not Utopia but Pandemonium that looks nearer to being achieved.

BIBLIOGRAPHY

The following books and journals/newspapers were consulted by the writer for this research. These include writings on various perspectives related to parental rape and also on laws of other countries regarding forced sex :

- Indian Penal Code, Sections on Sexual offences, especially sections 375-377; for placement of sex in the Indian legal perspective.

  Available with all leading publishers and all major libraries, including several copies at the Indian Law Institute Library, Bhagwan Dass Road, New Delhi-110001.

- Status of Women in Islam : A collection of papers on the eve of the Ten Day Dawn Celebrations in Iran.

  The following papers were consulted :
  - Women of Half of Body of Society
  - Islam and Women's Rights.
  - Women in a Quranic Society.

  By Islamic Propagation Organisation, P. O. Box 11365/7318, Tehran, Iran.

- A manual of Islamic Beliefs and Practises by Ali Muhammed Naqui; to assess the Islamic viewpoint on Father-Daughter sexuality.

  Available at the Iran Culture House Library, Tilak Marg, New Delhi - 110001.

- The Holy Koran

- The Constitution of Iran.

- Crimes & Punishments in New Perspective, an exclusive collection of Indian Law Institute Library, Bhagwan Dass Road, New Delhi-110001.

- American Code (Annotated) – a multivolume series by West Publishing Group, Washington, D. C., U.S.A.; for American Law On Rape & Related Issues.

    Available at the American Centre Library, K. G. Marg, New Delhi-110001.

- American Jurisprudence - Multivolume series; by Jurisprudence Publications; for US Jurisprudence on sexual assault. By Jurisprudence Publications, Washington D.C., U.S.A.

    Available with the American Centre Library, K. G. Marg, New Delhi-110001.

- The Penal Code of China; for Chinese law on rape.

    Available with the Chinese Culture Centre, Panchsheel Marg, Chanakyapuri, New Delhi-110021.

- The Supreme Court (USA) Yearbook; 1990-91 by Joan Biskpuc, Congressional Quarterly Inc. Washington D.C., U.S.A. - for facts of a prominent rape case for the International Case Book of Rape (Part 13/Section V)

    Available with the American Centre Library, K. G. Marg, New Delhi-110001.

- Significant Decisions of the Supreme Court : 1976-77 term (USA) by Bruce E Fein, Institute of a Public Policy Research, Washington D.C., U.S.A.

    Consulted for facts of a prominent rape case. Available with the American Centre Library, K. G. Marg, New Delhi-110001.

- Mahjubah, Islamic Magazine for Women :

    Female Genital Mutilation in Southern Nigeria; for sexual distortion of Women. Vol. 13, No. 8 (123) Aug. 1994).

- First seminar on Girls [Vol. 14 No. 2 (129) Feb. 1995]; for Introduction File of Iran.
- Women's Role in Productivity; for Introduction File of Iran (Vol. 13, No. 10 (125), Oct. 1994).

For information write to : Editor, Mahjubah, Islamic Thought Foundation, P.O. Box 14155-3987, Tehran-Iran. (Fax : (021) 898295).

The Hindustan Times :

- "Peculiar Paradox", Sunday Magazine, March 5, 1995, Page 1; for information on Pakistan's Law on Rape.
- May 23, 1994 (main paper) for information on Parminder Kaur Paternal rape case.
- July 20, 1994 (main paper) for information on Gandhi Nagar paternal rape case.
- August 20, 1994 (main paper) for Ram Avtar Shastri Paternal Rape case.
- April 15, 1995 (main paper) for Subrata Rai Paternal rape case.
- April 27, 1995, for information on Karam Chand Thakur Rape Case.
- "Sita to Phoolan" by Gargi Kaul, Sat. Magazine Section. Feb. 13, 1993; for assessment of factors contributing to the conversion of a submissive woman to a criminal in the post rape scenario.

INDEX

A

Adam 93
African regimes 271-77
aggressiveness 95
Ahura Mazda 72
AIDS 106, 131, 149
Alcibiades 215
Alexander the Great 215
Almighty Father 71
Amrita Singh 24
Anandi Lal, *Dr.* 13, 16, 19, 31-36, 88, 136
Anand Kapur 140
Anil K. Sharma 128
animal sexuality 99
Anti Sex Crime Force Programme 160
apathy in the jurisprudence 15-16
Archimedes 215
Artistic and Cultural Centre (Tehran) 199
Avesta 192
Aztecs 235

B

Bahonar, M.J. 188
Balwant Gargi 133
Benazir Bhutto 211
Bhanwari Devi Case 129-30
Bhutan 262-71
Bhutanese jurisprudence 265
Bhutani, *Dr. (Prof.)* L.K. 93-108
Bhutan's dual law 270
Bible 102, 189, 192, 307
Brahmacharaya viii
British Penal Code 250
Bureau of Women's Affairs (Iran) 199
Burka (burqa) vii, 141

C

capital punishment 78
Charles Dickens 77, 81
Charles Lamb 249
Chen Ling Chen 257, 258

child,
    perpetual, safe and trusted slave 140
child from a raped daughter's womb,
    birth of 45, 55
China 254-61
Chinese Jurisprudence 258, 260-61
Christopher Columbus 235
Christopher Thomas 210
Cimon 215
civilization 72, 94
Co-behaviour Programme 161
Cokar 287
corruption of minor 238
crime against women in Delhi 68
criminal law on rape 241-43, 260
criminal procedure law 260
criminological difference in women crimes and rape 59
criminological philosophy 26-27
critical law thought, development of 279-86
culprit and medical bill payment 271
culprit and prior romance relationship with the alleged victim 290
culprit-father 44
culprit in the man,
    search for 26-27

culprits be sympathized 27-28
culprit's crime making 25-26
culprit husband,
    reactions of 46, 54
cultural India 140-42
cultural stress participation 160
curb of police 60
Curriculum Access Programme 161
custodial rape 123-24, 181
Czar Ivan-IV 225

D

Dark Continent 273
Darwin's theory 103, 225
daughter,
    reasons of rape 41, 49
daughter-father sexuality 190-93
daughter's consent to sexual relationship with the father,
    anti view 55
    pro view 45
daughter's fundamental right 89
death penalty 258, 259
death sentence xii
Debate and Discussion Programme 160
Dowry Prohibition Act 76, 78
Draupadi 75
Dutta, K. 26

Index 315

E

Einstein 103
11 Point Implementation Charter 160-61
Elizabeth-I, Queen 184
Ethiopia 273-77
Ethiopian jurisprudence 277
Euclid 215
Evangelos Theopilou 217
Eve 93
examining parental rapes 142
execution 130-33, 281-82,
　Indian paradox 117
execution and rape 286-94
execution debate 75-83
execution question 63

F

false accusation 269, 271
Faruqi, L. 188
father-daughter relationship 87-88, 298
father-daughter sexuality 96-97
father's bail 65
father's blackmailing 12-14
father-son relationship 140
father's punishment,
　exemption of 42
female progeny,
　sexual evaluation of 40, 47

Fiction Programme 160
Fielding 120
fighting and kneeling,
　distinction between 155-57
fits and rape 32
5 Point Proposal 162-63
fixed terms imprisonment 258, 259
forcible rape 243
frustration 128-29, 130
full knowledge programme 160
fund and assistance 161

G

Gandhiji ix, x, 75, 156
Gandhi Nagar (East Delhi) rape case 12
gang rape 266
　married person 267
　minor 268
gang rape and murder 268-69
Gargi Kaul 19
Geeta 75, 102, 189, 192
George Eliot 184
Georgia law 287
Gorki 304
Great Britain 244-53
Greece 211-18
Greek Law 261
Gautam Buddha 190

H

Henry Fielding 119, 131
High Court case involving reduction of sentence on controversial grounds 16-17
highlighting victim's traumas, importance of 36
Hindustan Times 120, 121
Happarchus 215
Hippocrates 215
Hobbes 307
Home Ministry's Under Secretary rape case 12
homosexual hunger 140
homosexual incestual abuse 140
homosexuality 284-86
homosexual mate 140
homosexual parental abuse 142-43
homosexual rape 242
homosexual satisfaction 140
hospital 177, 178
hypocritic culprits 127-36

I

Iliad 103
illicit sex 202
incestual crimes 282-83
incestually raped girl, reactions of 33-34
incestual rape 252-53
increasing rape 60
indecent exposure 237
indecent liberties 239
Indian law, flexibility of 180
Indian Penal Code 174-79, 181
Indian sex behaviourism 157-58
Indira Gandhi vii
infant death 106-07
infant rape ix
Information Package 161
inharmony in law and public opinion 119
injury 268
intent 242
international case book 286-94
International synthesis 278
intoxication 242
Iran 193-204
Islam,
female/male differences 188-90
man/woman quality 186-88
Islamic Nations 182-211

J

Jawaharlal Nehru, Pandit 209
Jayanti Patnaik 14-15
Jeet Singh rape case 1-10, 20, 24, 83, 123, 135, 136, 298

Index

Jesus Christ 71, 107, 190
John Donne 249

K

Kal Yug 73, 80
Kama Sutra 94, 139
Khan, *Prof. (Dr.)* M.Z. 71-89
Koran *see* Quran
Keshav Chand rape case 12

L

Lamya Faruqi, L. 187
Lawrence, D.H. 26
life imprisonment 258, 259
Light House of Alexandria 103
London Mafia 103
Lord Krishna 71, 75
Lord Rama 71, 73, 75

M

maddening nervousness 148
madness 32
Mahabharata 75, 100, 174
Mahram 192-93, 202
male consent in sexual relationships 292-94
man against man 240-41
man against unchaste woman 240
man against woman 239-40

Mandeville 307
man rapes 283-84
man's sexual fantasy 102-06
marital rape 181, 279-81
Marriage Act *(1980)* 265
Martin C. Battestin 131
masturbation 104
Matheli Sharan Gupt vii
Mathew Hale, *Sir* 251, 280
Maurayan administration 124
Mayas 235
medicinal brain's consultation in law making 35
men hatred of victims 19
men in the cave,
    idea to estimate the power of sex 97-98
men rapes 35-36, 95
Mental Retardation Cure Institute 148
Mera Bharat Mahan xiii
Michailov, A. 226
minor rape ix
Mira Bai 184
Mnemosyne 215
moral education 161-62
morality issue 73-75, 160, 303
Moriarity, *Professor* 103, 106
Mother Teresa 184
Muses 215

N

Nalini Singh vii
National Commission for Women 14
naturalism 303-05
Neena Gupta viii
Nihar Ranjan Senapati 121
1982 minor rape case 15
Nobel Prize 236

O

Odyssey 103
Olympias 215
Om Prakash Parasher 25, 135
open execution 131
opinion poll 111-13
ordinary execution 131
Ordinary rape 124

P

Pakistan 204-11
Panchsheel 209
Pankaj Berry 133
parental incest awareness 122-23
parental law,
    insufficient law 135-36
parental rape ix, xi, 3-20
    passim, 39, 61-62, 180
parent's sexual abuse 12

Parminder Kaur *alias* Deepa rape case 10-12
peculiar rape law 202
people's comments 17-18
Personal Help Programme 160
Phoolan Devi 19
Plato 120, 215, 306
Poirot 103
police,
    reaction to rape and women exploitation 59
police protection 65
poll explanation 179
predestination 305
pregnancy theory 117-18
prevention clause 155-63
Private Counselling Centre 160
programme project team,
    formation of 163
Promilla Kapur, *Dr.* 39-56
prostitution 238
pseudo family bond 64
psychiatrist's reaction to the High Court case 35
psycho impacts on the victims 31-32
psycho treatment 42
P.T. Usha vii
public's awareness and concern 65
punishment consensus 147-48
Punishment Power Programme 160

Index

punishment structure 42, 51, 62, 169
punishment to culprit,
  psychiatrist's opinion 34-35
Purdah vii, 141
Pythagoras 215, 216

Q

Queen Victoria 104
Quran 71, 75, 85, 102, 183, 185, 188, 189, 201, 208

R

Ramayana 75, 100, 174
  cultural guiding light and immediate effect 118-19
Ram raaj 73
rape viii, ix, 16, 20, 31, 66, 203, 251-52
  psychiatric definition of 31
  punishment 129
  reactions of police 59
  social implications of 88-89
  under the Marriage Act,
    amendments for the offence 265-69
rape act,
  definition 266
  enacted by Bhutan nation Assembly 265
rape and murder 268

raped daughters,
  parents' reactions 33
raped daughters' psycho-structure,
  damage to 43
rape death 271
rape eradication,
  NGO intervention 163
rape in animals 98-100
rape in USA 237
rape law 202-03
rape murder 261, 271
rape prevention 120
Rape Shield Law 290
raping married person 266-67
raping minor 267
Real Life Project Programme 160
reformatory measures 119, 121
religion accusation 190
reporting 269
Rober A. Myers, *Dr.* 183
Royal Regimes 261-71
Russia 219-29, 254

S

salvation through sex 86
Sanja Chula 133
Sarojini Naidu vii
Sati Pratha 134
Sat Yug 73, 80

Self Proclaimed God Ram Avtar Shastri rape case 12
self-protection 66
sentence on controversial grounds, reduction by high Court 16-17
Seshan, T.N. 163
Seven Deadly Sins 167
17 Point Programme 153-55
sex vii, 93
    awareness 160
    abnormality of culprit 127-28
    education 119, 120, 157-61
    need for 157
    furnace 120-21
    hatred of 44, 53
    offences excluded from the rape category 237
    rule of nature and its breaking 139-40
    slaves 140
sexological difference between spouse 96-97
sexual assault 239, 243
sexual disease viii
sexual intercourse viii, 175
    without consent *see* rape
Sexual Offences Act *(1956)* 250
sex permissiveness and rape 86-87
sexual perversion 42, 53
sexual privacy 89
Shabana Azmi vii, viii
Sherlock Holmes 23, 103

16 Point Benefit Charter 158-59
slums,
    sex furnace 120-21
Smita Patil vii, viii
special Bhutanese terms 265
Special Committee question 18-19
special maritime and territorial jurisdiction 241
spiritualism 160
Social Banishment 135
social change 133-35
society 303
socio-communist regimes 254-61
Solon 215
Somersault regimes 219-29
statutory rape 243
stigma 66
stigma and rape 60-61
strengthening the family stride 83-86
stricter censor 163
subconscious antithetical establishment 26
Subrata Rai rape case 12, 25
suicide 142
    consequence of rape 34
Suneet Vir Singh 120, 121
Sun Temple 103
superintendent 177
Superpowers and developed regimes 229-53
superstitions and rape 88

Surat-al-Nisa 188
suspicion and belief 63

T

Theban Legend 94
Theodore Roosevelt 236
Tihar Jail 23
trauma eradication 162

U

Unchaste women and rape 244
UNFPA 199
U.N. Human Rights Commission 209
UNICEF 199
United States Code 241
United States of America 230-44
unnatural sexual offences 178
unnecessary paranoia 63
Upanishads ix, 174
Utopia 307

V

Vajpayee, A.B. 209
Vanaprastha viii
Vatsyayan 94
vedas ix, 71, 85, 101, 174
Ved Marwah 26

Victim counselling 243
Victim's mental condition 60
victim's security 65
Vietnam War 236
Vishwa B. 135

W

wife raped by husband 100-02
William Shakespeare 249
Wilson John 26
woman-man differences 185
women,
　general survey 183-85
women and Islam 182-90
women exploitation,
　reaction of police 59
women's/children's institution 177, 178

Y

Yamin Hazarika 59-68
Yellow River Civilization 88

Z

Zeno of Citium 215
Zeus 215
Zola 304